D1766715

Augustine and Psychology

Augustine in Conversation: Tradition and Innovation

Series Editors: John Doody and Kim Paffenroth

This series produces edited volumes that explore Augustine's relationship to a particular discipline or field of study. This "relationship" is considered in several different ways: some contributors consider Augustine's practice of the particular discipline in question; some consider his subsequent influence on the field of study; and others consider how Augustine himself has become an object of study by their discipline. Such variety adds breadth and new perspectives—innovation—to our ongoing conversation with Augustine on topics of lasting import to him and us, while using Augustine as our conversation partner lends focus and a common thread—tradition—to our disparate fields and interests.

Titles in the Series

Augustine and Psychology

Edited by Sandra Lee Dixon, John Doody, and Kim Paffenroth

LEXINGTON BOOKS
Lanham • Boulder • New York • Toronto • Plymouth, UK

Published by Lexington Books
A wholly owned subsidiary of The Rowman & Littlefield Publishing Group, Inc.
4501 Forbes Boulevard, Suite 200, Lanham, Maryland 20706
www.rowman.com

10 Thornbury Road, Plymouth PL6 7PP, United Kingdom

Copyright © 2013 by Lexington Books

All rights reserved. No part of this book may be reproduced in any form or by any
electronic or mechanical means, including information storage and retrieval systems,
without written permission from the publisher, except by a reviewer who may quote
passages in a review.

British Library Cataloguing in Publication Information Available

Library of Congress Cataloging-in-Publication Data
Augustine and psychology / [edited by] Sandra Lee Dixon, John Doody, and Kim Paffenroth.
p. cm. — (Augustine in conversation)
Includes bibliographical references and index.
ISBN 978-0-7391-7918-5 (cloth : alk. paper)
1. Augustine, Saint, Bishop of Hippo. 2. Christianity—Psychology. I. Dixon, Sandra Lee, 1955– II.
Doody, John, 1943– III. Paffenroth, Kim, 1966–
BR65.A9A843 2013
261.5'15—dc23

2012036849

♾™ The paper used in this publication meets the minimum requirements of American
National Standard for Information Sciences Permanence of Paper for Printed Library
Materials, ANSI/NISO Z39.48-1992.

Printed in the United States of America

Contents

Introduction

Kim Paffenroth

Our continuing series now turns to consider Augustine and psychology. Perhaps more than any other discipline—save philosophy and theology—the theory and analysis of how our souls or minds work, malfunction, and develop, is one in which Augustine was a noted and influential practitioner, and one for which he has become a notorious object of analysis. His examination of his own life in *Confessions*, as well as his pastoral care shown in his Letters and Sermons, show us someone with a level of introspection and sophistication few, ancient or modern, could match. But, necessarily, having laid before us the family dynamics of his parents' apparently strained marriage, and his own failings as son, father, and partner, his own life has been dissected many times, from many perspectives, in ways that can be illuminating, dismissive, or both. Having read through the essays that follow, I can say that the authors have ably continued the best parts of this tradition and have treated Augustine with the kind of respect that makes his thought clearer and more relevant to our present age and lives.

First, Todd Breyfogle explores Augustine's treatment of a fundamental aspect of human consciousness: How do we conceive the several experiences of the soul as both plural and unitary? Over and against the view that Augustine holds to a faculty psychology, the essay seeks to understand Augustine's treatment of remembering, understanding, and willing in terms of the integration and expansion (or disintegration and contraction) of the soul as a feature of a unified human personality. Augustine is concerned to understand how the apparently distinct activities of the soul contribute to the quality of the soul and its relation to the body, to itself, and to its origin and end. Putting central passages of the *De Trinitate* in the context of some of Augustine's earlier writings, the essay looks at three actions where the unity of remembering, understanding, and willing are perhaps most evident: how we learn,

1

how we pray, and how we love. In the end, Augustine's psychology is best understood in aesthetic rather than epistemological terms. The journey to simplicity is a journey in which the beauty of the soul comes to reflect more perfectly the beauty of the divine.

Our next contribution is a reprint, in which Sandra Dixon elucidates a basis for interpreting Augustine's writings through psychoanalytic concepts and categories. The chapter sets out Freud's concepts for interpretation, which he himself applied to dreams, behavior, speech, and works of culture. These concepts ground all his other interpretations, including the interpretation of family relationships which led to the well-known theory of the Oedipal complex. Readers of Augustine who object to heavy-handed psychoanalytic readings of the Oedipal complex in Augustine's *Confessions* will find in this essay a demonstration, both for the classroom and for scholarly reflection, of close study of Augustine's text with Freudian concepts as an interpretive tool. This study includes not only generating Freudian interpretations but also exploring how Freudian approaches intersect with other psychoanalytic schools' concepts in helping us consider possible psychological undercurrents in the text of the *Confessions*.

The next essay, a new one by Sandra Dixon, addresses two major topics, only one of which has received much attention previously. The less discussed topic is the scene in *Confessions* 9.7.15 in which Augustine describes himself and his mother as separated by their intentional responses to the conflict between Ambrose and the imperial family over the basilicas in Milan. Focused attention to this scene leads to reflection on literary and theological issues opened up by the passage and its placement in the text. Extending this reflection to other parts of Augustine's presentation of the years in Milan, readers can reflect in wider scope on his portrayal, primarily in Book 6, of his soul's struggle to relinquish his worldly success for what he saw as the true philosophy found in Christianity. The conflict of the basilicas also encourages psychological exploration of the possibility that the struggle he represents between himself and his mother speaks to the problems attendant on their efforts to remain in relationship, while also being distinct individuals who are constituted by their relationships. The second topic, much more discussed in recent years, concerns the extent to which we can discern flesh and blood people through the renderings of the characters in the *Confessions*, especially the characters of Monica and Augustine. The chapter argues that the literary nature of the *Confessions* does compel recognition of possible distinctions between the characters and the people, but that it also presses, especially at the close of Book 9, for the conclusion that the text supports delineation of the fragmented images, embedded in the characters, of people. Augustine's own desire for reconciliation and relationship with Monica and his father Patricius is one of the glimpses available to us, as is an intimation that Monica could act with notable independence herself, despite her desire for close connection with her son.

Our next essay is a reprint of a classic examination by Anne Hunsaker Hawkins of the family dynamics narrated in *Confessions*. It was an essay I came across early in graduate school, and it still impresses me with its sensitivity to literary and theological dimensions, as well as the psychological forces behind the text.

The following essay is also a reprint, of a short section from a book by the late Morton T. Kelsey. Like Hawkins's essay, it takes me back many years, even before graduate school, to when I first considered the overlap and interplay between the spiritual and intellectual elements of our lives and minds—and how both can now be considered by what we call psychology.

Paul R. Kolbet next argues that Augustine's Christian psychology is best understood as one particularly brilliant example of the philosophically informed therapies that were prevalent in the late antique world. Representatives of Greek and Roman philosophical schools commonly employed highly cognitive therapeutic regimes to assist individuals in imposing a rational order upon the instinctual push and pull of their emotions. They did so by artfully constructing words and ascetic practices to help individuals grow in self-knowledge and to act according to their newly acquired insights. To know oneself was to understand oneself within an ordered universe as a rational yet mortal human being rather than as a god or beast. According to Kolbet, seeing how Augustine used the psychology that he inherited makes it possible to appreciate, among other things, his pioneering analysis of the internal divisions that fragment the self. Furthermore, it is in his critique of philosophically articulated technologies of self-improvement that Augustine's worry becomes apparent that such therapies risk entrapping the self in its own rational point of view. For Augustine, psychic health required therapeutic practices that not only supplied self-knowledge, but also progressively freed the self from its own rational constructions as it increasingly found stability in divinely given love.

In her essay, Margaret R. Miles shows how the concept of self-deception, in which the same person is both the doer and the sufferer, has played many roles in Western thinkers' analyses of the human condition. What is self-deception, and why does it occur? Miles examines the diagnoses and prescriptions for self-deception of two "founders of [Western] discursivities," Augustine of Hippo and Sigmund Freud.

Dan Morehead, a practicing psychiatrist, observes how neuroscience has sometimes been utilized to refute ancient psychologies and more often to ignore them. Augustine's psychology has been explicitly questioned and critiqued in regard to cognitive neuroscience, raising the possibility that his psychological ideas will soon fall into complete irrelevance. However, Morehead argues that important aspects of his religious psychology can be readily interwoven with neurobiological accounts of the same human experiences. In the case of desire and its role in human life, Augustine's account has long been recognized as subtle and detailed, and his treatment of it matches that of neuroscience with surprising precision. The behavior of the dopamine system, so central to desire and positive motivation generally, is strikingly similar to Augustine's account of his own experience and of human nature. The accounts of Augustine and neuroscience are not merely parallel but are mutually illuminating subjective and objective treatments of a fundamental aspect of human nature. And if they accurately describe fundamental problems of human nature in this regard, then they are in a position to contribute toward a universally valid psychology of religion. A brief survey of other world religious literature suggests that Augustine's thought on the subject of desire in human life represents a useful connection with other religions as well as neuroscience.

In a reprint of an essay I wrote years ago, I consider Book 9 of *Confessions* and how to understand Augustine's weeping—or, more pointedly, his hesitation to weep—at his mother's death. Grief, perhaps more even than sexuality (though surely tied up with that, since both involve love and vulnerability), is the most basic experience shared by everyone, and which any proper psychology must explain and heal. As confusing as Augustine's personal account is, it finally reveals a useful and healthy perspective—almost in spite of himself and his overly intellectualized analysis.

William Parsons's essay aims at reconsidering the meaning and nature of Augustine's pivotal visions in Books 7 (at Milan) and 9 (at Ostia) for both Augustine's religious journey and, more directly, a psychoanalytic audience, which, perhaps affected by a cultural trend toward the spiritual, has become more open to the possibility and importance of what William James liked to call the "More." In order to properly assess psychoanalytic contributions to this topic from a balanced interdisciplinary perspective the essay proceeds by way of five short sections. The first surveys extant psychoanalytic interpretations of Augustine's mysticism. The second begins a critique of the latter by revisiting the history of psychoanalytic models for mysticism. The third broadens the critique based on the findings of literary-critical methods. The fourth completes the critique based on a textual and theological reconstruction of Augustine's mysticism. Finally, with such critiques in hand, the last section sketches out a new orientation which considers how psychoanalysis might be best utilized in creating a more meaningful, less reductive appreciation of Augustine's visions.

Finally, Raymond J. Shaw treats Saint Augustine's writings on memory as a theory of memory and compares them to current theoretical work. Like current theorists, Augustine divides memory into an equivalent of short-term and long-term memories, and long-term is divided into kinds that are strikingly modern. Some of his descriptions parallel the language of current theories, especially that of Endel Tulving. Further, Augustine writes about some memory phenomena, most notably memory for emotions and the structure of knowledge, in novel ways that could be the basis for important experimental work today. However, a theory built on introspection will miss important memory phenomena, and Augustine's theory suffers from that. Ultimately, considering that current theories are built upon decades of extensive empirical research, Augustine's contemplation of memory produced an extraordinary theory.

As in previous volumes of our series, the essays here represent diverse perspectives on Augustine, but all of them, I think, show his relevance to our lives today, just as they show how current methods of analysis and interpretation shed light on the fifth-century bishop. The conversation continues to everyone's benefit.

Chapter One

The Journey to Simplicity

Augustine and the Plural Experiences of the Soul

Todd Breyfogle

Augustine's approach to the study of the soul is empirical and yields a fundamental paradox: we experience the soul both as a plurality and as a unity. I discern distinct activities—remembering, understanding, willing—and yet I apprehend that there is a unified "I" who is discerning the distinct activities, and a single conscious identity that is being supported and informed by those activities. At the same time, Augustine suggests, I recognize a discord within my identity as I try to remember but cannot, or when I will something I know to be contrary to my understanding of what I ought to will. Furthermore, in the moment that I am conscious of my consciousness, I discern both a unity and a separation.[1] How am I to understand these plural experiences of the soul?

It is customary to emphasize Augustine's understanding of the discrete activities of the soul rather than their unity. These discrete activities are often referred to and mistranslated as "faculties."[2] The tendency to focus on the "faculties" of the soul is partly a consequence of an anachronistic imposition of medieval and modern faculty psychologies on the contours of Augustine's thought. The predisposition to emphasize the plural activities of the soul also stems from a theological impulse to attend to the emphasis Augustine himself places on the operation of memory, intellect, and will as an analogy for understanding Trinitarian relations. And yet the three persons of the Trinity are susceptible to the same empirical paradox—we affirm one God, Augustine says, and yet we encounter in scripture three distinct divine persons manifesting themselves. So, it would seem, the discrete manifestations of spiritual being—both human and divine—pose analogous problems. How do we conceive the plural experiences of spiritual reality as both plural and

7

unitary? Over and against the customary interpretation of Augustine as a faculty psychologist, this essay stresses Augustine's conception of the fundamental unity of the human soul amidst its plural expressions.

THE SOUL AND DIVINE BEAUTY RESPONDING TO EVODIUS

A circumscribed approach to Augustine's discussion of the nature and activity of the soul can be discerned in a series of letters he exchanged with his friend Evodius, bishop of Uzalis, in 414 and 415.[3] Evodius' letters, posing several questions to his friend, are short. Augustine's replies are progressively longer and more involved. The correspondence proceeds in three stages, moving from consideration of how physical beings perceive immaterial realities, to the character of Christ's soul, to the unity of the plural expression of spirit—the tripartite character of the human soul and the divine being.

Augustine addresses Evodius' initial concerns relatively straightforwardly. It should be no surprise, he writes, that physical beings have visions, dreams, and memories, for "every man has his own consciousness at hand as a teacher by whose help he may apply himself" to understanding the conjunction of matter and spirit in the human personality (*ep.* 159.5). The character of Christ's soul is more complicated. Does Christ's rational soul, Evodius asks, belong within the classification of souls of created beings, or of some other? And what happens to Christ's soul during his descent into hell? Here, Augustine's reply concerns the exegesis of scripture, and while he unquestionably affirms the incorruptibility and eternality of Christ's soul, he recognizes the ambiguity of scripture and invites further interpretations if what he has suggested is unsatisfactory (*ep.* 164.7.22).

The third set of considerations is again exegetical at root but centers on whether ignorance about the true character of the Trinity is an impediment to salvation. Surely, Augustine contradicts Evodius, God does not reject those who are ignorant of refined theological matters, and certainly not one as difficult as the Trinity. The purity of heart which allows a clear sight of God is not accessible in this life, Augustine maintains. Moreover, salvation is not reserved for the supremely intelligent only—it is not the contents of the mind which ultimately reflect God's love but rather the disposition of the whole soul.[4] Finally, Augustine argues, "the ineffable unity of the Trinity" is not discerned in the same way "as the unity of memory, understanding, and will in the soul of man" is discerned (*ep.* 169.1.2-3). How then, Augustine asks, could punishment be inflicted on those for whom the unity of the Trinity remains obscure?

In this last letter we see Augustine's increasing exasperation with Evodius' tendency toward hair-splitting inquisitiveness. Looking back at Augustine's reply in letter 164, one senses a stalling tactic. Augustine replies to one set of questions but not another, asking Evodius to resend a copy of the letter which has inexplicably "gone missing." In the opening of letter 169, Augustine is increasingly blunt, and lets his frustration show. He explains that he has written the first three books of the *The City of God* (*De civitate Dei*) and has two more to write to finish the first section. He has dictated "in volumes of considerable size" expositions on three Psalms, and further commentaries not yet begun are demanded of him. Further, he says, he is unwilling to be torn away from his book on the Trinity (*De Trinitate*), which is laborious and intelligible only to the few. In closing the letter, Augustine recounts other writings undertaken—a treatise to Jerome on the origin of the soul and tracts against the Priscillianists and Pelagians. "If you wish to have all these," he concludes, "send some one to copy them all for you. Allow me, however, to be free from distraction in studying and dictating to my clerks those things which, being urgently required by many, claim in my opinion precedence over your questions, which are of interest to very few" (*ep.* 169.4.13).

This correspondence is instructive in several ways in discerning Augustine's approach to understanding the soul. First, Augustine insists on a sense of proportion. Scripture is unclear, and the matter is only partially penetrable by the human intellect. We should be circumspect in how we spend our time in theological speculation and discourse, addressing issues that directly affect the faith and lives of many. Second, nonetheless, questions about the origin and nature of the soul are important if we are to understand both ourselves and our Creator.[5] Augustine's replies to Evodius are not mere indulgence. Where Evodius raises serious concerns Augustine takes time to address them, and between his stern rebukes at the beginning and ending of letter 169, Augustine offers reflections that echo the most mature passages of *De Trinitate*.

Third, Augustine sketches some fundamental contours for thinking and speaking about the unity and plural experiences of both the Trinity and the soul. The very fact that we learn, he insists, presupposes a change in something immaterial within us (*ep.* 159). While the origins of the soul remain obscure, he readily concedes, it is clear that the human personality—including the person of Christ—is not a soul imprisoned in a body but rather the unique conjunction of soul and body.[6] Further, the soul is immortal, subject to deformation but not destruction (*ep.* 164). The discursive character of time and language limit our ability to conceive and express the essential unity of the Trinity and the soul while at the same time comprehending our plural experience of them.[7] Piety demands and scripture teaches, Augustine says, that we believe in one God, Father, Son, and Holy Spirit. While scripture speaks of each separately, they are yet "an inseparable Trinity . . . just as when their names are pronounced in human language they cannot be named simultaneously, although their existence in inseparable union is at every moment simultaneous." Scripture presents "the Three to our apprehension separately, indeed, but in no wise separated (*haec separatim quidem, sed nullo modo separata tria illa demonstrant*)" (*ep.* 169.2.5).

To apprehend this, Augustine says, let us borrow an illustration from the activities of remembering, understanding and willing. "For while we can speak of each of these severally in its own order, and at a separate time, we neither exercise nor even mention any one of them without the other two (*Quamvis enim haec suis separatisque temporibus singillatim singula enuntiemus, nihil tamen horum sine aliis duobus agimus aut dicimus*)."[8] Like any analogy, Augustine cautions, the illustration of remembering, understanding and willing does not correspond in all particulars with the unity and plural expression of the Trinity. In the first place, "memory, understanding, and will exist in the soul, but the three do not constitute the soul (*quod tria haec, memoria, intellegentia, voluntas, animae insunt; non eadem tria, est anima*)." By contrast, the Trinity does not exist in God, but is God (*illa vero Trinitas non inest, sed ipsa Deus est*). The divine being and its operations are a marvelous simplicity (*simplicitas*). By contrast, the human soul and its operations are a unity but not a simplicity (*ep.* 169.2.6).

Second—and related—Trinitarian relations are independent. The Father understands in his own right, and not through the Son. By contrast, the respective activity of memory, understanding, and will are mutually dependent. The memory does not understand itself except by means of the understanding. But here Augustine corrects himself, adding a further refinement. It is more precise, he says, to speak not of remembering, understanding and willing as having a life of their own, but to keep in view "the soul itself" as the unit of operation. "The soul itself, in which these three are (*anima ipsa, cui haec insunt*), understands through the understanding, just as it remembers through memory and wills only through the will." The soul itself is both the combination of these three and something more than them. However we label the activity of the soul, the mention of each label, memory, understanding, and will, "is nevertheless accomplished only in the combined operation of all three, since it is by an act of memory and of understanding and of will that each label is spoken." To identify one requires all three. Remembering is not exclusively reflexive, nor is understanding, or willing. Only in the fundamental unit, the soul, do the operations constitute a unity (*ep.* 169.2.6).[9]

Augustine's terminology underscores the independence of the persons of the Trinity and the dependence of memory, understanding, and will on the soul. Augustine employs the language of persons (*personae*) in his discussion of the Father, Son, and Holy Spirit. The activities of the soul, by contrast, have no substantial term associated with them; they are simply referred to as "each" or "the three." What is clear in Latin, however, becomes awkward in English and so it is customary—for linguistic reasons, as well as the anachronistic application of philosophical terminology—for the three to be translated as "faculties." This conceptual terminology eases the readability of Augustine's prose in English but obscures his thought, as does referring to the three as "elements" or "components" of the soul or even, as I have been calling them, "activities." Augustine is careful, both here and in *De Trinitate* (and elsewhere), to avoid language which might reify unduly what is signified by the labels of memory, understanding, and will. The soul is a fundamental unity. Nonetheless, Augustine recognizes, as a matter of empirical observation of our own consciousness, that we experience the motions of the soul as plural.[10]

These letters between Augustine and Evodius recall their conversations together in Milan almost thirty years before. Not long after Augustine's baptism, Evodius had raised six questions about the soul, and from those conversations came *On the Greatness of the Soul (De quantitate animae)*, written in 387/88. The very notion of an immaterial soul, we know from *Confessiones*, had long troubled the young Augustine as he struggled to discern a realm of immateriality beyond material existence.[11] Further, as *Confessiones* again makes clear, Augustine struggled to understand the fundamental unity of body and soul in the human person—not a soul trapped in the prison of matter, but rather integrated with a body which, as part of divine creation, is good.[12] What concerns him most, however, in *De quantitate animae*, is what we might call the shape of the soul in its relation to beauty.

In *De quantitate animae*, Augustine outlines the seven degrees of the soul, their object, and their relation to beauty:[13]

The seven degrees represent a ladder of ascent which captures a number of transitions in the quality of the soul and its relation to the body, to itself, and to its origin and end. At the most basic level, the ascent runs from the physical (the body) to the immaterial (the soul) to the divine (God). This movement also reflects a shift from multiplicity and plurality (the soul seeing the body as something other than itself) to simplicity and unity (the contemplative rest in God). Further, the object of the soul's attention shifts, as it ascends, from external to internal to eternal. Finally, the seven degrees would

Table 1.1.

Degree	Object	Relation
1. *animatio*	of the body	beautifully of another
2. *sensus*	through the body	beautifully through another
3. *ars*	about the body	beautifully about another
4. *virtus*	toward itself	beautifully toward a beautiful
5. *tranquillitas*	in itself	beautifully in a beautiful
6. *ingressio*	toward God	beautifully toward beauty
7. *contemplatio*	in God	beautifully in beauty

seem to be themselves a kind of unity. The soul does not pass from one degree to another, leaving the previous stage behind. Rather, each progressive stage marks the consummation of the stage before. In the degree of *virtus*, for example, the soul acts toward itself beautifully as toward an object of beauty. In doing so, it treats the body beautifully, subsuming simultaneously the first three degrees. In contemplation, all seven degrees are fully actualized as the attentive soul rises up in beauty toward God as far as it is able under grace (though Augustine indicates that true contemplation in this life is rare and fleeting).

It is worth emphasizing here that Augustine's concern with the soul is not its activity or the plurality of the human consciousness, but rather the shape, or quality of the soul in its relation to beauty. The soul at rest (*tranquillitas*) is a soul unified in itself, beautifully in a beautiful—recognizing itself and enjoying itself as no longer at odds with itself. For Augustine, the Christian life—the philosophical life, for that matter—is a life in which the soul takes shape in its proper beauty.

The seven degrees of the soul have a numerical symmetry that Augustine discusses at some length. At the center, as a kind of pivot, is *virtus*, which in Augustine's analysis is central to the soul's ascent. *Virtus* is characterized by the soul's turning toward itself, having been prepared by *ars* (and here Augustine means "art" as both skills and aesthetic production), which prompts reflection about external beauty—what is appropriate or fitting. *Virtus* marks the pivotal directionality of the soul as it turns its attention from without, to within, to what is above—and then again to creation, which is without, as seen from above. The soul withdraws within itself, looks above itself, and turns outward again toward God and creation properly understood. Augustine describes the soul's delight in virtue as the fourth and pivotal degree:

> the more the soul becomes the cause of its own delight, the more it dares to withdraw from baser things and wholly to cleanse itself and to make itself spotless and stainless; it dares to be strong against every enticement that tries to move it from its resolution and purpose, to esteem human society, to desire for another nothing that it would not wish for itself; to obey authority and the laws of wise men, and to believe that through these God speaks to it. . . . But, there is nothing more purifying than fearing death and refraining from the allurements of this world. . . . The soul, however, is so great that it can do even this with the help, of course, of the Justice of the supreme and true God—that Justice which sustains and rules this universe; by which it is brought about that all things are, and not only are, but are in such order that they cannot be better. To this Justice, in the difficult task of purifying itself, the soul entrusts itself with complete filial devotion and trust to be helped and made perfect (*quant. an.* 73).

Virtus, then, stands as a pivot between the internal and external life, mediating between the visible-material (1-3) and the invisible-spiritual (5-7). It is the preparatory anchor which recognizes the "distinct and proper beauty" of each of the distinct degrees (*quant. an.* 78).

UNIFICATION OF THE SOUL THROUGH LEARNING, PRAYING, AND LOVING

As interesting as the plural experiences of the soul may be, Augustine's ultimate focus is the shape of the soul, its progress and expansion toward beauty in the form of contemplation. So, while the relations among memory, understanding and will are important—particularly as imperfect or partial thought experiments for coming to understand the Trinity—Augustine's fundamental concern is the direction of their unified activity—that is, whether the motion of the soul tends toward beauty in the form of contemplation, or toward disorder in pursuit of spiritual or physical distraction. Put another way, the experiential and analytical distinctions within the soul are significant only insofar as they help us understand whether the soul as a unity is increasing or decreasing in its approximation of divine beauty.

To see more clearly how Augustine thinks about the expansion or contraction of the soul, let us look at three actions where the unity of remembering, understanding, and willing are perhaps most evident: how we learn, how we pray, and how we love.

In his early dialogue, *De magistro*, Augustine initially describes the purpose of speaking as either to teach or to learn, to impart information to another or to solicit information by asking questions of another.[14] The activity of signifying through speech or gesture prompts the soul to learn, understood as the recognition of the thing signified already in memory. Here, understanding is clearly dependent upon memory, and Augustine's teaching approximates the Platonic doctrine of anamnesis. Signs help us remember or discern the truth that is already present but latent within us.[15] The written word is a sign which reminds us of the spoken word, which itself is a sign of the concept present to the imagination, which is itself a sign of the apprehension of the thing itself (*mag.* 1.1-4.7).[16]

Augustine's exploration of the process of teaching and learning emphasizes a continuum from external perception (by sight or sound) to internal perception (by image and then finally beyond image). This motion of learning mirrors the ladder which describes the motion of the soul toward beauty. Both begin with the recognition of physical objects before drawing within to the contemplation of spiritual objects. The physical senses are clearly active in the initial stages of reading or hearing. Memory is clearly active in the discernment and representation of mental images. Willing accounts for the attention by which we concentrate on the external and internal perceptions of what we are learning. Understanding describes the state of the apprehension of the thing itself. But the question remains, when we finally learn something, is it a part of the soul (the mind/understanding) that apprehends the thing itself, or the soul as a whole?

There is a terminological ambiguity, perhaps insurmountable, which unavoidably complicates any interpretation of Augustine on this matter. In *De Trinitate*, Augustine notes that some Latin authors distinguish between *anima*, the term to describe that which animates each living thing, and *animus*, the term specific to the rational-animating principle of human beings only (*trin.* 15.1.1).[17] Animus, then, might be held to refer to "rational soul" or simply "reason" or "mind" as well as simply "soul" as particular to human beings. Complicating the matter is the fact that Augustine himself is not always consistent in applying the distinction.[18] Regardless, the translation of animus as either "soul" or "mind" is a linguistic difference that begs the question, Is it the mind or the whole soul that apprehends the thing being learned?

A paradox in the mystery of learning in *De magistro* helps illuminate whether Augustine thinks the mind or the whole soul apprehends the thing being learned. If a teacher supplies signs, and those signs remind me of something I already know, in what way can the teacher be said to have taught? The same paradox obtains with respect to learning itself. "When a sign is given to me, it can teach me nothing if it finds me ignorant of the thing of which it is a sign; but if I'm not ignorant, what do I learn through the sign?" (*mag.* 10.33).[19] Augustine's solution is to speak of the "inner teacher" who dwells in the "inner man":

> Regarding each of the things we understand, however, we don't consult a speaker who makes sounds outside us, but the Truth that presides within over the mind itself (sed intus ipsi menti praesidentem consulimus veritatem), though perhaps words prompt us to consult Him. What is more, He Who is consulted, He Who is said *to dwell in the inner man* (qui in interiore hominem habitare), does teach: Christ—that is, the *unchangeable power and everlasting wisdom of God*, which every rational soul does consult (quam quidem omnis rationalis anima consulit), but is disclosed to anyone, to the extent that he can apprehend it, according to his good or evil will. If at times one is mistaken, this doesn't happen by means of a defect in the Truth consulted, just as it isn't a defect in light outside that the eyes of the body are often mistaken—and we admit that we consult this light regarding visible things, that it may show them to us to the extent that we have the ability to make them out (*mag.* 11.38).

The data of memory are verified against the wisdom of the teacher who presides over the mind to the extent that will inclines toward good or evil. The more the soul has opened itself to the divine according to the scale of beauty, the more perfectly the plural activities of the soul are in tune with each other and with their respective potentials. Moreover, the touchstone of the entire activity of learning is not simply knowledge, but wisdom—mere content knowledge is partial without discernment as to its proper use, the context of its application, and its suitability to the divine will. [20]

When the light of the mind is active, when the inner light shines brightly, it is not just the mind that is illuminated but the whole of the inner man. "When we perceive something by the mind," Augustine says, using "mind," "intellect," and "reason" interchangeably (*Cum vero de iis agitur quae mente conspicimus, id est intellectu atque ratione*), "we gaze upon them immediately in the inner light of Truth, in virtue of which the so-called inner man is illuminated and rejoices (*in illa interiore luce veritatis, qua ipse qui dicitur homo interior, illustratur et fruitur*)" (*mag.* 12.40). Augustine's illumination theory does not simply articulate an epistemological position but also reflects a broader psychology. [21] Learning is not something by which the mind populates the memory, it is an activity which illuminates the entire soul, causing it to rejoice.

Further, Augustine describes this illumination which comes, when we learn, as a form of contemplation: "Our listener, if he likewise sees these things with his inward and undivided eye, knows what I'm saying from his own contemplation, not from my words" (*mag.* 12.40). Learning is a divine disclosure in which the soul—having turned inward toward itself, comes to rest in itself, and inclined itself (knowingly or not) to the source of all wisdom—has a brush with eternity in the moment of contemplative understanding. [22]

Throughout his discussion in *De magistro*, Augustine's concern is not so much the possession of knowledge as it is the moments of sight (or insight), illumination, contemplation, and discernment. [23] Indeed, Augustine places a great deal of weight on the soul's ability to discern (*cernere*) being in the first instance a function of the mind (*mens*) but describing more comprehensively the activity of the soul (*mag.* 12.40–13.41). The failure of discernment is a kind of imbecility toward God characterized by the soul's eye being divided within itself. It is in the undivided eye of the soul—the moment of attention when remembering, understanding, and willing are unified in activity and in time—that the fruits of contemplation are enjoyed. Learning, fundamentally, is a spiritual experience in which the soul delights in its expansion into the divine. [24]

The culmination of learning in a moment of contemplation approximates the activity of prayer. At the same time, learning would seem to be predicated on a kind of prayer. At the beginning of *Confessions*, Augustine asks a series of epistemological questions that underscore the relation between knowledge and prayer: "Grant me Lord to know and understand which comes first—to call upon you or to praise you, and whether knowing you

precedes calling upon you. But who calls upon you when he does not know
you? For an ignorant person might call upon someone else instead of the
right one. But surely you may be called upon in prayer that you may be
known" (*conf.* 1.1). Granting that prayer and knowledge of God may constitute a special case, the epistemological concerns recall Augustine's discussion of the use of signs in learning. If we seek an object of knowledge, it is
because we already have some intimation as to its existence and character.
Augustine shows this explicitly in *Confessions*, which itself is an extended
prayer, the dialogue of a single soul with its many impulses, memories,
intellectual insights, and difficulties of will.[25] The inclination to pursue
knowledge is itself a kind of prayer which requires the attention of the whole
soul.

In his treatise on the Sermon on the Mount, Augustine outlines what it
means to pray. Christ tells his disciples, Augustine notes, to enter into their
"bedchambers" to pray. "What are those bed-chambers but just our hearts
themselves," Augustine continues (*s. dom. m.* 2.3.11). If the door to our
bedchambers is open, then distracting thoughts and images from without rush
in to "assail the inner man." So the injunction to pray to the Father in secret is
both a warning against proud hypocritical prayer for public admiration and a
call to retreat into the solitude of one's heart, purifying it from distraction.
The purpose of prayer is not to "exercise the tongue," Augustine says, but to
"cleanse the heart" (*s. dom. m.* 2.3.12).

It makes no sense, Augustine says, to use words to pray to God when he
not only knows what we need but also what it is we are going to say. Why
then do we pray? "Here, in the first place, the answer is, that we ought to
urge our case with God, in order to obtain what we wish, not by words, but
by the things which we cherish in our mind, and by the orientation of our
thinking, with pure love and simple feeling or desire (*sed rebus quas animo
gerimus et intentione cogitationis cum dilectione pura et simplici affectu*);
but that our Lord has taught us the very ideas in words, that by committing
them to memory we may recollect those ideas at the time we pray" (*s. dom.
m.* 2.3.13). Prayer—specifically here the Lord's Prayer—is a collection of
signs committed to memory to help rouse and stimulate the soul to recollect
itself into a particular quality. Memory, understanding, and willing are each
involved, but it is the soul itself which is active in prayer.

Augustine's description of prayer is almost poetic. What constitutes
prayer is what we cherish, the orientation of our thinking, the purity of
delight and simplicity of feeling (*affectus*). Augustine writes:

> the very effort involved in prayer calms and purifies our heart, and makes it
> more capacious for receiving the divine gifts, which are poured into us spiritu-
> ally. For it is not on account of the urgency of our prayers that God hears us,
> who is always ready to give us His light, not of a material kind, but that which

is intellectual and spiritual: but we are not always ready to receive, since we are inclined towards other things, and are involved in darkness through our desire for temporal things. Hence there is brought about in prayer a turning of the heart to Him, who is ever ready to give, if we will but take what He has given; and in the very act of turning there is effected a purging of the inner eye, inasmuch as those things of a temporal kind which were desired are excluded, so that the vision of the pure heart may be able to bear the pure light, divinely shining, without any setting or change: and not only to bear it, but also to remain in it; not merely without annoyance, but also with ineffable joy, in which a life truly and sincerely blessed is perfected. (*s. dom. m.* 2.3.14)[26]

Prayer, then, calms the restless heart, purifies it, and renders it more capacious. Again, Augustine stresses the quality of the soul—its openness, its purity, its serenity—rather than its internal activity. Prayer turns the heart, purifies the spiritual sight of the inner eye, and prepares it to receive and bask in the divine light.

Augustine interprets the first line of the Lord's Prayer in such a way as to reinforce the soul as the location, as it were, of the divine indwelling. "Our Father who art in heaven" cannot specify a physical location, says Augustine, for God is not contained in space. Rather, God dwells in his temple, which is to say, God is present in the righteous, those who are of humble heart. "Hence, when it is said, Our Father which art in heaven, it is rightly understood to mean in the hearts of the righteous, as it were in His holy temple. And at the same time, in such a way that he who prays wishes Him whom he invokes to dwell in himself also; and when he strives after this, practices righteousness—a kind of service or worship by which God is attracted to dwell in the soul" (*s. dom. m.* 2.5.18).

Of the seven petitions contained in the Lord's Prayer, three refer to eternal life and four to temporal life. But all seven aim at the same cleansing of the heart understood not only as purity but also as the freedom from division. Augustine quotes from scripture (Matthew 6:22-23): "The candle of the body is the eye: if therefore your eye be single, your whole body shall be full of light. But if your eye be evil, your whole body shall be full of darkness. If, therefore, the light that is in you be darkness, how great is that darkness!" Augustine draws out what he thinks this means:

And this passage we are to understand in such a way as to learn from it that all our works are pure and well-pleasing in the sight of God, when they are done with a single heart (*si fiant simplici corde*), i.e. with a heavenly intent, having that end of love in view; for love is also the fulfilling of the law (plenitudo legis caritas; Rom 13:10). Hence we ought to take the eye here in the sense of the intent itself, wherewith we do whatever we are doing; and if this be pure and right, and looking at that which ought to be looked at, all our works which we perform in accordance therewith are necessarily good. (*s. dom. m.* 2.13.45)

Augustine's formulation here is condensed later in his more pithy statement "love and do what you will" (*Io. ev. tr.* 7, 8).[27] The fruit of prayer is the fullness of love; and increase in love is the fruition of prayer. Prayer heals the heart, Augustine continues, by ridding it of its service to two masters. Prayer allows us to "disentangle the upright intention of his heart from all doubleness: for thus he will think of the Lord with a good heart, and in simplicity of heart will seek Him" (*s. dom. m.* 2.14.48). The purity of heart that comes from prayer is to love one thing.

To be united in love in the first instance is to be united within, to participate in temporal life with a unity of soul that is focused on God and so not at odds with itself. Augustine writes: "Faith moves us, hope raises us, charity unites us" (*conf.* 13.9).[28] In love, the three theological virtues are united: faith seeks understanding; hope anticipates our union with the divine; love unites the soul in its own beauty in reference to the beauty from which it came. In the love of learning and the love intrinsic in prayer, "we are being changed from form to form, and are passing from a blurred form to a clear one" being "transformed from an ugly form into a beautiful one" (*trin.* 15.3.14).[29]

Love is, simply, the form of the soul.[30] The purpose of learning and prayer, for Augustine, or for any activity of the soul, is to become conformed to the love from which the soul has its being. At one level, this simplicity of soul is the soul in an attitude of loving attention.[31] Memory, understanding, and will intersect both internally and in the activities of learning and prayer. Their intersection yields a single moment of the soul's contemplative gaze of love—the end of our learning and the fulfillment of our created natures, a recapitulation of the pure form of unbroken attention that is the eternal Sabbath rest (*Gn. litt.* 4.18.31-32; cf. *conf.* XIII.35.50-38.53). Love, then, is the activity that begins to restore the form of the soul to the simplicity of its created nature.[32]

The several outward and inward trinities described in *De Trinitate*—the formulations of the plural relationships within the soul—are all directed toward the unified moment of the simplicity of the soul's contemplative gaze of love. That is, Augustine's analysis of the plural experiences of soul are intended to lead the soul up the ladder of beauty articulated with Evodius in the *De quantitate animae* of almost thirty years before. Augustine's purpose in investigating and reflecting on the plural experience of the soul is to lead the soul to the attentive awareness of its internal unity and its unity with God in love.

In *De Trinitate*, the reader is twice led to cross the threshold between corporeal and incorporeal attentiveness. The ascent of the soul which begins in book eight and culminates in the inner vision of book ten is interrupted with a return to the external vision of the "trinity of the outer man" of book eleven, before the reader is again brought to the spiritual climax of book fourteen.[33] As the soul moves from external to internal vision, the object of attention becomes the soul itself and what is most immediate to it, viz., itself: "Here you have the mind seeking to know itself and all afire with this studious concern. So it is loving. But what is it loving?" (*trin.* 10.2.5-6). It is loving itself. Consistent with our reading of *De magistro*, Augustine insists that everything known is a word impressed upon consciousness (*animus*), even as he struggles to find a word to express the "knowledge with love" (*cum amore notitia*) which resides in memory.[34] "So when the mind knows and loves itself, its word is joined to it with love" in a kind of presence or attention.[35] Love, then, may be understood as the soul's simple moment of presence to itself (*trin.* 10.3.12) in which it comes to know itself in its totality as both subject and object.[36] By the time the soul is led to ascend again in book fourteen, love has replaced will in the internal trinity as the soul comes "to remember and understand and love him by whom it was made," thereby becoming wise (*trin.* 14.4.15).[37]

There is never a time, Augustine maintains, when the soul does not remember, know, and love itself.[38] In its expansion to simplicity, the soul comes to love itself properly, and consequently, "the man who knows how to love himself loves God" (*trin.* 14.4.18). In an extensive quotation from Cicero's *Hortensius*, Augustine makes clear that he sees learning as a progressive sharpening of the mind in contemplative wisdom (*trin.* 14.5.26). All this the soul learns "by a wholly intimate instruction from within" in which it recognizes that its ascent or expansion is entirely by God's gracious doing (*trin.* 14.4.21).

The renewal of the soul deformed by sin does not take place in one moment of conversion but over time as the image of the divine is restored day by day, as the soul transfers its love from temporal things to eternal (*trin.* 14.5.22-25). "For the soul has a single nature, and it has both the wisdom of the flesh when it follows inferior things, and the wisdom of the Spirit when choosing the superior, just as water's single nature both freezes from cold and melts from heat" (*exp. prop. Rom.* 49).[39] Book fifteen of *De Trinitate* renders the single nature of the soul in its clearest form. "To put it in a nutshell we can say: 'It is I who remember, I who understand, I who love with all three of these things—I who am not either memory or understanding or love, but have them" (*trin.* 15.6.42). Significantly, echoing the pattern of his early dialogue *Soliloquia*, Augustine ends *De Trinitate* first with a soliloquy addressed to his soul and then with a prayer addressed to God, "Let me remember you, let me understand you, let me love you. Increase these things in me until you refashion me entirely. . . . So when we do attain to you, there will be an end to these many things which we say and do not attain, and you will remain one, yet all in all, and we shall say one thing praising you in unison, even ourselves being also made one in you" (*trin.* 15.6.51).

In learning, praying, and loving, the soul comes to attend to its plural structure not from amidst its restlessness but from within its newfound simplicity, which Augustine describes perhaps most poetically and forcefully in this way:

> But I am scattered in times whose order I do not understand . . . until that day when, purified and molten by the fire of your love, I flow together to merge into you. Then shall I find stability and solidity in you, in your truth which imparts form to me (*conf.* 9.29–30).[40]

NOTES

1. See, e.g., *sol.* 2.1ff. These ambiguities are most apparent throughout *conf.*, though they also permeate Augustine's discussions in *mag.*, *c. acad.*, *lib. arb.*, and *trin.*

2. See, most prominently, L. Zuzne, *Names in the History of Psychology* (New York: John Wiley and Sons, 1957), who incorrectly attributes the origin of faculty psychology to Augustine. B. Bubacz, *St. Augustine's Theory of Knowledge* (Lewiston, NY: Edwin Mellen Press, 1981,); A. Dihle, *The Theory of the Will in Classical Antiquity* (Berkeley: University of California Press, 1982); E. Gilson, *The Christian Philosophy of Saint Augustine*, trans. L. E. M. Lynch (New York: Random House, 1960); and R. H. Nash, *The Light of the Mind: St. Augustine's Theory of Knowledge* (Lexington, KY: University of Kentucky Press, 1969) represent fine Augustinian scholarship with which I differ in matters of emphasis, not on fundamental conclusions.

3. *epp.* 158–164, 169.

4. "For if Christ died for those only who with clear intelligence can discern these things, our labor in the Church is almost spent in vain" (*ep.* 169.1.4).

5. At *sol.* 2.1 Augustine prays that he be granted two things, to know his own soul and to know God.

6. The debate over the origin of the soul in Augustine is voluminous. See R. J. O'Connell, *St. Augustine's Early Theory of Man* (Cambridge: Harvard University Press, 1968); idem., *Imagination and Metaphysics in St. Augustine* (Milwaukee: Marquette University Press, 1986); idem., *The Origin of the Soul in St. Augustine's Later Works* (New York: Fordham University Press, 1987); G. J. P. O'Daly, *Augustine's Philosophy of Mind* (Berkeley: University of California Press, 1987); idem., "Did St. Augustine Ever Believe in the Soul's Pre-existence?", *Augustinian Studies* 5 (1974) 227–235; idem., "Augustine and the Origin of Souls," in *Platonismus und Christentum. Festschrift für Heinrich Dörrie* (Munster: Aschendorffsche Verlagsbuchhandlung, 1983) for detailed coverage of the most essential issues of debate as well as bibliography.

7. On the limits of the discursive character of language, see T. Breyfogle, "Intellectus," in *Augustine Through the Ages: An Encyclopedia*, ed. Allan Fitzgerald, O.S.A. (Grand Rapids: Eerdmans, 1999) 452–454; idem., "Memory and Imagination in Augustine's *Confessions*," in *Literary Imagination, Ancient and Modern: Essays in Honor of David Grene*, ed. Todd Breyfogle (Chicago: University of Chicago Press, 1999) 139–154.

8. The English translation in NPNF erroneously inserts the notion of faculties, translating "we can speak of each of these faculties severally in its own order."

9. Memoria and intellectus do have qualified reflexive qualities in that the memory can remember itself, just as the intellect can think about itself. Indeed, in *conf.* 10, memoria expands to be synonymous with the whole of the conscious and unconscious awareness. But neither memoria nor intellectus can embrace the whole soul on their own.

10. See P. Burnell, *The Augustinian Person* (Washington, DC: The Catholic University Press, 2005) ch. 2, pp. 54–70, for a fundamental discussion of what he calls "the faculties of the human personality" while rejecting a standard faculty psychology.

11. See, e.g., *conf.* book 3.

12. *ep.* 166, written to Jerome in 415, advances an elaborate argument about the soul's incorporeality, though we see him working with the same assumption from his earliest writings, including *sol.*, through such fundamental works as *conf.* and *Gen. litt.*

13. *quant. an.* 79; for other early accounts, comparable in overall scope but differing in some details, see *Gn. c. man.* 1.25.43, *vera rel.* 26.49; see also R. Hazelton, "The Devotional Life," in *A Companion to the Study of St. Augustine*, ed. R. W. Battenhouse (New York: Oxford University Press, 1955).

14. Peter King, trans., *Augustine: Against the Academicians and The Teacher* (Indianapolis, IN: Hackett, 1995) is a fine translation with useful notes and an essay on *De magistro*.

15. Cf. *sol.* 2.35: Those trained in liberal disciplines "disinter the knowledge buried in forgetfulness in themselves."

16. Augustine's dialogical approach in *mag.* enacts the very use of speech and signs even as he and his interlocutor, his son Adeodatus, learn together what learning is.

17. My quotations are from Edmund Hill, trans., *The Trinity / Augustine* (New York: New City Press, 1998), whose translation and commentary are extremely insightful and stimulating. (References to *trin.* list Hill chapter divisions before the *PL* paragraph designation.)

18. Cf. *c. acad.* 3.35, where life, character, and mind seem interchangeable.

19. See D. Chidester, "The Symbolism of Learning in St. Augustine," *Harvard Theological Review* 76 (1983) 73–90, for an examination of the symbolism of learning in Augustine.

20. For explicitly theological accounts of Augustine's understanding of wisdom as it relates to Christology, see G. Madec, "Christus, scientia et sapientia nostra. Le principe de cohérence de la doctrine augustinienne," *Recherches augustiniennes* 10 (1975) 77–85; and R. Williams, "Sapientia and the Trinity: Reflections on *De Trinitate*," in Bernard Bruning, Mathijs Lamberigts, and J. van Houtem, eds. *Collectanea Augustiniana: Mélanges T J van Bavel*, Vol 1; Bibliotheca Ephemeridum Theologicarum Lovaniensium XCII–A (Louvain: Leuven University Press, 1990) 317–332.

21. On Augustine's theory of illumination, see Breyfogle, "Intellectus"; Bubacz, *St. Augustine's Theory of Knowledge*; Nash, *The Light of the Mind*; O'Daly, *Augustine's Philosophy of Mind*.

22. See O'Daly, *Augustine's Philosophy of Mind*, 208, on Augustine's varied terminology of introspection.

23. B. Longergan, *Insight: A Study of Human Understanding* (New York: Philosophical Library, 1970), is useful for thinking about the notion of insight in Augustine's epistemology.

24. See P. Hadot, *Philosophy as a Way of Life: Spiritual Exercises From Socrates to Foucault*, Arnold Davidson, ed., Michael Chase, trans. (Oxford: Blackwell, 1995), for philosophical learning as a kind of spiritual exercise.

25. See R. McMahon, *Augustine's Prayerful Ascent: An Essay on the Literary Form of the Confessions* (Athens: University of Georgia Press, 1989), for an insightful examination of *conf.* as prayer.

26. *quia ipsa orationis intentio cor nostrum serenat et purgat, capaciusque efficit ad excipienda divina munera, quae spiritaliter nobis infunduntur. Non enim ambitione precum nos exaudit Deus, qui semper paratus est dare suam lucem nobis non visibilem sed intellegibilem et spiritalem; sed nos non semper parati sumus accipere, cum inclinamur in alia et rerum temporalium cupiditate tenebramur. Fit ergo in oratione conversio cordis ad eum qui semper dare paratus est, si nos capiamus quod dederit, et in ipsa conversione purgatio interioris oculi, cum excluduntur ea quae temporaliter cupiebantur, ut acies simplicis cordis ferre possit simplicem lucem divinitus sine ullo occasu aut immutatione fulgentem, nec solum ferre sed etiam manere in illa, non tantum sine molestia sed etiam cum ineffabili gaudio, quo vere ac sinceriter beata vita perficitur.*

27. Cf. *ep.* 167.6.4: *lex itaque libertatis lex caritatis est*; also *en. Ps.* 67.17.

28. See also *sol.* 1.1.3.

29. *Transformamur ergo dicit, de forma in formam mutamur, atque transimus de forma obscura in formam lucidam; quia et ipsa obscura, imago Dei est . . . a deformi forma formosam transformatur in formam.*

30. For an extended discussion of the notion of love as form and formlessness, see Hans Urs von Balthasar, *Love Alone is Credible*, trans. D. C. Schindler (San Francisco: Ignatius Press, 2004).

31. See *trin.* 9.3.18: "the mind's self-knowledge is commensurate with its being . . . its self-love is commensurate with its self-knowledge and its being" (trans. O'Daly, p. 211).

32. Mind/soul is commanded to know itself so that it may "contemplate itself and live in conformity to its own nature" (*trin.* 10.2.7).

33. On the relation between the structure and content of *trin.*, see J. Cavadini, "The Structure and Intention of Augustine's *De Trinitate*," *Augustinian Studies* 23 (1992) 103–123; L. Ayres, "The Christological Context of Augustine's *De Trinitate* XIII: Toward Relocating Books VIII–XV,"*Augustinian Studies* 29:1 (1998) 111–39; idem., "The Discipline of Self-Knowledge in Augustine's *De Trinitate* Book X," in *The Passionate Intellect: Essays on the Transformation of Classical Traditions, Presented to Professor I. G. Kidd* (New Brunswick: Transaction Publishers, 1995) 261–296.

34. In introspection, the link between knowledge (*notitia*) and love (*amor*) becomes clear (*trin.* 10.16). See also O. M. T. O'Donovan, *The Problem of Self-Love in Saint Augustine* (New Haven: Yale University Press, 1980) 60–92.

35. *trin.* 9.2.15: "*Verbum est igitur, quod nunc discernere et insinuare volumus, cum amore notitia. Cum itaque se mens novit et amat, iungitur ei amore verbum eius. Et quoniam amat notitiam et novit amorem, et verbum in amore est et amor in verbo, et utrumque in amante atque dicente.*"

36. *Gn. litt.* 7.21.28: "When it [the soul] knows itself in its searching, it knows itself as one whole subject, and so as one whole object; for not as one thing knows another, but as a totality, does it know itself" (cf. *conf.* 13.2–4, 10).

37. See also *trin.* 14.1.14: to remember oneself is to be present to oneself.

38. See, e.g., *lib arb.* 2.7: we understand we exist and are alive, and understand that we understand that we exist and are alive.

39. See P. Fredriksen, *Augustine on Romans* (Chico, CA: Scholars Press, 1982).

40. Cf. von Balthasar, *Love Alone Is Credible*, 126.

Chapter Two

Teaching Freud and Interpreting Augustine's *Confessions*

Sandra Lee Dixon

This chapter will highlight two words of the overall topic, "teaching Freud" and interpreting Augustine's *Confessions*. I emphasize "teaching Freud" because the literature on the psychological study of Augustine, largely psychoanalytical as it is, rarely cites Freud at all.[1] Yet Freudian ideas abound, especially in the articles from the 1960s that launched research on this topic. If we claim to teach Freud, we should, I believe, let students sharpen their minds on the words, at least in translation, of Freud himself. Moreover, self-discipline in the psychological study of Augustine is crucial, as historians and theologians will remind us.[2] If we do not start by disciplining ourselves in our use of theory, I have little hope that we will do so in the interpretation of Augustine's writing.

I proceed both in this essay and in class by thinking of the conclusions of psychoanalytic theory and practice as tools of investigation for understanding a perplexing phenomenon. To employ them deftly, one must, of course, know how they are put together. So we spend time taking them apart and examining the pieces. Then we can reconstruct the tools and test more fully our understanding by using them to produce something different. For those of us who like this sort of project, Freudian theory offers a marvelous means of investigation and Augustine's *Confessions* a wonder of material to reconceive in Freudian terms.

The rest of this chapter will explain more specifically how I try to apply these conceptualizations in class. I will describe the setting and my assumptions about the students and how they learn. Then I will discuss how we examine Freud's conclusions as a prelude to the psychological interpretation of Augustine's *Confessions*. I will remark on the teaching of the *Confessions* itself and give an example of how a class might proceed with the psychoanalytic interpretation of the text. Engaging the students in trying to analyze Freud's own writing and apply it to Augustine's *Confessions* will raise major scholarly questions in the study of Freud and in the contemporary psychological study of the *Confessions*.

THE CLASS AND THE TEACHER

A seminar format best serves my purpose. By "seminar format" I mean that the students are to have read the assignment seriously (increasing their ability to do so during the academic term), that discussion of the text (books open and quoted) predominates, and that the teacher asks questions, coaches the students, and guides them through and back to the text. The demand on the teacher is high in this form of teaching, of course, because one has to be ready to propose contrasting or complementary passages without knowing in advance the issues that will arise.[3] But the texts I suggest from Freud are short; reading notes last from year to year, and so do the diagrams.

I favor drawing diagrams to explicate Freud's theory. My own diagrams deepen my familiarity with the text and give me a framework for fielding suggestions from the floor.[4] I also often give the chalk to the students and ask them to start drawing on the board, usually with suggestions from their classmates. This makes them nervous at first, but after I voice my appreciation of their efforts—even those we improve together as a class—they show more freedom and agency.

If the class is larger than a seminar, similar exercises can work by dividing the class up into small groups, each with a passage to diagram. The teacher decides which order the groups should follow in putting their diagrams on the board. The class discusses the diagrams and suggests modifications, possible connections between them, their relationship to the text, and so forth.[5]

Even teachers who do not feel comfortable with the style outlined above may want to know what texts can work, why, and to what ends. The texts I recommend below can certainly be adapted to other modes of presentation.

CHOOSING THE EARLY FREUD

I use the early Freud in my class on psychobiography. I usually choose *On Dreams*, his condensation of his masterpiece *The Interpretation of Dreams*, and I supplement it with *Five Lectures on Psycho-analysis*. A practical advantage of these books is that they are short. Using the *Interpretation of Dreams* instead of *On Dreams* would be academically more rigorous but would require much more of the course's duration just to advance a basic understanding of Freud's ideas.

The theoretical justification for these choices starts with the commonly voiced concern that Freud's ideas are culturally conditioned and cannot apply to other cultures. Concern about culture is one of the major questions in the psychological study of Augustine.[6] While Freud's ideas are culturally conditioned, the concepts in his early works, covering what is known as the "first topography," have been thought to apply more readily across cultures than the ideas of the more familiar "second topography," or id-ego-superego model of the mind.[7] In addition, many of the ideas of the first topography appear in the later schools and offshoots of psychoanalysis. Yet many students have never seen them explicated and these readings urge students to explore this part of Freud's work more fully.

The first topography is so called because Freud himself compared the mind to the layers of the ground. The underground is an image for the unconscious (ucs.)—not readily apparent, full of hidden activity, capable of making variations in the surface. The surface is an image for the conscious (cs.) aspects of mental life—in full view, easily accessed, a source of pressure and material for the area underground (the unconscious processes of the mind). The first layers of the soil are analogous to the "pre-conscious" (pcs.) processes—not readily apparent but not difficult to expose, connecting the visible to the deeply buried, affected by both upper and lower layers. The pre-conscious in Freud's view includes the processes and patterns that could become conscious but often do not, such as the words of a song one knows. The unconscious, on the other hand, is inaccessible without a great deal of work and energy, and it makes its processes felt obliquely or in strange outcroppings on the surface.[8]

The processes that formed this topography, according to Freud, resemble the ones geographers and geologists know: the processes of physics.[9] That is to say, the topographical model includes the idea that pressures could build in the system of the mind, contents could shift, new formations could obtrude into consciousness. These processes will receive further attention below in the discussion of teaching *On Dreams*.

Freud derived the second topography, the id-ego-superego model of the mind, from the first. The second topography depends on further abstraction from the data that Freud interpreted to formulate the first topography. The first topography used concepts that were themselves abstracted from his psychoanalytic practice. With these concepts he described and coordinated an understanding of the processes he believed to underlie the conscious words spoken by patients in analytic sessions. The second topography adds abstractions in order to conceptualize the results of the first topography's processes. These abstractions in turn allow more influence of Freud's own culture on the development of his ideas.[10] Culture would flow through the patients' conscious and pre-conscious to affect the unconscious and the patterns of the id, ego, and superego. As Freud and his followers gave content to these abstract constructs from their work in European culture, they sketched out theoretical constructs and used the constructs to interpret new data. As they did so, more and more interaction could occur between the theory and the psychoanalysts' own culture.

Even scholars rejecting the universality of Freudian formulations of the id, ego, and superego can still agree that childhood urges can undergo repression in response to cultural pressures. They can agree that the urges remain active, respond to other pressures, and emerge in different forms. They can discuss the interaction of culture and psyche in these terms without having to import the conclusions of the second topography. Proponents of the first topography can emphasize it and downplay the second.

WORKING IN CLASS WITH THE EARLY FREUD

The pedagogical value of *On Dreams* and *Five Lectures on Psycho-Analysis* is that they allow the students to see Freud's range of concerns and why he thinks we should believe his conclusions. Attending to the context Freud sets for his argument, and to which he returns, enhances its plausibility greatly. In reading *On Dreams* one must linger for a few moments on the indicators of context in order not to forget them. Recognizing them lets students draw together different strands of Freud's theory, especially his emphases on science and meaning.

Regarding context, notice that Freud starts the book: "During the epoch which may be described as pre-scientific, men had no difficulty in finding an explanation of dreams."[11] Here he introduces several important themes of the book: science and what counts as scientific, explanation, and dreams. Then follows a list of the aspects of dreams that might be explained, now that the scientific era has arrived. Before the end of the second paragraph, Freud has the reader crossing from explanation to interpretation of meaning. Such interpretation will occupy our study of Augustine: "what stands in the foreground of our interest is the question of the *significance* of dreams."[12]

Interpreting dreams is not the concern of this paper,[13] but interpreting the text to discover possible indicators of unconscious processes is.[14] We will follow Freud as he "seeks to discover whether dreams can be interpreted, whether the content of individual dreams has a 'meaning,' such as we are accustomed to find in other psychical structures."[15] Here one might ask, "what 'other psychical structures'?" This can serve as a question for the class, because sharp students will have noticed an answer two pages later, at the beginning of chapter two: "I had been led to fresh conclusions on the subject of dreams by applying to them a new method of psychological investigation which had done excellent service in the solution of phobias, obses-sions and delusions, etc."[16] "Phobias, obsessions, delusions, etc.," are the other psychical structures, and they, like dreams, appear meaningful to Freud. Here the teacher can underscore an important question in the study of Freud: What are the different conscious phenomena that Freud identifies as coming from similar unconscious processes?

Freud now begins a process of thinking by analogies.[17] He examines dreams as analogous to psychological pathologies. In addition, he implicitly puts the analogy back in the context of what counts as scientific by including words evocative of medical research: "The numerous analogies that exist between dream life and a great variety of conditions of psychical *illness* in waking life have indeed been correctly *observed* by many *medical investigators.*"[18]

Freud soon gives a sample of one of his own dreams so he can demon-strate dream interpretation as related to both the function and the meaning of dreams. A diagram, as aesthetically rich or impoverished as you like, can set out the dream's main components in the center of the chalkboard. It should include especially the objects: a dining table (a rectangle), spinach (circle with wavy lines in it), Frau E.L. (whose identity Freud is purposely obscur-ing), Freud next to Frau E.L. (circles labeled Frau E.L. and SF will do nicely), a pair of eyes or eyeglasses. Then the class can pick out Freud's free associations to the dream.[19] These can be added to the diagram in rays spreading out from the key dream elements in the center. The advantage of this process is that it leads the students to take the work of analysis seriously. The analytic process is more crucial for this part of the exercise than are the conclusions of Freud's dream analysis.

Further theoretical ideas can be mapped onto the diagram as one follows Freud through the text. When the class studies chapter four, where Freud discusses condensation, the diagram will already give a visual image of his points: "the dream work has carried out a work of compression or *condensa-tion* on a large scale. . . . From every element in the dream's content associa-tive threads branch out in two or more directions."[20] The few elements of the dream and the large number of rays of associated material make the dream's condensation evident.

The students may now raise a key question about Freud's ideas: Why do the dream elements seem insignificant compared to the amount of material associated with them? Freud's discussion in chapter five of "displacement" answers this question. He says, "What stands out boldly and clearly in the dream as its essential content must, after analysis, be satisfied with playing an extremely subordinate rôle among the dream thoughts."[21] Students grasp his point because they can see on the board that what was important about the dream elements no longer looks important in the whole. Importance, which Freud thinks of as energy (in analogy to physics),[22] has been displaced from its original home in the dream thoughts onto the distorted elements that appear in the dream.

But students may persist in asking the important question of why such rigmarole should take place at all. The answer shows up in chapter eight of *On Dreams*. Freud says that the elaborate process of dream formation happens because of the feature shown by analysis of his dream that pertains to all dreams: "I should eventually arrive at thoughts which would surprise me, whose presence in me I was unaware of, which were not only *alien* but also *disagreeable* to me, and which I should, therefore, feel inclined to dispute energetically."[23] The students, thanks in part to the diagram, are prepared to see the "alien" and "disagreeable" nature of the dream thoughts: Freud's own discomfort about whether he was "selfish" or "unselfish," indebted or forced to pay too highly for whatever he got.[24] In terms of the first topography, the unpleasantness of the dream thoughts lends pressure to push them from the pre-conscious to the unconscious. The pressure, repression, then causes them to take different forms. A result is "overdetermination," the representation of one unconscious thought by many conscious outcroppings, and the relationships of each outcropping to many unconscious thoughts.

Once the processes and the most basic material shaped by them are understood, some students will be ready to consent to Freud's conclusion: "The dream thoughts . . . are not clothed in the prosaic language usually employed by our thoughts, but are on the contrary represented symbolically by means of similes and metaphors, in images resembling those of poetic speech."[25] This sentence links dream interpretation to the interpretation of Augustine's *Confessions*, for it is creative, poetic speech (not the "free association" suggested by Kligerman).[26]

Two key, related thoughts must be borne in mind in the Freudian interpretation of symbolic speech. First is the idea that dreams, with the representations that compose them, are wish fulfillments. That is, they represent the fulfilling of some desire that has not been fulfilled in ordinary waking life. Second, the representation stands not only for the fulfilled wish but also for the desire still awaiting satisfaction. Any fulfilled wish hints at the original longing.[27] Thus, in Freud's own dream, he wished to be seen as "unselfish" and as having paid for whatever he got, but the lingering sense that he was not seen as he wanted is also portrayed in the dream.

Freud treats the famous psychoanalytic ideas of repressed sexuality and infantile sexuality only quite late in the discussions in both *On Dreams* and *Five Lectures on Psycho-Analysis*. In *On Dreams* he notes that the theory of repression does not require that sexual desires be most liable to repression, but allows that they could be. Primarily, he appeals to fact: "No other group of instincts has been submitted to such far-reaching suppression by the demands of cultural education." He adds quite simply that "we have become acquainted with infantile sexuality, which is often so unobtrusive in its manifestations and is always overlooked and misunderstood."[28]

No discussion of the Oedipal conflict follows. Teaching Augustine's *Confessions* will gravitate toward it. For a straightforward presentation we turn to the *Five Lectures on Psycho-Analysis*, a collection of lectures that Freud delivered at Clark University in 1910. In brief, "the child takes both of its parents, and more particularly one of them, as an object of its erotic wishes. In doing so, it usually follows some indication from its parents, whose affection bears the clearest characteristics of a sexual activity, even though of one that is inhibited in its aims." This last sentence indicates Freud's broad understanding of "sexuality" and his emphasis that not all sexuality leads to sexual intercourse.[29] Instead, as the text says, it can be "inhibited in its aims" and manifested as parental affection. Freud's explanation of the Oedipal conflict continues:

> As a rule, a father prefers his daughter, and a mother her son; the child reacts to this by wishing, if he is a son, to take his father's place, and, if she is a daughter, her mother's. The feelings which are aroused in these relations between parents and children . . . are not only of a positive or affectionate kind but also of a negative or hostile one. The complex which is thus formed up is doomed to early repression; but it continues to exercise a great and lasting influence from the unconscious. It is to be suspected that, together with its extensions, it constitutes the *nuclear complex* of every neurosis, and we may expect to find it no less actively at work in other regions of mental life.[30]

These "other regions" include dreams and creative activities, like imagistic writing.

When students are naysayers, as some should be if they are grappling with the material, they are raising the big questions of doubt about Freud's ideas. Returning to the context of Freud's theory can help. Freud as a medical practitioner cared greatly about whether his ideas worked. Evidence for their working comes from *Five Lectures on Psycho-Analysis*. The first lecture includes the description of the very startling medical case that led Freud and his senior collaborator Breuer toward the ideas of psychoanalysis. The famous "Anna O.," described in the lecture, had a strange set of symptoms which were relieved by her talking about them. Like good scientific investigators, Breuer and Freud took seriously the evidence—her feeling better—and tried to understand what might allow such change and how they could more surely produce it.[31] By reading excerpts of Freud's summary of the "talking cure," the teacher can help the students understand why Freud thought the scientific analogy to geology ever made sense and why pursuing it by analogy into a field like dream interpretation might be useful: he was trying to extend a technique that could relieve serious physical and psychological disorders.

FREUDIAN DREAMWORK AND AUGUSTINE'S STORIES

To use these methods on the study of Augustine and his *Confessions* one must remember that the application of those ideas to the material in the *Confessions* is itself an analogy.[32] This effort may make vivid for the students perennial questions in the appropriation of Freud for religious studies: How analogous is everyday thought to psychological disturbance? How analogous is creative writing to the symptoms of psychological distress or to dreamwork? If we agree with Freud, we will say that the analogies extend very far indeed. Or we may think they do not extend very far at all. Or we may believe that the results vary depending on the material. Raising these issues, interpretation of the *Confessions* proves useful for reflecting on how widely and well Freud's ideas apply. Application of Freud's ideas to Augustine's *Confessions* can follow a procedure in class similar to the elucidation of Freud's ideas themselves. Based on careful reading of the book, students can begin to diagram relationships between events in Augustine's life or ideas in his text. Then they can create a diagram of Freudian inferences. One student, or even several, will usually raise some psychological problem in understanding Augustine or his text. Their standard queries include, why does he look at God as he does? What's his relationship to his mother? Why was he so hung up on sex? Good starting points all. A few suggestions on the practicalities of handling the text, then an example, will show how the work can proceed.

The text of the *Confessions* reveals immediately that the book is not primarily designed as a chronological narrative, although it does loosely follow the course of Augustine's life from his birth to his age at writing, roughly his mid-forties. Therefore, consulting the timelines or introductions often included at the front of classroom editions of the *Confessions* can help both students and instructor.[33] One's own notes about locations of specific life events in the text will be crucial. In addition, several short, good introductions to Augustine's life can orient the reader to Augustine's time period and culture.[34]

Other important notes regard translations. Unless the professor can read Latin, the best approach is to have more than one translation at hand. All the recent editions available for classroom use, and many of the older ones, will do. A brief comparison of specific passages will be sufficient to show that leaning heavily on the English words would be ill-advised (e.g., IX.i.1). The class can tune its critical skills by asking what to make of the differences in translations, a question closely related to a major issue in psychoanalysis: What is the importance of specific words compared to major themes, visual images, typical symbols, and behaviors? Students will usually conclude that they should work with what is common to the translations, such as the broad outlines of particular events, invocations of God or the mother church, and laments about Augustine's own sinfulness. The translations can be easily coordinated because the "books" (what we would call chapters) of the *Confessions* are divided and the parts are numbered.[35]

An example of psychological interpretation one could try in class starts with Augustine's illness and near-baptism (*Confessions* I.xi.17), proceeds to the incident of the baths (II.iii.5–8), and relies on the biographical sketch of Monica (IX.ix.19–22) for support. The example combines several advantages: it starts with Augustine's childhood as psychoanalysis would encourage; it raises in good psychoanalytic fashion his relationship with his mother and father; it forces the interpreter to deal seriously with various parts of the book but does not require knowledge of every aspect of it.

Starting with I.xi.17, I would ask the class what features of the story of the boy Augustine's illness and near-baptism they notice. The answers will recap the story: his mother Monica was a Christian; when Augustine got very ill he asked to be baptized, even though he was just a child; his mother arranged for a baptism, but it did not take place once he quickly recovered; Monica and the rest of the family were Christian, except Patricius, Augustine's father; Patricius did not interfere with Monica's raising Augustine as a Christian; Augustine thinks Monica was better than Patricius, but Monica obeyed Patricius anyway because, according to Augustine, she thought God commanded her to do so; Augustine complains that his family did the wrong thing by not having him baptized in spite of his recovery.

The theme of division between Augustine's parents, one of the issues in published psychological studies, is fairly strong in this passage.[36] Three columns can be set up on the board, one labelled "Monica," one further right labelled "Both," one beyond that labelled "Patricius," with room left for a diagram of the Freudian interpretation. Under "Monica," the class will want words like "Christian (I.xi.17)"; "better than husband (I.xi.17)"; "obeyed husband (I.xi.17)." Under "Patricius," they will place "not Christian (I.xi.17)"; "worse than wife (I.xi.17)"; "accepted wife's obedience (I.xi.17)."

The list will lengthen when one turns to II.iii.5-8. In this incident Augustine's father comes home from the public baths, where he has seen signs of passage through puberty in Augustine's physique, and tells Monica that they may soon have grandchildren. Monica feels much less joy and warns Augustine in private about the dangers of adultery. Augustine scoffs, at least inside himself, at her admonitions. The students might want to put under the column "Monica," ideas like "worry about Augustine's sexuality (II.iii.6)"; "not telling her husband about what she said to Augustine (II.iii.7)"; "thought education might turn Augustine toward God (II.iii.9)." Opposite phrases would belong under "Patricius": "happy about Augustine's sexuality (II.iii.6)"; "telling Monica how he felt about Augustine's sexual maturing (II.iii.6)"; "ambitious *only* for Augustine's worldly success (II.iii.9)"; "catechumen in Catholic Church (II.iii.6)."

The area between the columns can house a list of Monica's and Patricius' points of agreement: "importance of Augustine's education (II.iii.8)"; "hope for Augustine's worldly success (II.iii.8)" (although Augustine insists that their reasons were different, the hope itself was similar). More such points will come out in the examination of the biography of Monica in IX.ix.19-22: no quarrels in marriage (IX.ix.19); both baptized Christians by end of life (IX.ix.22); she was virtuous and gentle (IX.ix.19 and 20) and he was kind (IX.ix.19).

Yet IX.ix.19-22 is also a good place to find further divisions between Monica and Patricius. For instance, she was patient and reasonable in her discussions (IX.ix.19). He was hot-tempered and, when irritated, not suscep-tible to reason (IX.ix.19).

After setting up such a chart, one can reintroduce the psychoanalytic questions. First, is there anything on the chart that Augustine might find unpleasant enough to have repressed? On a new diagram, the responses can be set out horizontally below a broad, dark horizontal line. This line repre-sents the repression barrier,[37] the power of mental regulation holding back from consciousness the unpleasantness retained in the unconscious. The stu-dents might suggest placing below the repression barrier Patricius' variability between anger and kindness, as well as the distress that Augustine might have felt as a child about the division between his parents.

The class can then reflect on that visual presentation of repression and guide their psychoanalytic exploration with the following questions: (1) What is the wish associated with each repressed thought or feeling? (2) According to Freud's description of condensation and displacement, what is a plausible series of transformations of the original wish? (3) What is the resulting disguised expression? (4) How does this later expression include both the unfulfilled wish and its desired fulfillment?

If my experience serves as a guide, the students can answer question 1— What is the wish?—if they take a few minutes to discuss it. Question 2 on the unconscious processes of transformation will probably elude them until they try to take an educated guess about what the resulting disguised expression might be—that is, until they answer question 3. Once they make some guess-es about the later disguised expressions, they can try to trace a plausible path of condensation and displacement. This analysis resembles what they saw in Freud's analysis of his own dream.

For instance, if the students concentrate on Patricius' variability between anger and kindness, they might identify the unfulfilled wish as a longing for a more reliably kind father. Some student will probably already know that Freud saw God as an exalted father figure.[38] So they can try out some images of God in Augustine's *Confessions* and see if the figurative language shows both the unfulfilled wish for a reliably kind father and its fulfillment. A good passage to suggest that they examine in order to see the disguised portrayal of Augustine's repressed discomfort comes in II.ii.4. In this somewhat startling passage, Augustine claims that God punished him mercifully to bring him back to the only true pleasure, God's own self. He even claims that God kills human beings so that they will die closer to God. In these thoughts we have hints of a father figure's shifts of mood—punishment can be joined to the idea of anger, bitterness affects pleasure, a desire for closeness emerges between the one who threatens and the one who receives the threat. These thoughts represent the repressed elements of thought and feeling about a father both irascible and kind. Below the repression barrier on the board, one could add an arrow from Patricius' variability between anger and kindness so that it points to a newly added word "threat." The arrow could pass thence to the added word "fear," then on to "punishment" (also added). Here the class would be explicating the condensation at work in the images in II.ii.4.

But the powerful figure portrayed in II.ii.4 is not unpredictably variable, as Patricius was. Instead, Augustine assures us that God was always present, always well intentioned, reliable in disciplining people, ever seeking a beneficial outcome. Similar language appears elsewhere in the *Confessions*[39] and provides support for aspects of this interpretation of his conscious representation of God. The arrow in the diagram could turn upward from "punishment" to break through the line of the repression barrier and point to words, written in the diagram's area for consciousness, like "present," "well-intentioned," "reliable." Perhaps a summation of Augustine's idea in II.ii.4, "God's well intentioned punishment" could surmount them all. This part of the diagram would clarify that the elements spelled out from the condensed image have been displaced, as Augustine's feelings related to Patricius have attached themselves to images of God.

Concern with a father's anger, punitiveness, and long-term positive disposition toward his son is, of course, one of the major components of the classic formulation of the Oedipal conflict.[40] Could the students suggest a plausible transformation of such experience, according to Freud's rules of dream interpretation, leading to Augustine's decision to recount Monica's admonitions against his committing adultery? Could his emphasis on her concern serve as a transformed expression of Patricius' interference with Augustine's Oedipal sexual urges toward Monica? That is, if Patricius impeded Augustine's Oedipal advances, and the paternal prohibition was repressed, could it be transformed by being displaced onto Monica in Augustine's portrayal of her admonition to him?

Readers will want to know that the interpretation just proposed is dramatically at odds with any elaborated thus far in psychological studies of Augustine.[41] I advance it because most of those already published have relied heavily on the second topography and thereby introduced many considerations of doubtful relevance to Augustine's life. The Oedipal interpretations to date have not been tied closely to Freud's actual writings, either. Consider the following scenarios, suggested by historians of Augustine's world. While the father in late Roman antiquity could be a very threatening influence, [42] he also would spend a lot of time outside the home. Moreover, the boy near the age Freud indicated for the Oedipal conflict—that is, around 5 or 6—was allowed a lot of freedom to play outdoors. The mother who also wanted a reputation as a good wife, however, was not allowed to spend much time out in the open. This social pattern permitted the boy to loosen the bonds of infantile love for his mother without great risk of threat from his father. Therefore, the pressures at Augustine's time that would have affected the unconscious would not necessarily have led to the patterns of thoughts and feelings explicated through the second topography, specifically not the dynamics of the superego imputed to Augustine. [43]

These considerations could lead to practice with the concept of "overdetermination." One could point out that each bit of unconscious material should have more than one conscious expression. If any interpretation is to withstand scrutiny, then more representations of a similar concern should be discernible through Freudian interpretation of the text. The class could search the *Confessions* for other clues to Oedipal concerns.

But one need not emphasize the Oedipal line of thought. For the purpose of teaching Freud, the object is to study the passage according to the principles of Freudian dream interpretation and discover how well any hypothesis accounts for the material in the *Confessions*. For instance, the class could turn to the distress that small children can feel about divisiveness in their parents' relationship. Which symbols and images in the text might represent a wish fulfillment about his parents' relationship? What is the wish? What is the fulfillment? Two interesting bits of text related to this problem appear in IX.xiii.36 and 37. In the first, Augustine tells us that his mother asked on her deathbed that she be remembered at Christian worship. In the second passage Augustine asks the reader to remember both her *and* Patricius. Given that he has just finished telling us that Monica had given up her desire to be buried by her husband (IX.xi.28)—that is, was willing to be separated from him— why does Augustine reintroduce Patricius? How could these little elements of Augustine's story relate to his other representations of divided and united mother and father figures? What unconscious thoughts might give rise to them?

USING THE SECONDARY LITERATURE AND ASSEMBLING NEW CONCLUSIONS

I have not recommended one definitive Freudian or post-Freudian interpretation of Augustine. The investigative approach outlined above may raise for students, as well as their teachers, the crucial question of whether there can be a unitary psychological understanding of a person or a work. A quick look at the secondary literature will indicate that various psychological interpretations of Augustine have already evolved.

The exercises suggested in this essay prepare the students for insightful reading of the secondary literature. Graduate students can observe in the secondary literature how an area of investigation may expand and critique itself. Undergraduates might well be overwhelmed, either by confusion or by the "rightness" of some specific author's position. They can get their bearings from Freud's statement, cited above, that the unconscious base for conscious expression in dreams is something "not only alien but also disagreeable" to the person's consciousness. Whether this is Oedipal and derivative from a sexual drive, or pre-Oedipal and drawn from relationships in early childhood, as later studies using post-Freudian schools of psychoanalysis would say, is not crucial for undergraduates. The alien nature and disagreeableness, the ensuing repression, transformation, and disguised expression are the factors on which they should focus.

Students can follow the changes in viewpoint over time if the secondary literature is taken chronologically. The study by Kligerman[44] shows Freudian theory and findings adopted as second nature and used largely without careful reference to Freudian texts. Fredriksen's introduction of psychologies concentrating on the pre-Oedipal phase of life, its elaborations by Capps, and Miles's[45] blending of pre-Oedipal concerns with close textual study will expose students to further critiques, including commentary based on historical and cultural knowledge, considerations of genre, and theological themes. Laurence J. Daly offers a theoretical shift by relying on Erik Erikson's ideas to interpret Augustine.[46] William B. Parsons draws out similarities of Erikson's thought and the object relations perspective of Ana-Maria Rizzuto to propose that Augustine's psychological conflicts might have been transformed by a process of maturation, rather than frozen in a largely changeless unconscious.[47] Volney Gay offers a well argued interpretation from the viewpoint of Kohut's pre-Oedipal self psychology.[48] Browning suggests ways to link Freudian and pre-Oedipal interpretations.[49] Diane Jonte-Pace's attention to rhetoric and culture, as well as to the notion of the subject of psychohistory, fosters well-rounded critique.[50] My own work draws primarily on the theory of Kohut in combination with theories of culture, and along the way tries to address some of the major problems in earlier studies.[51] Any of these interpretations can be scrutinized rigorously if the basic rules of unconscious psychological transformation are kept in mind as one approaches both the theory of choice and Augustine's text.

The editors of *Hunger of the Heart* tell us that their volume of essays on the psychological study of Augustine emerged a quarter century after Capps was a student in Dittes's seminar at Yale Divinity School on "Continuities between the life and thought of selected religious figures."[52] During the twenty-five years between their class's study of theologians other than Augustine, Dittes wrote his own "Continuities Between the Life and Thought of Augustine," Pruyser edited the initial series of articles in the *Journal for the Scientific Study of Religion*, Capps edited the twenty-year follow-up, and several authors of later articles on the topic participated in a seminar offered by Don S. Browning at the University of Chicago in the 1980s that used Augustine's *Confessions* as a case study for the application and assimilation of theories of ego psychology. Few of us have been "right" about Augustine in more than a passage of our papers or an insight in an essay. But many of us have been inspired, and we have learned our psychological theory by the effort of applying it. Moreover, we encountered a great man—Augustine— even if we cannot specify definitively the vicissitudes of his mind. We have explored Freud's thought and that of his successors and come to recognize how their conclusions are put together and how they work. I encourage you and your students to continue the investigation.

NOTES

*This chapter originally appeared in *Teaching Freud*, ed. Diane E. Jonte-Pace, American Academy of Religion Teaching Religious Studies Series (Oxford, New York, et al.: Oxford University Press, 2003), pp. 121–136; reprinted here with permission.

1. A quick count in *The Hunger of the Heart: Reflections on the "Confessions" of Augustine*, edited by Donald Capps and James E. Dittes, yields eight footnote references to Freud's writings in over 350 pages, including many of the widely cited psychological studies of Augustine (Society for the Scientific Study of Religion Monograph Series, no. 8; n.p.: Society for the Scientific Study of Religion, 1990).

2. Paula Fredriksen, "Augustine and his Analysts: The Possibility of a Psychohistory," *Soundings* 61 (Summer 1978), 209–214; James J. O'Donnell, *Augustine: Confessions, II: Commentary on Books 1–7* (Oxford: Clarendon Press, 1992), 71; Margaret More O'Ferrall, "Monica, the Mother of Augustine: A Reconsideration," *Recherches augustiniennes* 10 (1975): 35.

3. See William M. Welty, "Discussion Method Teaching: How to Make It Work," *Change* (July/August 1989): 41–49, especially 42.

4. Ibid., 43.

5. One might work this out on computers in technologically advanced classrooms. Certainly one could create Web pages with icons for different parts of the theory and ask the students to arrange them. In such an exercise, giving up the mouse would parallel giving up the chalk. Copies of Web pages could easily be saved for other class periods. They could be left on a server for students to access between classes, transfer to their own computers, revise, and bring back to the next class. I have not yet tried these suggestions, but my point is that visual representation of the text may be quite adaptable to technological advances.

6. Lawrence J. Daly, "Psychohistory and Augustine's Conversion Process: An Historiographical Critique," *Augustinian Studies* (1978): 252–253; Sandra Lee Dixon, *Augustine: The Scattered and Gathered Self* (St. Louis, MO: Chalice Press, 1999), pp. 9–13, 15, 19–22; Diane Jonte-Pace, "Augustine on the Couch: Psychohistorical (Mis)readings of the Confessions," *Religion* 23 (1993): 75–78.

7. Gananath Obeyesekere, *The Work of Culture: Symbolic Transformation in Psychoanalysis and Anthropology* (Chicago and London: University of Chicago Press, 1990), pp. xx–xxi, 63, 84, 243–244, 250–255.

8. Sigmund Freud, "The Unconscious," ed. and trans. James Strachey, *S.E.* 14, 172–173.

9. *On Dreams*, trans. James Strachey (New York: W. W. Norton, 1952 [1901]), p. 63 (*GW* 2–3: 222) for metaphorical allusions to geology; see language on opposing forces in Sigmund Freud, "Five Lectures on Psycho-Analysis," ed. and trans. James Strachey; *S.E.*, 11.

10. Obeyesekere, pp. 244–245 and 250–254.

11. *On Dreams*, p. 11.

12. Ibid., p. 12. Emphasis in the English, not in the German (*GW* 2–3: 189).

13. Some scholars have chosen to interpret dreams in the *Confessions*, but they neglect the fact that the dreams Augustine reports are his mother's dreams, not his own. We have his ideas associated to them, not hers. Therefore interpreting them is a tricky business, best treated with extraordinary reserve; see Dixon 1999, pp. 98–99.

14. The line between explanation and understanding is hard to draw, but suffice it to say that I am avoiding the idea that psychoanalytic interpretation can fulfill strict standards of causality implied in the word "explanation." Paul Ricoeur tries to steer a course through these related but still distinct terms: *Freud and Philosophy: An Essay on Interpretation*, trans. Denis Savage (New Haven and London: Yale University Press, 1970) 65–66, 91–97, 358–363, 375.

15. *On Dreams*, p. 12, *GW* 2–3:190.

16. Ibid., p. 15, *GW* 2–3:192; see also p. 83, *GW* 2–3:235.

17. For an example later in the book, see p. 95, *GW* 2–3:243.

18. Ibid., pp. 15–16, *GW* 2–3:192. My emphasis.

19. Ibid., pp. 19–28, *GW* 2–3:194–200.

20. Ibid., p. 41, *GW* 2–3:209. Similarly for his comments on overdetermination on p. 49, *GW* 2–3:213.

21. Ibid., p. 52, *GW* 2–3:215.

22. Ricoeur, pp. 73–77, 86, 93–94.

23. *On Dreams*, p. 85, *GW* 2–3:236.

24. Ibid., p. 25, *GW* 2–3:198.

25. Ibid., pp. 60–61, *GW* 2–3:221. The teacher needs to understand that these symbolic representations are not what Freud means when he talks about "fixed" symbols.

26. Robert McMahon, *Augustine's Prayerful Ascent: An Essay on the Literary Form of the "Confessions"* (Athens, GA, and London: University of Georgia Press, 1989); Charles Kligerman, "A Psychoanalytic Study of the *Confessions* of St. Augustine," *Journal of the American Psychoanalytic Association* 5 (1957), 471 (reprinted in *Hunger of the Heart*). Freud's further comments about "considerations of representability" (Freud, 1901, *SE* 5, 659) can also be understood to apply to Augustine's use of symbols in the *Confessions*. He was a rhetor by training and needed to consider representability consciously even while his unconscious may have been affecting it without his awareness.

27. *On Dreams*, pp. 89–90, 101,*GW* 2–3:238, 247.

28. Ibid., p. 106, *GW* 2–3:250–251.

29. *Five Lectures on Psycho-Analysis* (1910), *Standard Edition of the Complete Psychological Works of Sigmund Freud*, ed. and trans. James Strachey, vol. 11, p. 47. Freud is explicit earlier in the text about understanding sexuality broadly (p. 46).

30. Ibid., p. 47. Emphasis in original.

31. Ibid., pp. 11–16.

32. Ricoeur, *Freud and Philosophy*, pp. 164–165, 172.

33. *Confessions*, trans. with an Introduction and notes by Maria Boulding, ed. John E. Rotelle, The Works of Saint Augustine: A Translation for the 21st Century, vol. I/1 (Hyde Park, NY: New City Press, 1997), also available from Vintage Books (1999); Saint Augustine, *Confessions*, trans. with an Introduction by Henry Chadwick, World's Classics (Oxford and New York: Oxford University Press, 1992); Saint Augustine, *Confessions*, trans. and with an Introduction by R. S. Pine-Coffin (New York: Dorset Press, 1961), also available from Penguin; Rex Warner, trans., *The Confessions of St. Augustine*, with an Introduction by Vernon Bourke (New York: New American Library, Mentor Books, 1963).

34. Two good references are Henry Chadwick, *Augustine*, Past Masters, gen. ed. Keith Thomas (Oxford: Oxford University Press, 1986) and James J. O'Donnell, *Augustine*, Twayne World Authors #759 (New York: Macmillan, 1985). See also O'Donnell's marvelous World Wide Web site at http://www9.georgetown.edu/faculty/jod/augustine/. Garry Wills' *Saint Au-*

gustine (New York: Lipper/Viking, 1999) has received excellent reviews. Peter Brown's *Augustine of Hippo* (Berkeley: University of California Press, 1969) may still be the best read, but it is already influenced by Brown's own understanding of psychoanalysis; statements, especially about Augustine, his father, and mother, should not be read as facts unadorned by interpretation.

35. Unfortunately, two numbering systems have come down through the manuscript traditions. The instructor would do well to have one edition with both systems (e.g., Chadwick's translation) and then coordinate it with other editions that use only one of the systems. In any case, if one avoids using page numbers, then the class can accommodate most of the editions procured in sundry fashions.

36. Kligerman, "A Psychoanalytic Study," 470.

37. *On Dreams*, p. 94, *GW*, 2–3:242–3.

38. Sigmund Freud, *Civilization and Its Discontents*, trans. and ed. James Strachey (New York: W.W. Norton, 1961 [1930]), p. 21.

39. For example, see also IV.xvi.31, V.ii.2, VI.xvi.26; by extension, God not as punitive but as healing through the use of painful medical techniques (VI.vi.9).

40. For example, see *Civilization and Its Discontents*, pp. 73–75; *The Ego and the Id*, *S.E.* 21, 129–33.

41. James E. Dittes, "Continuities Between the Life and Thought of Augustine," *Journal for the Scientific Study of Religion* 5 (October 1965), 130–140 (reprinted in *Hunger of the Heart*); Kligerman, "Psychoanalytic Study"; Phillip Woollcott, Jr., "Some Considerations of Creativity and Religious Experience in St. Augustine of Hippo," *Journal for the Scientific Study of Religion* 5 (Spring 1966), 273–283; see Dixon, *Augustine*, pp. 69–78.

42. Brent D. Shaw, "The Family in Late Antiquity: The Experience of Augustine," *Past and Present* 115 (May 1987), 18, 21–22, 31, 40; A.-G. Hamman, *La vie quotidienne en Afrique du Nord au temps de saint Augustin*, nouvelle éd. (Paris: Hachette, 1979), p. 103.

43. For fuller treatment, see Dixon, pp. 69–78. These complications add to the criticisms of Fredriksen, O'Ferrall, Daly, and Jonte-Pace, cited above. The critiques and evidence in sum prevent my recommending the early articles on Augustine (Dittes, "Continuities Between the Life and Thought of Augustine"; Kligerman, "Psychoanalytic Study of the *Confessions*"; Woollcott, "Some Considerations") as good models of psychoanalytic interpretation. They have an important place, however, in the story of how the psychoanalytic study of Augustine developed.

44. Kligerman, "Psychoanalytic Study of Augustine."

45. Fredriksen, "Augustine and his Analysts"; Capps, "Augustine as Narcissist"; Margaret R. Miles, "Infancy, Parenting, and Nourishment in Augustine's *Confessions*," *Journal of the American Academy of Religion* 50 (September 1982) 349–364.

46. "St. Augustine's *Confessions* and Erik Erikson's *Young Man Luther*: Conversion as 'Identity Crisis,'" *Augustiniana* 31 (1981), 183–196.

47. William B. Parsons, "St. Augustine: 'Common Man' or 'Intuitive Psychologist'?", *Journal of Psychohistory* 18 (Fall 1990), 155–179.

48. Volney Gay, "Augustine: The Reader as Selfobject," *Journal for the Scientific Study of Religion* 25 (March 1986), 64–76.

49. Don S. Browning, "The Psychoanalytic Interpretation of St. Augustine's *Confessions*: An Assessment and New Probe," in *Psychiatry and the Humanities*, vol. 2, *Psychoanalysis and Religion*, edited by Joseph H. Smith, associate editor Susan A. Handelman, (Baltimore and London: The Johns Hopkins University Press, 1990) 136–159.

50. "Augustine on the Couch."

51. Dixon, *Augustine: The Scattered and Gathered Self.*

52. "Preface," p. ix. The following lines correct a misstatement in the first published version of this article. The author apologizes to James Dittes, who pointed out a misreading in the first publication of this chapter and was assured it would be corrected in the future.

Chapter Three

Reading Augustine, Monica, Milan with Attention to Cultural Interpretation and Psychological Theory

Sandra Lee Dixon

INTRODUCTION

A brief story from Augustine's *Confessions* allows us to think theologically and rhetorically about the *Confessions*, supports psychological interpretations already widely cited in the scholarly literature on Augustine and psychology, lends credence to reinterpretation of some of those same scholarly themes, and encourages the introduction of a set of psychological considerations that are less bifurcated than the terms most often cited earlier from psychoanalytic theory, notably the opposition of "autonomous" and "dependent." This brief story appears in Book IX of the *Confessions*, as Augustine is recalling how in the months after he had committed himself to Christianity he cried when he listened to hymns in the church of bishop Ambrose in Milan. He tells a tale of how the singing of hymns rooted itself in the liturgy there. During a time when Ambrose and his congregation were besieged by the imperial forces, Ambrose had endorsed singing to sustain the spirit of his people. Augustine summarizes the situation they had faced:

Justina, mother of the boy-emperor Valentinian, had been persecuting your faithful Ambrose, in the interests of the Arian heresy by which she had been led astray. His God-fearing congregation, prepared to die with their bishop, your servant, stayed up all night in the church. Your maidservant, my mother, was among them, foremost in giving support and keeping vigil, and constant in her life of prayer. As for us, we were still cold, not being yet warmed by the

39

fire of your spirit, yet we too were stirred as alarm and excitement shook the
city. (*Conf.* IX.vii.15)[1]

The story refers to a standoff between the church and the imperial powers
that other sources attest and that scholars take as historical. As Ambrose
resists the emperor, the church experiences increasing power and independence, which Ambrose asserts later in his episcopate as well.[2] The reader is
well aware from the prior books of the *Confessions* that Augustine's occupa-
tion is the city's professor of rhetoric, who also served as premier speech
maker for the emperor in this capital city, a position that historian Peter
Brown characterizes for us as a "Minister of Propaganda."[3] So Augustine at
this point in the story is a government official and presumably allied with the
emperor. Yet these few lines also depict him as a son who feels the emotion
and energy of the capital's upheaval but whose feelings about his mother's
dangerous vigil with the bishop and his congregants merit no remarks, despite the pathos of the *Confessions*.

Taking a step back from the emotional tensions of the scene, students of
Augustine will admonish readers who are too caught up in this brief worldly
event that Augustine's endeavor in the *Confessions* is primarily theological.
The theological dimensions of the scene burst out of it: some characters are
faithful, others heretical; the heretical have been "led away" from true Christian beliefs and the potentially faithful may yet be moved by God's Spirit, but
neither is an independent soul calmly making rational personal decisions; the
devoted Christians too join their souls with others of like commitments and
seek connection with God; the faithful, who are courageous under threat of
death, locate themselves inside the church while the cold, as well as the
heretical, stay outside where they can wield power or, not so bravely, ac-
quiesce to it. The movement of the scene also fits with a pattern noticed in
the composition of the *Confessions*: its books have been referred to as *exercitationes animi*, exercises of the soul, designed to bring the reader's soul
along with Augustine, as a character in the book, as he recognizes and confesses the sinful movement of his soul away from God and its gradual return
under God's guidance to his creator and redeemer.[4] In reading closely and
meditating on this scene and its resolution as Ambrose overcomes the imperial family's wishes, the soul can move through a short *exercitatio animi*,
absorbing concepts about sin and shame and where to find courage and life
with God.

Not only do all these elements of the story admit of fuller interpretation,
but as we step back even further from the short sketches of the "affair of the
basilicas," as the standoff is known, we see that the placement of the story in
the *Confessions* as a whole both makes sense and seems strange. It makes
sense, as suggested above, in Augustine's discussion of music in the church
and as a contrast of his current life in the church with his previous life outside

it when he elaborated worldly eloquence rather than listened to psalms and hymns. Yet the placement seems strange when we recognize that other events that would have occurred at the time of the crisis in Milan are retold in Book VI. Similar characters and themes turn up there: Monica has left the family homeland in North Africa and joined Augustine in Milan; she has found her way to the church; she has established herself as one of Ambrose's congregants, even one worthy of his praise; and Augustine is ambivalently related to Ambrose's ministry—recognizing his mother's devotion, appreciating Ambrose's rhetoric, slowly being moved by it, being noticed by Ambrose as the city's rhetor and as Monica's son, but also left aside at the door to Ambrose's receiving room once the formality of initial introductions had transpired (VI.3.3). Why not tell the story of the conflict with the empress in these chapters, or further in Book VI as Augustine displays himself struggling with how to live with integrity as a high ranking civil servant who also loves the truth he has seen in philosophy and has decided to ally himself tentatively with the Catholic church? The question is bothersome especially as Augustine's narrative indicates that Ambrose's preaching had shown him that philosophical truth reflected in the church's scriptures and teachings. Surely the drama of Augustine outside and Monica and Ambrose inside the church, along with the tensions of profession and family connection, belongs among the scenes of success, self-doubt, self-promotion, and self-recrimination that shape Book VI.

While these notions help raise questions on the incident of the basilicas, Augustine's projects as a theologian and a creative writer, psychologically attuned according to the understandings of the soul in his own time, need not crowd out the psychological efforts developed a millennium and a half later. Psychologists of the twentieth and twenty-first century have seized on tales that segment feelings from behaviors and diminish tensions by holding back narratives of familial distress. The psychology most sensitive to these sorts of narrative gaps has been psychoanalysis, the early Freudian kind as well as its heirs and offshoots. Often psychoanalysis has acted on a reductive impulse by treating the only aspect of importance in a story as the unconscious factors that the psychoanalytically trained listener can laboriously trace out from the overt story, which psychoanalysts call the "surface content." But by the late twentieth century, an epistemological argument for maintaining both psychoanalytic insights and the properly cultural value of symbolic works, including literature like the *Confessions*, had caught much attention. Its full elaboration resides in Paul Ricoeur's *Freud and Philosophy*, but Ricoeur himself advanced elements of it in other essays.[5] This careful working with cultural artifacts and practices, on the one hand, and psychoanalytic interpretations, on the other, enriches studies of a range of religious practices and figures.[6] It has momentum as one area of a field called "cultural psychology," and it is the method that I will use in this essay to draw us deeper into the strangeness of the incident of the basilicas as Augustine depicts it in his tales of his life, his mother's, and his family's, in Milan.

I will use the method of interpretation grounded by Ricoeur's hermeneutics to argue that the story of the crisis of the basilicas and its place in Augustine's story of his years in Milan unfold several familiar and important theological themes at the same time that they support the identification of difficulty in closeness and separation for Monica and Augustine on which psychoanalytic writers often comment. Strictures on this claim will become evident, but it should be seen as addressing both the characters Monica and Augustine in the *Confessions* and the extension we might make from Augustine's sculpting of those characters to our ideas about the Monica and Augustine who lived in late-fourth-century North Africa and Italy. At the same time that this argument about text and person emerges from prior scholarship from various schools, it also challenges some particulars claimed by psychoanalytic writers. Especially in doubt is their insistence on Monica's supposed dependence on Augustine and their emphasis on the limitations of her life circumstances, from which they infer various weaknesses of personality or character.

If we mull over empathically and critically the narratives that Augustine sets out, we see several middle grounds appearing. One is that Augustine portrays a Monica who devised ways to live creatively in the midst of serious strictures on women's life chances. This point can hold whether his flesh-and-blood mother was creative or not. Another middle ground is that his narratives suggest that characters stood up for their understandings of the good that would have been in conflict, even though those understandings conflicted within each character and famously differed between the mother and son we view in the *Confessions*. Third, characters in the *Confessions* are not simply well-constructed literary types, such as sinners who have fallen away from God but are now being drawn back by God to Godself; they also can fairly be read as rough-edged approximations to human beings who in their misunderstandings and personal quirks grate on one another while God, in Augustine's view, works out the divine purposes in them and among them. The middle ground here is not positivist. It does not support the idea that we can "'recover her [Monica] pure and simple from texts' . . ."[7] or that we could recover any of the characters in the *Confessions* in that way.

The view that forms the "middle ground" for which I argue in this essay holds that Augustine the writer of the *Confessions* was a person; that people create works of culture—including theological, literary, and philosophical works—from the experiences of their own lives; that creativity exceeds recitation of one's own life even when it relies on elements of one's own life; and that the creative process opens up possibilities of understanding that deserve thoughtful consideration. Rebecca Moore has already striven for such a middle ground in her effort to sort out what seems probable about the flesh-and-blood Monica from Augustine's representation of her in the *Confessions* and his early dialogues written ten years before it at Cassiciacum.[8] She contextualizes her discussion in an interdisciplinary framework, as I set mine. With her help, and that of many scholars in a number of fields, I aim to set free the play of signifiers[9] for our reflection on Monica and on Augustine, both as characters and in pinhole views as living, breathing human beings. This depends on setting free the play of signifiers that Augustine makes available in his texts—specifically, the *Confessions*.

To understand how I loosen the play of signifiers from the text, the reader must understand how I reply to a number of objections waiting to leap from the scholarly literature. The first appears several times in this volume; Elizabeth Clark states it well: "Augustine the rhetorician leaves us no avenue by which to secure an 'objective' historical narrative from the literary construction that he here weaves."[10] Granted. Yet this difficulty in dealing with a highly skilled rhetorician's creations can invite us to think carefully about what kind of interpretation we can design. Some of us will want to pursue the literary interpretation of the text. Some of us will want to understand as best we can the characters with which the work presents us. Some will want to understand the author. Some will emphasize Augustine's theology or philosophy. All of these efforts will meet limitations. In this pursuit, we work with probabilities, inferences, arguments, judgment calls, and shifting perspectives toward our own understandings. We attempt to speak to our questions, even transgressive ones, and maybe even answer them. Thus we can make available points of view for future and better understandings.

A second objection would be that psychoanalytic approaches, which I will use, have proven useless. Some critics will hold that psychoanalytic arguments must be useless because they rely on the notion of a repressed unconscious and that no such thing exists. Others will hold that past psychoanalytic discussions, and distinctly those of Augustine, have been too heavy-handed and reductive, so that Augustine, his characters, his artistry, and his theology have all been obscured. My response to both these points depends on one major idea: the notion of the unconscious is a hypothesis that we use to help us make sense of behaviors, ideas, and other outcroppings of human thought that we cannot understand otherwise. The understanding we derive depends not just on the notion of the unconscious but also on its connection with rules for interpreting its outcroppings and careful attention to the material that is being presented, along with an effort to open ourselves to that material and to notice how it affects us. None of this effort guarantees a persuasive interpretation, but we continue with what Ricoeur calls "the hermeneutic wager" in an effort to enter into the material that presents itself to us.[11] The possibility of closing our eyes and ignoring our perplexities remains available and almost incessant in the face of the fact that no one can understand everything. But in this essay, the psychoanalytic way of working will suggest some aspects of the text, as well as demands on the reader and on the effort to understand the text, that have been given short shrift in previous discussions of Augustine and psychology.

While many more objections may be raised to this endeavor, a short paper cannot encompass responses to all of them, and its case may be better made in its creativity and thoughtfulness than in its defense against all detractors. So let us turn to the "surface content," as the psychoanalytic interpreters would call it—what Ricoeur would think of as the cultural work of the text. As we enter into the accounts of Augustine and Monica in Milan, we will think especially about literary ideas about the placement of the incident of the basilicas and some theological implications of this part of Books VI and IX.

ANALYSIS OF THE COMPLEX AND MULTI-DIMENSIONAL "SURFACE"

The literary and theological points of the structure of Books VI and IX intertwine. Both reverberate with Augustine's rhetorical skills. They give us scenes, images, and ideas in which to revel, with language that delights in English as well as in the Latin original, not to mention in many other tongues. Yet a basic disentangling of strands can help us deal with the startling text by Augustine, the creative genius shaping a relatively new form of prose, the introspective autobiography.[12] What James J. O'Donnell writes about the first nine books of the *Confessions* as a whole applies to Books VI and IX and inspires the piece by piece examination: "their distinctive feature is not the lively biographical interest they evoke, but rather the complexity of the confessional mode, the allusiveness, and the indirectness of the text's construction." As they do evoke "lively biographical interest," we can look first at literary matters to lay a groundwork for seeing later how they play in "the indirectness of the text's construction."[13]

A BASIC LITERARY TECHNIQUE: HEIGHTENING TENSIONS THROUGH ACCENTUATING CONTRASTS

As mentioned previously, prominent elements that reappear in the story of the basilicas appear in Book VI of the *Confessions*, but Augustine does not recount the confrontation of bishop and monarch until Book IX. Augustine's intentions about this dispersal of parts of his life in Milan into different books of the *Confessions* remain his secret, if he ever thought about the issue in this way at all. But for us now, several points about the literary structure arise. First we can reflect briefly on the coherence of the two books as they stand. Then we can look at the tensions of Book IX and how the story of Augustine outside the church while his mother and Ambrose were inside increases anticipation of a resolution.

Book VI draws the reader into the highs and lows of life in Milan, especially, but not only, for the character Augustine.[14] Monica arrives in Milan, after having been deserted by Augustine two years before on the shores of Carthage, where she wept copiously about his tricking her into not accompanying him as he sailed away to advance his career in Italy (V.8.15). She is more stoic now, at least about good news (VI.1.1). She meets Ambrose and becomes his congregant and receives more recognition from him than does her civically more prominent son. As she tries to carry over the North African custom of feasting at the tombs of the dead Christians, we find that Ambrose has already forbidden this practice in Milan because the attendees tended toward over-indulgence instead of temperate remembrance. She receives the notice of the outstanding bishop but also the news of his disapprobation of her custom (VI.2.2).

Augustine's highs and lows happen for him, the literary character of his book, in a busy social world. He gives a major speech but harbors personal anxieties, wondering on the way to the declamation whether a drunken beggar is better off than he. Nor does he treat this as a private worry: "I groaned and pointed out to the friends who were with me how many hardships our idiotic enterprises entailed. . . . Yet while all our efforts were directed solely to the attainment of unclouded joy, it appeared that this beggar had already beaten us to the goal, a goal which we would perhaps never reach ourselves" (VI.6.9). He parts from his concubine of over fifteen years in hopes of a high-class and financially advantageous marriage but lets the reader know that he suffered from his longing for her and his attachment to sexual satisfaction (Vi.15.25).[15]

Augustine discusses his friend Alypius, another noteworthy character in the *Confessions* with some relationship to a flesh-and-blood person, whose correspondence as bishop of Thagaste with Augustine gives evidence of at least a shadowy point of reference for the character in the *Confessions*. Shown as a brilliant young lawyer in Book VI (7.11-10.16), Alypius has a stellar career ahead of him—except that he suffers disappointment in practicing law in a society beset with bribes. The high moral evaluation he receives from Augustine the author for resisting those bribes contrasts with a low of personal dignity that Augustine recounts from their past years in Carthage. There Augustine the rising young professor of rhetoric was the privileged young Alypius' teacher. Alypius had enjoyed the gladiatorial shows, widely judged disreputable by highly educated and esteemed people. Book VI reminds us of their excitement and the shame attached to reveling in them and to the character Alypius' struggle to give them up. And then more fun with stories intervenes as we read also about the time Alypius was arrested on the false accusation of thievery, a tale which comes to a happy ending.

So part of the enjoyment of Book VI derives from the ongoing contrasts it contains, especially between the highs of worldly interests—participation in public arenas (literally), aspiration to higher social status, chances for wealth, as well as sexual access and profitability—and personal fault, shame, loss, and disappointment. Someone puzzling about the lack of mention of the affair of the basilicas could simply say that perhaps the book is already full.

But what about book VII? This book also discusses Augustine's time in Milan but focuses largely on the character Augustine's intellectual struggles with the problem of evil. Success crowns the struggles as he achieves a comprehension of evil that will reappear in works written by Augustine the author between the years in Milan and the time he wrote the *Confessions*. Better yet, from the point of view being developed in the *Confessions*, the character Augustine ascends to an intellectual vision of God, the pinnacle of the Neo-Platonic philosophy that supports his understanding of evil. This is a book much more of mental than of physical activity. And much the same can be said about book VIII, except that the word "mental" might need supplementing by the idea of activity of the soul and not a more narrow sense of intellectual activity that the English word "mental" can connote.

So finally in Book IX we find the story of the affair of the basilicas, along with the character Augustine's wrestling with his ideas, his feelings, and his past actions in the language of the biblical psalms. Augustine as the personage in the *Confessions* who is most devoted to rhetoric here revels in the phrases of specific Psalms, reevaluating his life and seeking his future through the words—and quite possibly through the music associated with them also. Augustine describes himself in transition to a fuller life in the church, which also becomes the repository for the long years of personal distress in the relationships he has allowed to figure in the story. Here the extended and volatile distresses will repose, as the *Confessions* go on to talk about Augustine's life in the church and major issues of the church, including its final repose. But the relationships will no longer figure directly in the work.

Augustine the writer brings the narrative of his past life to a close in Book IX with a succession of emotional waves. They bear less obvious consequence for the character's life story than those set out in Book VI, but like the episodes in Book VI the scenes in Book IX highlight contrasts. From Augustine's meditations while he stayed somewhere in the vicinity of Milan putatively in the months after his decision to become a baptized Christian, we look at him in church as he responds tearfully to the psalms. Then we see him in the affair of the basilicas notably outside the church in contrast to his mother inside. Then shifting from the scene of Ambrose and his congregation under threat we witness the transporting of saints' relics that confirm Ambrose's spiritual power and his victory over the emperor's mother in her persecution of Ambrose through the power of her son (IX.7.16). As Augustine's writing leads us out of this conflict, it confronts us quickly with his mother's death (IX.8.17). But this startling moment too calls forth contrasting thoughts as Augustine the author moves directly to sketch the life of Monica (IX.8.17–IX.9.22). Then he paints for us the images that try to convey Monica's and Augustine's mystical experience at Ostia (IX.10.23–26). Finally, he returns to the topic of her death, as well as personal and communal responses to it, and the prose juxtaposes the strong sorrow the character Augustine felt with the cultural prohibitions he had assimilated against displaying such emotion in public (IX.11.27–13.26). Even in the midst of filial reconciliations with his deceased parents, he inserts a brief contrast: his mother in the story has asked him and his brother to remember her at God's altar, and rather than doing just this Augustine the author enjoins his readers to remember both of his parents (IX.13.36–37). As author, he does not simply comply with the character Monica's request but distinguishes his urging of his readers from her wishes by including his father also.

This recollection of his parents at God's altar presents an interesting consideration for our literary efforts. If we have distinguished Augustine and Monica as characters from Augustine and Monica as human beings that one could have met in, say, the cathedral in Milan, in this passage we find Augustine linking the Monicas and Augustines very closely, for as far as we know, Monica the character made the request, while Augustine the author and human being asks us as readers to help fulfill it. Before we pursue further interpretations that might associate the characters more closely to the people whose names they bear, let us move to another set of interpretations that fit in the "surface content" of the text.

THEOLOGICAL AND MORAL PHILOSOPHICAL POINTS

Just as our consideration of literary issues treats only a few themes from an immensely complex text and from phalanxes of critical concepts, our theological reflections will proceed from a few major points. In both analyses, the aim is not to imply that all the important points are being made. Rather, it is to indicate that these considerations are recognized and valued. In order to continue the dialogue of surface content and psychological depth with yet another interpretation, psychoanalytically derived, none of the perspectives can make all its points. Nor could it if we chose only one interpretive angle, because the text is too rich and the scholarly tradition too deep to encompass in a single work. Nonetheless, we can also find theological themes that intersect with the literary contrasts already expounded.

The first theological theme for our consideration adopts a Neo-Platonic motif, the ascent of the soul to the One, which the Christians responding to Neo-Platonism called "God." This motif implies linearity, a rising from low

to high. Yet Augustine writing the *Confessions* sometimes focuses on the low
and the high so that they appear as a contrast without the variegated shades of
the middle range of the ascent. His prose brings the extremes closer to the
reader by describing the lows and the highs, usually metaphorically. His
metaphorical images interweave so closely that they call to mind poetry;
indeed sometimes translators choose verse to render the text, especially passages about the ascent to God. As writer, Augustine also uses metaphors to
evoke the low place from which one starts the ascent. But sometimes he
brings the metaphorical idea of "low" very close to a prosaic kind of human
experience.

A famous passage regarding the rhetor Augustine's "lows" pertains to an
incident in Milan set out in Book VI. Augustine was at the "height" of his
worldly success in government. And yet he felt himself sinking. As Augustine prefaces Book VI, setting the scene for the whole, he notes: "I had sunk
to the depth of the sea, I lost all faith and despaired of ever finding the truth"
(VI.1.1). Demonstrating the interaction of his rhetorical strategies with his
theological commitments to the importance of scripture, the first part of the
quotation refers to Psalm 67:23 (68:22), unsurprisingly as the book of Psalms
often called forth Augustine's interpretive labors throughout his priesthood
and episcopacy. So how did this "sinking" to the depths look in the life he
depicts his younger self living back in the days of government service in
Milan? Augustine presents himself as the city's orator on the way to "deliver
a eulogy upon the emperor . . ." Approaching an occasion for consorting with
society's higher-ups, the lower rungs of society catch his eye: "I noticed a
poor beggar, drunk, as I believe, and making merry. I groaned and pointed
out to the friends who were with me how many hardships our idiotic enterprises entailed. . . ." He develops the contrast of Augustine the government
official and the beggar through an allusion to the form of a philosophical
dialogue, and thereby shows us that his situation would not elicit admiration
from philosophically informed non-Christians: "If anyone had questioned me
as to whether I would rather be exhilarated or afraid, I would of course have
replied, 'Exhilarated'; but if the questioner had pressed me further, asking
whether I preferred to be like the beggar, or to be as I was then, I would have
chosen to be myself, laden with anxieties and fears. Surely that would have
been no right choice, but a perverse one?" (VI.6.9). So despite being elevated
among the great in the public mind, Augustine the character sinks toward the
depths of poverty, irrationality, and dishonor from the point of view of the
author appraising the character's youth. Throughout several more chapters of
Book VI, we see him depicted as someone who cannot make an honorable
worldly case or a Christian one for his ambitions or his desires for sex
(11.18-16-26). So if God is on high, to whom he might ascend, the character
Augustine in Book VI lies very low and far away indeed.

The affair of the basilicas took place within a year and a half of the time just mentioned.[16] For both, Augustine was still a catechumen in the Roman Catholic church who had not decided on Christian baptism. And so we return theologically to the passage with which this chapter opens. A point common to pagans and Christians of the time deserves note. Augustine says of Ambrose's flock that while the empress persecuted Ambrose, "His God-fearing congregation, prepared to die with their bishop, your servant, stayed up all night in the church." He thereby indicates not only that they accepted possible martyrdom, and hence were admirable to Christians, but that they also rose to the highest standard for pagans. Non-Christian philosophers too praised the ability to face death without fear. Augustine, as he pictured himself not joining Ambrose's congregants, passes judgment on himself as a character in the *Confessions*: Augustine the character lacked both the courage and wisdom sought by everyone whose ideals he had adopted. The character of his mother, however, appears among the courageous and wise, and moreover in a prominent place: "Your maidservant, my mother, was among them, foremost in giving support and keeping vigil . . ." ("*sollicitudinis et vigiliarum primas tenens*"). This picture fits with a literary "topos of woman-as-wisdom," as Clark has pointed out, and supports his theological point that the untutored could reach heaven, even for an exquisite moment in an earthly ascent (as in the Ostia vision). One need not be a philosopher to reach heaven.[17] The wise person Augustine depicts in the character Monica did not sit in the basilica reading philosophy but remained "constant in her life of prayer." Taking the Latin "*orationibus vivebat*" more literally, we can mull over the possibility that he draws her for us more as living in prayers or by means of prayers.[18]

These thoughts might seem to be an overreading of the placement of the character Monica in the basilica with Ambrose during the time of dire threats, but they seem less so when we realize that later in Book IX Augustine comments again in two ways on her lack of a fear of death. First, he recounts that she had given up her desire to be buried in North Africa where she had had a tomb prepared for herself by the body of her husband. Second, he remarks that he himself had heard from his friends that she had mentioned to them that she had "contempt for this life" and believed that death would be to the good (IX.11.28).[19]

We see the image of the faithful Christian that Augustine sets up through the character Monica. What might Augustine the writer want us to reflect on about Augustine the character in this *exercitatio animi*? At least this: that whatever else his character was doing, he emphatically did not show courage and wisdom in the face of possible death, he did not face martyrdom, we should not envision him as a leader in the church—or even a supporter of the church—and he was not living by prayers. He says explicitly that he was not warmed by the Holy Spirit, that he was "cold, away from the heat of your spirit" ("*nos adhuc frigidi a calore spiritus tui*"). One of the rhetorical contrasts follows as Augustine states of his character, "*excitabamur.*"[20] The word connotes being heated up, in opposition to being "*frigidi,*" or overtly "cold." Yet when he was "stirred," as Boulding translates the word, he was carrying on the emotion in the city. Rather than actively living, as Augustine presents Monica, Augustine the young Roman official is portrayed in the passive voice: was "stirred as alarm and excitement shook the city" ("*excitabamur tamen civitate attonita atque turbata*"). The character passively responds to the feeling of the city. By the contrast with Monica's character's disposition to engage events with and in the church, Augustine the writer implies that the worldliness of the conflict—its drama and high stakes and important personages—moved Augustine the rhetor. Perhaps the character was also, like the city, "*attonita*"—"stunned" or even "frantic"—and "*turbata*"—"confounded" and "agitated"—given his feeling for God's servants (as he calls both Ambrose and Monica) or the church building where he had often listened to Ambrose. But overall the *Confessions'* author is saying theologically about the character Augustine that if the soul's true aim is to ascend to God, at this time his soul veered off target.

Yet the episode of the basilicas appears in Book IX following a picture of Augustine the convert crying in church over the Psalms on which he has meditated for several chapters. Moreover, Augustine the author will soon move on to fill in the character Monica and highlight the admiration of the characters of her son and his friends for her. So whatever the author's intention about the story, it serves in this place to heighten the theological point that God had brought him a very long way after he accepts entrance into the Catholic Church. He pictures himself now listening and "how intensely was I moved by the harmonies of your singing church" (IX.6.14). And soon he will be the mourner for his mother, not yet ready to bear her death as heroically as he thought a good Christian—or pagan—should (IX.12.33). But Augustine the author will move the story forward so that his character becomes reconciled with his mother's death.[21] Not only that, but as the author he can serve her in the church, by remembering her, God's servant, at the altar, where he also now serves (IX.13.37). So the narrative about the basilicas helps position the church as the place where people, even relatively uneducated mothers, may live in prayer, both during their lives and afterward. None of the pre-conversion life is forgotten—it appears when the author recounts the story of the basilicas in the midst of his depiction of a fuller Christian life after baptism. But none of it impedes any longer the good of people living in unity, as he will so wish for years later in his many controversies, notably with the Donatists whom he saw as tearing the church apart and rigidly insisting on disunity. Clearly in these passages individuals, family members, friends, and church resolve the narrative tension and suggest a pattern for human life when they acknowledge their sins and past weaknesses and reunite, sharing their lives with each other and, in full awareness and gratitude, with God.

TRANSITION TO PSYCHOANALYTIC READING

The affair of the basilicas may appear as too brief a tale in the *Confessions* to bear much interpretation. Yet for someone with either psychological or historical interests the brevity itself can prompt inquisitiveness. Sources agree that in Milan in 386 C.E., the events had the city in turmoil. Ambrose himself corresponded to his sister about it and made a very public issue of it in his preaching.[22] His biographer, the aristocratic and pious Paulinus, also mentions it. Evidence for some of the elements of tension on which Augustine does not comment in the *Confessions* comes from the legal code: not long before the confrontation between Ambrose and the imperial family a law was promulgated that the Arian faith of the empress and her son would be legal and that anyone who interfered with its practice would be executed.[23] Augustine briefly mentions it twelve years later in Letter 44.4.7. In that letter he describes the church as having been surrounded by armed soldiers. While further interpretation cannot explain why Augustine said so little about it in the *Confessions*, it may niggle at the reader as part of what O'Donnell calls "the allusiveness, and the indirectness of the text's construction."[24] Yet O'Donnell's erudition leads him to puzzle over the placement of the incident: "Why this episode is inserted here is not immediately evident . . ." Further comments lead him nowhere in particular: "All that said, it would still be easier to find here a story dating from after A[ugustine]'s baptism and involving him directly in church affairs . . ."[25] Who can disagree?

Several possible explanations present themselves, nonetheless. One could argue that Augustine as author also sidesteps detailed description of other major events in his life—such as the actual making of his speeches in public arenas with the pomp of state occasions, or his encounters with prominent church leaders other than Ambrose and Simplicianus,[26] or even, on the personal side, his baptism itself. An obvious explanation of all these omissions is that he focuses instead on confession. He aims to use confession to move his audience toward ascent to God, and concentration on public political events would likely distract the reader from the goal of his *exercitationes animi*. With respect to baptism, one might insist on its status as initiation into a specialized Christianity and not a ceremony to be disclosed to the unbaptized masses.[27] But these sorts of arguments carry with them two problems. One problem arises from the fairly obvious ability of Augustine the author to make worldly and unusual episodes into key elements of his story. Perhaps most famously, he expounds on stealing some pears with his friends when he is an adolescent (*Conf.* II.4.9–10.18).[28] If that story can serve the author's purposes, surely he could make instructive points from the incident of the basilicas. The second problem arises from circularity in the rejoinders: if the answer to why Augustine does not elaborate on the affair of the basilicas is he wishes to emphasize other issues, the purported answer only restates the question.

Someone with psychoanalytic interests should nonetheless recognize that an answer to the "why" question risks legitimate scholarly censure. First, authors' intentions are famously hard to pinpoint. Second, the meaning of the text may well exceed or deviate from the author's intention, especially when the writing depends heavily on symbols, because symbols themselves carry multiple meanings, and these can take on configurations that authors themselves may have missed. Third, as deconstructionists discerned from psychoanalytic theory, the lacunae in texts can be revealing. Many interpretations have been launched from reflection on ideas that drop into the gaps at the interstices of authors' intentional lines of argument. Finally, if a psychoanalytic interpretation proposes an answer to a "why" question, it probably is making a claim about causes. That is, the answer to "why" is "because," and usually "because" refers to a cause assumed in psychoanalytic circles to exist in the activity of the unconscious, outlined according to a mechanistic model. But I am following Ricoeur in insisting on the interaction of conscious and unconscious life in creative works, so causality from the unconscious most likely will miss the point of the cultural and psychoanalytic interpretation.

The answer to the "why" question is not settled, then. Nonetheless, the value of the question lies in its prompting further attention to the incident and the contribution it makes to our effort to understand the nexus of Augustine as author, Augustine as character, Monica as Augustine's mother, and Monica as character. The startling brevity of the story effects a disruption of narrative that readily draws the attention of scholars schooled in psychoanalytically based interpretations. If we take Ricoeur's suggestion seriously that the same symbols can carry meanings that point toward cultural innovation— the investigation of one's own heart and the assistance it can receive from music once one has entered the church—and toward a past that is now at least partially unconscious, we can undertake an interpretation that allows us to use tools of thought from psychoanalysis, to respect and even amplify the story as Augustine would seem to want to use it, makes the account at home in Book IX, and helps us think about the larger problem of how people can attempt to understand one another through written records.

INTERPRETATION INFORMED BY SCHOOLS OF
PSYCHODYNAMIC THOUGHT

Two major psychoanalytic concepts spring to mind in regard to this separation by Augustine the author of episodes he implies were contemporaneous. The concepts are repression and splitting. They require two others, condensation and displacement, for us to interpret the text. All of these concepts perdure at least implicitly through later extrapolations from psychoanalytic thinking. The concepts therefore will facilitate a glimpse of a variety of psychological interpretations of Augustine's text and some further considerations of his time in Milan, especially the conflict of Ambrose and the imperial family during the affair of the basilicas.

"Repression" designates the pressure that the psyche exerts against recollection of experiences that overwhelmed it. Freud explicitly plays out the metaphor of pressures, as in a physical system.[29] And as in a physical system, conscious choice is not relevant to the psychological process. Rather, repression is the outcome of forces responding to force, so that an experience that shakes the psyche too harshly undergoes repression. Repression results in the non-appearance of vital links between features of a story or a dream or a memory. Freud in his early psychoanalytic work believed that as the analyst pulled memory forth against the patient's resistances, which are evidence of the repressing force in the psyche, a more complete recollection and even a cure of hysterical symptoms could result.[30]

The other operation of the psyche that we may consider is "splitting." The idea also is Freud's, and like the concept of repression, it has served other psychoanalysts. It may be understood in a number of ways, but for our purposes we can see it as a more specific form of repression. The term "splitting" is often used when the connections between a thought and the feelings one would expect to go with it, or between a person's story and his or her usual presentation of self, do not appear in conscious self-expression.[31]

The *Confessions'* passage on the affair of the basilicas can illustrate the concept of splitting. The author tells us that his mother's character in the story was inside the cathedral with people prepared to die with their bishop—and other sources confirm the dire circumstances, although no congregants' names appear.[32] His mother was not only there but in a leading role. What moved the character Augustine, however, was not his mother's danger, but the mood of the city. Wait. What? He had no feelings about her presence there? A quick, if inadequate, psychoanalytic reading would hold that the character exmplifies a split of feelings about his mother's danger in the basilica from his thoughts about her situation. Does a similar psychological division appear in the author's calm narration of the events described as upsetting the whole city? Perhaps he could not assimilate his distress when the civil turmoil occurred. Maybe he still risked being overwhelmed by it when he wrote the *Confessions* over ten years later.

The question of what Augustine repressed might seem a little less obvious, but a starting point might be that he depicts a character who could not acknowledge the extent of his entanglement with career advancement and high society. How difficult might a rising star in late antiquity find the admission, even to himself, that the ties he depicts to a life of posturing and flattery actually had involved him in calculating his position as a government official and putting it ahead of his filial relationship to his mother? The son and mother relationship bore considerable weight at the time, even if somewhat differently from relationships between mothers and sons today.[33] The possibility he pictures, that he allowed familial bonds to approach an irremediable break, may have been too difficult for him to recapitulate fully in the midst of the stories in Book VI about his professional trials and personal longings. That the longings took so many forms—idealized with respect to philosophy and Christianity, more earthly with respect to his concubine, marriage, and habitual sex—would only create an image of him more inextricably caught in a tangle of overwhelming contradictions.

More careful consideration of psychoanalytic theory itself makes us wary of such quick interpretations. The point Ricoeur so carefully helps us notice is that the concepts of psychoanalysis depend on rules of interpretation. One of these rules is that the unconscious memories appear in consciousness in distorted form. If they move undistorted toward consciousness, repression increases in order to submerge the upsetting content. Under repression, the ideas and feelings are still active, although the person cannot discern their activity. The energy of thoughts and feelings forced down under repression leads them to collide. Collision, as traffic accidents and physics both tell us, can lead to deformity of the pre-collision structure. So as they collide, the ideas and feelings break into new shapes. These acquire some of each original idea's or feeling's characteristics—like another car's lines and paint left on the bumper of one's unfortunate auto. This combining of features is what Freud calls "condensation." He affirms that it pervasively forms symbols in dreams, symptoms, and creative work.[34]

Similarly, in the mode of comparison to physics, collisions among unconscious contents of the mind transfer energy; at least one of the cars ends up in an unintended place because of the collision and while it moves there, it accrues energy from the other car's movement. This transfer of energy Freud calls "displacement." Freud's explanation of displacement, however, attenuates the mechanical metaphor from physics and leads us to replace the auto collision with electrical energy. Freud talks about the vividness of conscious images that have received displaced energy from repressed psychic contents. A person might expect that vividness would indicate importance of the image, but the diversion created by the vividness allows the main repressed content to stay hidden. He claims from his clinical practice that displacement more than other psychological processes makes "the connection between the dream content and the [unconscious] dream thoughts unrecognizable."[35] Displacement, like condensation, distorts the psychic images of traumatic events, as well as ideas and feelings.

So based on the rules of psychoanalytic interpretation that enjoin us to expect repression and perhaps splitting, and to interpret them through the application of concepts like condensation and displacement, we should expect combinations of repressed memories to appear in the symbols in Augustine's texts. To remark "He is splitting" or "He is repressing" only suggests a staring point for interpretation. How might we proceed more methodically in interpretation?

Psychoanalytically oriented interpretations of Augustine's *Confessions* have frequently noted Augustine's and Monica's difficulties in closeness and separation. The studies that rely heavily on Freud's ideas have highlighted the Oedipal conflict, the time when a boy of about age five or six wants to displace his father in his mother's affections and harbors fantasies of murdering his father and marrying his mother. The studies of the *Confessions* have seen this desire emerge in distorted form in comments of Augustine like, "My mother did all she could to see that you, my God, should be more truly my father than he [Patricius] was" (1.11.17). They have also construed this comment as evidence of Monica's own incestuous desires toward Augustine. In the normal resolution of the Oedipus conflict, the boy gives up his murderous conscious fantasies with respect to his father and identifies with him, but relinquishes the sexual claim that he fantasized himself (however inchoately) advancing with respect to his mother. The loss implied in these conscious fantasies overwhelms the child sufficiently that they become part of the unconscious and emerge in new combinations and distortions from their collisions with other unconscious contents. Psychoanalytic discussions have argued for various views on whether Augustine gave up his identification with his father and at about what time the identification or lack of it caused him trouble. He is thought to have an unsteady resolution of the Oedipus complex and therefore to be perched on the verge of conversion to his mother's faith, as he would have been vulnerable to identifying with her rather than with his father.[36]

Alternate models of the mind associated with psychoanalysis concentrate on the effects of repression in the very early childhood years, before the child's Oedipal conflict. One of these models, self-psychology, has served scholarly interpretations of Augustine. Self-psychology holds that in the first months and year of life, a welcome narcissism develops in children. It comprises two parts: grandiosity, or the positive sense of one's own goodness, and identification with one's parents as idealized imagos (or internalized but imprecise images of the parents). The grandiosity in optimal cases scales

back through the child's confrontations with actual limits to his or her striv-
ings so that the child eventually forms more realistic ambitions, fueled indirectly by the narcissistic energy that was repressed as the grandiosity waned.
The idealized parent imagos also scale down to more realistic proportions
and persist as ideals that align with one's parents' ideals or relate to the ideals
that the child built up around impressions of the parents. When the optimal
outcomes do not occur—probably because of sudden and great or relentless
and small disappointments—repressed grandiosity transforms into shame,
coldness, haughtiness, self-preoccupation, sarcasm, rage,[37] or hypochondria.
Traumatic disappointments in ideals—traumatic either because of sudden-
ness and scale or unremitting small but damaging events—would emerge
from the unconscious as a longing to idealize people. Studies have cited
Augustine's frequent language about shame in the *Confessions* to support
claims that he suffered injuries to his grandiosity. They also note his vig-
nettes about lack of parental empathy with injuries to his grandiosity, such as
when his parents and other adults would laugh at his anguish about being
beaten by his schoolmasters (I.9.14).[38] Such injuries could be repressed and
emerge in sarcasm, rage, coldness, and so forth. Scholars have also noted his
apparent searching for idealizable male figures, especially Ambrose, but also
Faustus the Manichean and others, who would allow his disappointments
about Patricius' idealizability to come to consciousness. The disappointments are seen as emerging, transformed through condensation and displacement, as a recurrent wish for an idealized father figure or as hopelessness
about potential improvements in difficult situations.[39] I have relied on some
of these interpretations to advance my own in the past and still find them
worthwhile.[40]

The assumption embedded in many of these interpretations is that Augustine needed to separate himself from Monica to achieve an adult male autonomy or a coherent self in which modulated forms of both grandiosity and
idealizing led to energetic health and productivity, but the separation failed,
and thence followed many difficulties. Fairly often, the blame for his failure
lands on Monica—that she was too persistent and clingy for him to escape.
But a different set of assumptions helps elucidate another possibility: that the
issue was not simply how Augustine could become independent or how
Monica could let him go, but that they struggled with remaining in relationship to one another while they also lived out their individuality. This idea of
conflicts that stem not from insistence on "either-or" but "both-and" concerns about independence and closeness emerges from Jean Baker Miller's
idea of "being in relationship."[41] Miller argues for paying attention to the
prospect that throughout a girl's years growing up she will develop capacities
to live in relationship while she is also developing a self. These two develop-
ments, according to Miller, are not opposites but mutually constitutive: the
self forms in relationship and comes to fruition in relationships, and relation-

ships happen between selves. Miller believes that this discovery applies to men also and that the theories of male psychoanalysts like Erik Erikson overemphasized the separation of child from mother, and indeed of person from others, in the process of attaining adulthood.[42] A close look at Miller's argument shows that she, like other psychoanalytically informed authors, expects that feelings and information that the mind cannot handle are repressed and later emerge in disguised formations.[43] The difference of her ideas from theories like Erikson's lies in the repressed material. She sees repressed distress about problems of being in relationship, not only either-or problems of autonomy or dependence.[44] Her ideas have been elaborated and refined in research on "relational-cultural theory."[45]

The affair of the basilicas helps us to see several important issues related to psychoanalytic readings of the *Confessions*, only one of which has been highlighted before. A point remains from both Freudian and later psychoanalytically derived accounts that Monica and Augustine as portrayed in the *Confessions* had difficulty with how emotionally close or how distant they were from each other. This idea fits well with the surface content of the text, especially if one has a psychoanalytic hermeneutic to help one talk about it. Otherwise, the seemingly obvious surface content can dissolve by the application of truisms of everyday psychology. For instance, one could comment on the disparity of their life chances given the difference in their sexes or more shallowly on young men always wanting to get away from their mothers. But for us the apparent splitting off of Augustine's expression of feelings from his comments about his mother's location in the affair of the basilicas alerts us to reflect on his psychological processes as author, whether in psychoanalytic, self-psychological, relational-cultural, or some other theory's terms.

First, the placement and language of the account of the basilicas could easily allow repressed distresses about the relationship with his mother to escape in distorted form. Their energy may be displaced onto other issues, like the greater amount of prose devoted to the finding of relics that were related, but not historically central, to the affair of the basilicas. The shape of the distresses—How close shall we be? With what consequences for my work, my other relationships, my commitments in thought?—can emerge quietly, if a bit disruptively, in the structure of the text. Book VI, after all, never directly addresses whether Augustine and Monica might need some more separation. Quite the contrary in fact. Book VI only shows them reunited and her working for a marriage (VI.13.23) for which Augustine the author claims that his character longed (VI.6.9). But the marriage arrangements in the social world of the time also necessitated the departure of his concubine, and losing her causes him distress, that, as he depicts it, did not die but festered (VI.15.25). If anything of this order actually had happened to Augustine the author over a decade before he wrote the *Confessions*, he might have felt anger with his mother for playing a part in the arrangements that led to his concubine's leaving. Such anger would be irrational, in that Augustine himself had been seeking marriage. Nonetheless, the operation of the unconscious need not be rational; the rage might indicate a blow to his unconscious need for affirmation for his grandiosity, a blow like the realization that his reasonable, socially acceptable calculation of the value of marriage did not protect him from the pain of parting from his longtime lover. So if when he composed the *Confessions* he minimized expression of distress about Monica's possible fate in the basilica and placed the incident far from the marriage arrangements mentioned in the text, the tone and placement could represent the rage and coldness.

When one considers the social facts of the situation, this reading only becomes more tenable: the author shows us a situation in which Augustine the character had serious responsibility for the financial support of his household, in which social conventions about marriage and family honor could press on him, and in which the government threatened its officials with death—and hence certainly with the end of their financial care for their families—if they interfered with the emperor's and empress's worship preferences. These factors alone could cause major distress. An empathic reader could go so far to say that Augustine's separating facets of the story seems psychologically more bearable than the tremendous emotional strain of allowing them all to come to consciousness together.

The second threat that might be reflected in the story is that Augustine—both character and author—not only tried to escape from his mother but that he also feared losing her. A startling level of independence on the part of Monica the character appears in this story. The distinction of Catholic mother and pagan father, of which past psychoanalytic interpreters have made much, may have had implications, even in his early childhood, for the possibility that she could act as her own person, without constant reference to her son. In regard to the Christian faith and church, as well as some aspects of household life, the author allows us to see the character Monica taking a direction distinct from Patricius'. In Book I (11.17), Monica arranges for Augustine's baptism and Patricius does not interfere. Is her habit of church attendance in Milan indicative also of a habit earlier in life (VI.2.2)? This possibility is not far-fetched given that Augustine presents her to us as having grown up in a devout household, growing toward greater piety, and acquainted with her bishop in North Africa. Could Augustine thus have lived with an infantile fear that she might in fact choose the church and abandon him? Or, as children sometimes fear, go away—in this case to church—and not come back?

Interestingly, a child's fear about his mother's absence figures in *Beyond the Pleasure Principle*, one of Freud's texts that Ricoeur explicates to formulate his proposal on the interaction of culture and psyche. Freud tells a story of his grandson playing a game with a spool when his mother left the house for the evening. The child would roll the spool out of sight and draw it back, and say, "*fort . . . da*" ("gone . . . there)." Freud interpreted this behavior as symbolizing the mother's absence and exercising playful control by pulling the spool back when the child could not retrieve the actual mother.[46] For Ricoeur, the vignette supports the idea that losses (even small ones like a mother's short absence from her toddler) prompt the use of materials at hand to help people picture the overcoming of the loss. Not only do children do this, but culture itself develops from the interaction of creative geniuses with cultural materials to embody their own losses ("*fort*") and concomitantly picture the resolution ("*da*") of the unhappy situation.[47]

If we look at the few sentences about the affair of the basilica, we see Augustine the author picturing Monica as having jeopardized precious aspects of not only her own life but Augustine's. In the author's description of the conflict between the bishop and imperial family, the character Monica willingly risked death rather than stay with the characters Augustine and Adeodatus. Augustine tells us in the story of her death that Adeodatus, her grandson, grieved loudly for her (IX.12.29). What if she had died by violence in the basilica? Augustine the author creates a possibility that Augustine the character then would not only have lost his mother, sometime near when he also lost or contemplated losing his concubine, but he would have had to care for an adolescent son, without the help of the grandmother whom, the story posits, Adeodatus loved and had seen daily for several years. So the incident of the basilicas leads to consideration of not only how closely entwined Monica and Augustine, characters or living people, were but also how separately he imagined they could act. The author shows us Monica as a character who actively chose a potentially drastic separation. Nor, we should note, does he picture her hiding in the back of the church and whimpering for her son. The author did not create a mother character whose personhood dissolved when she insisted on parting from her family and living by her faith. How was he to live *in* relationship with this person?

The affair of the basilicas seems to capture the feared loss of being-in-relationship with his mother and to join it to a series of culturally shaped images of restoration of relationship in the rest of Book IX.[48] Soon after the short passages in the *Confessions* on the conflict, Augustine depicts an apex for his relationship with his mother: their shared mystical experience at Ostia (IX.10.23-26). After that he discusses her death and his grief, and again he shows them in relationship, in a way rarely if ever noted in psychological studies of the *Confessions*: "in that last illness she would at times respond with a caress to some little service I rendered her, calling me a devoted son, and with deep affection would declare that she had never heard from my lips any harsh or rough expression flung against her." A variety of readings might call into question the factuality of this reading: Should we believe about the character of Augustine that he rendered his mother little services when she was ill? Or did he stay with the menfolk and discuss philosophy? Did this same character actually live so many years, so eager to advance in his worldly success outside the home and away from the realm of women, without ever "any harsh or rough expression" slipping out toward his mother? We could multiply questions, but these issues do not undermine the point of the reading informed by Miller's psychological view. They instead reinforce it because they allow us to see that whatever the reality that an observer might have seen, Augustine the author's representation of the characters' relationship emphasizes being together and having a close relationship in spite of its impending end. This permits, in a creative cultural work so full of separations as the *Confessions*, the representation of both the loss experienced with his mother's death and the creative image of a resolution written over a decade later as a sketch of their tender moments together. Not only does the scene represent both loss and closeness, but so does the author Augustine's reflection a few lines later on his mother's death: "Being now bereft of her comfort, so great a comfort, my soul was wounded; it was as though my life was rent apart, for there had been but one life, woven out of mine and hers" (IX.12.30). While this sentence has been taken to indicate too close a narcissistic enmeshment of Augustine and Monica, it may also be seen, with Miller's help, as picturing nearly overwhelming sorrow about separation yet assuagement of it in the face of death, which cannot be physically resolved in a reunion of those whom it separates. These lines evoke being-in-relationship in spite of the most final end of being-in-relationship as we know it.

At the end of Book IX, Augustine famously asks his readers to remember at God's altar both of his now-dead parents, where he, the priest and bishop, also will remember them. He starts from his thoughts of the loss of them in daily life and extends his phrases toward the restoration of relationship with them but even more toward communion with the whole of the Church, heavenly as well as earthly. Such images allow painful earthly grief to rise to the surface of the mind in manageable proportions; simultaneously it uses and affects elements of culture by posing a literary vision of relationship in spite of separation. It thereby speaks to readers over the centuries as they meditate on the theological doctrine of the church eternal, as well as psychologically on grief and life's finitude. It thus can speak to deep-seated fears about having and losing our being in our relationships. Moreover, its effectiveness in its place in Book IX is amplified by its literary evocativeness about both theology and psychology. Reducing any two of the three—literature, theology, psychology—to being only about the third would diminish the power of the passage.

The writer Augustine's request that his audience remember Monica and Patricius at God's altar leads the sophisticated reader to a strange hermeneutic juncture. We have learned about Augustine the author's use of characters, such as Monica, to make theological points. We realize that he may incorporate them into the design of the *Confessions* for various literary purposes, such as heightening various tensions to carry the narrative forward. Yet we read a segment of the *Confessions'* prayer asking "that as many of them as read this may remember Monica, your servant, at your altar, along with Patricius, sometime her husband." Does he want us to remember that lively character Monica and her more hazy but still vaguely visible husband figure at God's altar? The unlikelihood of this inference increases as we read the next sentence: "From their flesh you brought me into this life . . ." He thus associates the Monica and Patricius of the *Confessions* all the more closely with flesh and blood people. This may, of course, just be Augustine-the-author trying to reinforce the verisimilitude of his fictionalized account, but he immediately goes on to undermine an overly literal reading, saying of this conception and birth, "though how I do not know." Rather than a literal statement of ignorance about biological reproduction, this phrase hints at a theological speculation on the mysteries of personhood and a theme that Augustine as theologian will discuss later in his commentary on Genesis as he ruminates on the origin of the soul.[49] But here in *Confessions* IX Augustine continues writing more allusively about various kinds of family relationships that Christians have in the Church: "Let them remember with loving devotion these two who were my parents in this transitory light, but also were my brethren under you, our Father, within our mother the Catholic church, and my fellow-citizens in the eternal Jerusalem . . ." (IX.13.37). So the passage's reminder of flesh-and-blood people still carries multiple meanings about how to think about them, even on the conscious level.

One of the meanings, I claim, is to give us some sense that the characters of Monica and Patricius are not to be relegated to fiction simply because we cannot always tell what words are only literary device and what carry representations that might correspond more closely to people Augustine actually knew. Augustine the writer seems to believe that he has told us enough about his flesh-and-blood parents that we can remember them at God's altar. So the prose turns us two ways in conscious thought at this point—toward once-living beings and toward elaborated ways of knowing them and seeing them in a theological light. The theological light might distort the person on the street as much as any other aid to our sight, but we have a request and an authorization here to consider that we might know something about Monica-*not*--the-character, and Patricius likewise. What to accept as a feature of someone we might have met and what to see as more strictly literary is not clear, as Clark insists.[50] But Augustine invites us to remember people, not simply characters, and we may join from a variety of perspectives in Moore's effort to sketch out what we might think is probable about Monica the person.[51]

What I would emphasize from the affair of the basilicas is that the Monica spotted through pinholes in the representation of her character by Augustine may well have been much more independent of Augustine than our psycho-analytic lenses and mid-twentieth-century patriarchy have encouraged us to notice. Moreover, her son in childhood and in adulthood might not only have experienced her as seeking too much closeness to him but as frightening in her ability to leave home in order to align herself with God's servants in the church. While the bishop writing the *Confessions* might admire someone who would follow scriptural injunctions (Matt. 10:37, attributed to Jesus, "he that loveth son or daughter more than me, is not worthy of me" [Douay-Rheims]), what repressed anxieties of Augustine the child might have been attached to this representation? What might Augustine the writer have been unable to speak regarding his mother's fidelity to something other than him and his family? "Gone . . . there" can intrude on our relationships unexpect-edly in the most secure situations humanly possible. Living simultaneously with the prospect of "gone and there" together in our lives may be one of the many tasks that Augustine's *Confessions* captures for our *exercitatio animi*. This exercise can take us from his shame at not joining in her courage or biblical faith to understanding that God intervenes to help us deal with threats, as the story of the discovery of martyrs' relics seems to indicate, and that our return to being in relationship widens in the best instance to include ourselves and our immediate loved ones in the family of God.

THOUGHTS ON AUGUSTINE AND PSYCHOANALYTICALLY BASED PSYCHOLOGIES

Reading the *Confessions* with psychoanalytic ideas in mind is arguably the predicament of every educated reader at the beginning of the twenty-first century. Some readers may wish that the intellectual course of Europe had never proposed this possibility. Others may feel considerable gratitude that shifts in psychological thought over the prior century have allowed us to use some psychoanalytic concepts—like repression, splitting, condensation, and displacement—without necessarily having to drag in others—like the Oedi-pal complex, sexual bases for every repression, and the id-ego-superego model of the personality. Some readers may still find the Oedipal or more strictly Freudian readings most persuasive.

Yet a reader might experience confusion about many topics related to psychoanalytic readings, even ones thoroughly articulated with cultural con-siderations. Here I think of three major doubts. First, which of these psycho-analytically derived theoretical readings is right? Second, what about other psychologies, like the Aristotelian psychology of habit that crops up in *Con-fessions* Book VIII as Augustine the author portrays the young character

Augustine moving from his bondage to lust toward conversion? And finally, what about the problem that psychoanalysis is constantly under attack and in many ways displaced in psychiatry, especially in the U.S., by the use of other therapeutic modes, some relying on advanced neuroscience?

As we ponder the first question, one of the key features of psychoanalytic understanding comes to our aid: symbolic formations of the mind, like symptoms or dreams or modes of speech, bear the marks of many collisions of unconscious ideas, feelings, and memories. The technical term that applies is "overdetermination." No product of the psyche finds a single source for its determination. All are determined many times over. The interpreter seeks unconscious meanings that interact with conscious meanings, images, events, and relationships. The correspondences and distortions are multitudinous. After years of psychoanalytic practice, Freud himself came to see as illusory his initial hope that retrieving a traumatic unconscious memory would effect a cure of his patient's symptoms. Instead, the therapy required "working through," the return of the memory in disguised form over and over before the patient could become less enthralled by it and more able to recognize it and adjust his or her action to other ways of viewing the surrounding circumstances.

To answer the second question, note that other psychologies, like Aristotle's on habit, some of which Augustine himself employed, have their place in the interpretive strategy opened up by Ricoeur. They are works of culture to be explored through a variety of hermeneutics and to be left in peace, away from psychoanalytic challenges or reductionism, so that we can understand them on their own terms and in a variety of other conscious lights. If one chooses to bring them into conversation with psychoanalytic thought, then Ricoeur's approach to the interpretation of symbols may carry over to the other psychologies, construed as symbolic structures. But nowhere does Ricoeur say that one must conduct the psychoanalytic investigation, only that one may. I agree. Setting free the play of signifiers does not require every set of signifiers be tried to eliminate the others from the playing field.

The answer to this second doubt about using psychoanalytic theories leads us to the third and its greater implications. What shall we think about psychoanalytic readings of Augustine's writings if neuroscience supplants psychoanalytically based interpretations of the psyche? This question takes a place in a larger debate facing our culture as neuroscience continues to offer us wondrous ways of getting to know our minds and our lives. In respect to some psychological functions, neuroscience propels us toward understanding better how our brains work. How that understanding links up to what our lives and thoughts and feelings mean to us is not always clear, however. And to some large extent, this was what intrigued and motivated Freud's theorizing. His early research with people with hysterical or obsessive-compulsive symptoms pursued solutions where neurology had failed.[52] The claim he made was that neurological complications were relieved by interpretation of meaning. But nothing constrains us to look for meaning only where neuroscience fails us. As we learn how the brain works, what its products mean to us in relation to our past lives will still pose conundrums. For a while, at least, psychoanalytic modes of thought may give us a way to address them. As we engage other modes of understanding meaning in human lives, the connection of meaning to neuroscience will continue to require exploration. If we were to pinpoint with the help of neuropsychology a moment in Augustine's infancy when Monica's and Augustine's oxytocin levels were low (that is, they were short of the body's chemical that promotes personal attachment), we would still have much to learn to understand how that event affected their experience of their lives.

This brings us to a final consideration raised by the effort to review the conflict of the basilicas and the pressures of Augustine's life in Milan. One potential benefit of the psychoanalytic mode of inquiry, especially as it is complemented by the study of culture and cultural psychology's efforts to elucidate the interaction of psyche and culture, is that it insists on a functioning mind. Definite lines between the mind, the author, and the character of autobiographical writing may never establish themselves, but reading the book without a search for the author is an eerie exploration, even if also a fascinating and enlightening discipline. This statement is not a call for a simple reading of an author from a completed text. But it is a suggestion that as all interpretive stances have their advantages and shortcomings, we might do well to allow or even encourage some readings of authors as well as texts, especially where the authors use their own name and purport to tell their own story to make a point. The links of the *Confessions* to Augustine's life can be indirect, but the conflict of the basilicas reminds us that he embeds hints in his text about serious business in the world. The pressures that Augustine, both author and character, berates himself for minding (Books VI and VIII) receive a grounding in the allusion to the affair of the basilicas. The conflict demonstrates that he places his character in a social world of high stakes political activity. Read historically, in a literary manner, theologically, with a philosophical bent, or psychologically, the passages about life at the pinnacle of an empire humble us. Who was this bishop, this author? Who are we with our interpretive tools? What could we learn from one another? Why feel sure—why even try to be sure—that psychologically, or any other way, we "got him right"? Why back off from investigating closely the possibility that—despite all our suspicious hermeneutics, worries about hegemonic discourses, embarrassment of intertexts—we have encountered representations of a remarkable man, and a remarkable woman? Exactly who he is, who his mother is, who knows? But then who knows that about anyone, including oneself? After all we, just as Augustine portrayed himself, may discover ourselves as "land hard to till and of heavy sweat" (*Conf.* X.16.25). Or, as the historian of culture Karl Weintraub said with full intentionality to his wife in his dedication of *The Value of the Individual: Self and Circumstance in Autobiography*, "*individuum ineffabile est.*" The deeper question this statement poses, especially at the beginning of a book on the historical development of the concept of the self as individual, is how we can understand singularity, especially the individuality of a person. Nonetheless, in the "Acknowledgements" Weintraub seeks with admiration, generosity, and gratitude to characterize this wife, *ineffabile* though she may be.[53] Such acknowledgements of a person propose, despite their potential distortions, a great enterprise. Let's go on with it.

NOTES

1. Augustine, *Confessions*, trans. Maria Boulding, Preface by Patricia Hampl, Vintage Spiritual Classics (New York: Vintage, 1997). This translation will be used unless otherwise indicated. For the Latin text I have used James J. O'Donnell, *Augustine, Confessions, vol. I, Introduction and Text* (Oxford: Clarendon Press, 1992).

2. See, for instance, Andrew Lenox-Conyngham, "The Topography of the Basilica Conflict of A.D. 385/6 in Milan," *Historia* 31:3 (Third Quarter, 1982) 363.

3. *Augustine of Hippo: A Biography*, new ed. with an Epilogue (Berkeley and Los Angeles: University of California Press, 2000) 59.

4. Karl Weintraub, *The Value of the Individual: Self and Circumstance in Autobiography* (Chicago and London: University of Chicago Press, 1978) 37, 39–42.

5. *Freud and Philosophy: An Essay in Interpretation*, trans. Denis Savage (New Haven, CT: Yale University Press, 1970), and "Art and Freudian Systematics," trans. Willis Domingo, in *The Conflict of Interpretations*, ed. Don Ihde, Northwestern University Studies in Phenomenology and Existential Philosophy, gen. ed. James M. Edie (Evanston, IL: Northwestern University Press, 1974) 196–208.

6. Jeffrey Kripal, *Kali's Child: The Mystical and the Erotic in the Life and Teachings of Ramakrishna*, 2nd ed. (Chicago and London: University of Chicago Press, 1995), and "Why the Tantrika is a Hero: Kali in the Psychoanalytic Tradition," in *Encountering Kali: In the Margins, at the Center, in the West*, ed. Rachel Fell McDermott and Jeffrey J. Kripal (Berkeley and Los Angeles: University of California Press, 2003) 196–222, and references therein for other scholars interested in the same line of thought. Another exemplary exponent of this way of working is Gananath Obeyesekere, explicitly in *The Work of Culture: Symbolic Transformation in Psychoanalysis and Anthropology* (Chicago and London: University of Chicago Press, 1990), xviii–xix, and prototypically in *Medusa's Hair: An Essay on Personal Symbols and Religious Experience* (Chicago and London: University of Chicago Press, 1981).

7. Elizabeth Clark, "Rewriting Early Christian History: Augustine's Representations of Monica," in *Portraits of Spiritual Authority: Religious Power in Early Christianity, Byzantium and the Christian Orient,* ed. Jan Willem Drijvers and John W. Watt, Religions in the Graeco-Roman World, ed. R. Van Den Broek, H. J. W. Drijvers, H. S. Versnel, vol. 137 (Leiden: Brill, 1999), 21.

8. "O Mother, Where Art Thou? In Search of Saint Monnica [sic]," in *Feminist Interpretations of Augustine*, ed. Judith Chelius Stark (University Park: Pennsylvania State University Press, 2007) 149–162. This volume contains a number of thought-provoking chapters dealing at length with Monica and questions of rhetoric and interpretation.

9. See Ricoeur, *Freud and Philosophy*, 174, and "Art," 207–208, for a similar idea, one of entering "into the movement of the signifier" through its derivatives.

10. Clark, "Rewriting," 9–10.

11. Ricoeur, *The Symbolism of Evil*, trans. Emerson Buchanan (Boston: Beacon Press, 1967) 355.

12. Weintraub, *Value of the Individual*, 1; Brown, *Augustine*, 158–161.

13. *Augustine Confessions III: Commentary on Books 8–13, Indexes* (Oxford: Clarendon Press, 1992) 154.

14. See Eric Plumer, "Book Six: Major Characters and Memorable Incidents," in *A Reader's Companion to Augustine's Confessions*, ed. Kim Paffenroth and Robert P. Kennedy (Louisville, KY, and London: Westminster John Knox Press, 2003) 89–105, for a strong argument about the interest of the book.

15. See Plumer, "Book 6," 104 and 240, n. 25, for a thoughtful adoption of Margaret Miles' view that Augustine had a "sexual addiction." See also Margaret Miles, "Infancy, Parenting and Nourishment in Augustine's *Confessions*," *Journal of the American Academy of Religion* 50 (1982) 349–364, especially 358.

16. James J. O'Donnell, *Augustine, Confessions, vol. II, Commentary on Books 1–7*, 356–357, and *Augustine Confessions III: Commentary on Books 8–13, Indexes*, 111–112.

17. Clark, "Rewriting," 15–20.

18. Henry Chadwick's translation simply renders *orationis vivebat* as "living in prayer" (*Confessions*, trans. With an Introduction and Notes by Henry Chadwick, World's Classics [Oxford and New York: Oxford University Press, 1992]).

19. Clark, "Rewriting," 20.

20. O'Donnell, *Augustine Confessions III: Commentary on Books 8–13, Indexes*, 110.

21. For a fine and much fuller discussion of reconciliation in Book IX, see Kim Paffenroth, "Book Nine: The Emotional Heart of the *Confessions*," in *A Reader's Companion to Augustine's Confessions*, ed. Kim Paffenroth and Robert P. Kennedy (Louisville, KY, and London: Westminster John Knox Press, 2003) 146–154.

22. Ambrose, Letter 20, *Patrologiae Latinae*, 16 (printed as Letter 60 in *Fathers of the Church*) and *Sermon against Auxentius on the Giving Up of the Basilicas*, in *St. Ambrose: Select Works and Letters, Nicene and Post-Nicene Fathers of the Christian Church*, sec. series, vol. X, trans. and ed. Philip Schaff and Henry Wace (New York: Christian Literature Company, 1896).

23. Lenox-Conyngham, "Topography," 353, citing *Codex Theodosianus* XVI.1.4.

24. O'Donnell, *Augustine Confessions III*, 154.

25. See O'Donnell, *Augustine Confessions III*, 110.

26. O'Donnell, *Augustine Confessions III*, 110; for Simplicianus, see *Conf.* VIII.2.3.

27. James J. O'Donnell, *Late Have I Loved Thee*. Videorecording. Santa Fe, NM: Della Robbia Productions, c1992.

28. For a thoughtful interpretation of this incident, see (among many others) Danuta Shanzer, "Pears Before Swine: Augustine, *Confessions*, 2.4.9," *Revue des etudes augustiniennes*, 42 (1996) 45–55; and Robert J. O'Connell, *Saint Augustine's Confessions: An Odyssey of Soul* (Cambridge: Harvard University Press, 1969).

29. Sigmund Freud, *Five Lectures on Psychoanalysis*, Standard Edition of the Complete Psychological Works of Sigmund Freud, ed. and trans. James Strachey (London: Hogarth Press and the Institute of Psycho-Analysis, 1957 [1910]) 11:22–26.

30. Freud, *Five Lectures*, 27–28.

31. For a more detailed explanation of splits in the psyche as understood by the later twentieth-century psychoanalyst and founding self-psychologist Heinz Kohut, see Sandra Lee Dixon, *Augustine: The Scattered and Gathered Self* (St. Louis, MO: Chalice Press, 1999) 121–125.

32. Ambrose, Letter 20; Lenox-Conyngham, "Topography."

33. Gillian Clark, *Augustine, The Confessions*, Landmarks of World Literature, gen. ed. J. P. Stern (Cambridge: Cambridge University Press, 1993) 58–59; Moore, "O Mother," 154; Kim Power, *Veiled Desire: Augustine on Women* (New York: Continuum, 1996) 27–28.

34. For easy reference, see *On Dreams*, trans. and ed. James Strachey, with an Introduction by Peter Gay (New York and London: W.W. Norton, 1989) ch. 4.

35. *On Dreams*, 34.

36. E. R. Dodds, "Augustine's *Confessions*: A Study of Spiritual Maladjustment," *Hibbert Journal* 26 (1928) 459–473; Charles Kligerman, "A Psychoanalytic Study of the *Confessions* of St. Augustine," *Journal of the American Psychoanalytic Association* 5 (1957) 469–484. A

strong critique of these studies appears in Larissa Carina Seelbach, "*Das weibliche Geschlecht ist ja kein Gebrechen . . .": Die Frau und ihre Gottebenbildlichkeit bei Augustin* (Würzburg: Augustinus-Verlag, 2002) 84–89; and Seelbach, "Psychoanalytische Deutungsversuche zur Persönlichkeit Augustins—Beispiele und Anfragen," *Theologie und Glaube* 93 (2003) 240–261. For a paradigm sketch of such criticisms, see Paula Fredriksen, "Augustine and His Analysts: The Possibility of a Psychohistory," *Soundings* 61 (1978) 207–208.

37. Heinz Kohut, *The Restoration of the Self* (New York: International Universities Press, 1977) 137.

38. For an especially sensitive treatment of this topic see Donald Capps, "The Scourge of Shame and the Silencing of Adeodatus" in Donald Capps and James E. Dittes, eds., *The Hunger of the Heart: Reflections on the* Confessions *of Augustine*, Society for the Scientific Study of Religion Monograph Series, No. 8 (West Lafayette, IN: Society for the Scientific Study of Religion, 1990) 71–92.

39. Heinz Kohut, "Forms and Transformations of Narcissism," in *The Search for the Self: Selected Writings by Heinz Kohut*, ed. with an Introduction by Paul Ornstein (New York: International Universities Press, 1978) I:437; Don S. Browning, "The Psychoanalytic Interpretation of Augustine's *Confessions*," in *Psychoanalysis and Religion*, ed. Joseph H. Smith and Susan Handelman, Psychiatry and the Humanities, 11 (Baltimore and London: Johns Hopkins University Press, 1990) 136–159; Paul Rigby, "Paul Ricoeur, Freudianism, and Augustine's *Confessions*," *Journal of the American Academy of Religion* 53:1 (March 1985) 93–114.

40. See, among others, William R. Beers, "The *Confessions* of Augustine: Narcissistic Elements," *American Imago* 45 (1988) 107–125; Donald Capps, "Augustine as Narcissist: Of Grandiosity and Shame," in Donald Capps and James E. Dittes, eds. *The Hunger of the Heart: Reflections on the Confessions of Augustine*, Society for the Scientific Study of Religion Monograph Series, No. 8 (West Lafayette, IN: Society for the Scientific Study of Religion, 1990) 172–184; Sandra Lee Dixon, *Augustine*, and "The Many Layers of Meaning in Moral Arguments: A Self Psychological Case Study of Augustine's Arguments for Coercion," Ph.D. diss., University of Chicago, 1993; Fredriksen, "Augustine and his Analysts," 206–227.

41. Jean Baker Miller, "The Development of Women's Sense of Self," in *Women's Spirituality: Resources for Christian Development*, ed. Joan Wolski Conn, 2nd ed. (New York and Mahwah, NJ: Paulist Press, 1996), 170. Development of Miller's idea of being-in-relationship is the work of Linda Land-Closson in her analysis of the life of the twentieth-century Benedictine, Bede Griffiths, "Strings of Relationship and Community: A Dialogue between the Life of Bede Griffiths and the Theories of Jean Baker Miller," Ph. D. diss., Joint Ph.D. Program in Religious and Theological Studies of the Iliff School of Theology and the University of Denver, 2008. I am grateful to Dr. Land-Closson for helping me discern its possibilities for psychological investigation of historical figures, although the responsibility for applying it to Monica and Augustine is mine alone.

42. Miller, "Development," 167–174.

43. Miller, "Development," 178–179.

44. Miller, "Development," 169.

45. Jean Baker Miller Training Institute at the Wellesley Centers for Women, "Relational-Cultural Theory," http://www.jbmti.org/Our-Work/relational-cultural-theory, accessed June 15, 2012.

46. *Beyond the Pleasure Principle*, Standard Edition of the Complete Psychological Works of Sigmund Freud, ed. and trans. James Strachey (London: Hogarth Press and the Institute of Psycho-Analysis, 1957) 18:17.

47. *Freud and Philosophy*, 285–286; Ricoeur elaborates this understanding in his reading of Freud's study of Leonardo da Vinci (*Freud and Philosophy*, 176).

48. See Paffenroth, "Book IX."

49. *De Genesi ad litteram* (*Literal Commentary on Genesis*), X.

50. Clark, "Rewriting," 21.

51. Moore, "O Mother," 150–151, 153–156.

52. Freud, *Five Lectures*, Lecture 2.

53. Weintraub, *Value of the Individual*, x.

Chapter Four

St. Augustine: Archetypes of Family

Anne Hunsaker Hawkins

THE MATERNAL NEXUS

The *Confessions* could be said to be a long, sustained fugue on the complementary motifs of restlessness and rest, or hunger and satisfaction, where resolution is achieved in conversion. The theme of rest and refuge is represented in Augustine's Heavenly Jerusalem, "Mother of us all," and the corresponding theme of restlessness is represented as unceasing and often tormented motion—the hunger of body, mind, and heart for satisfaction. We have observed the restlessness of body in the outer narrative of literal journeys, the restlessness of mind in the inner movement from philosophy to philosophy, and the restlessness of heart in the well-known theme of the *cor irrequietum*. But beyond this, hunger is itself a chief metaphor in the *Confessions*—a metaphor that relates the restlessness of body, mind, and heart alike to the archetypal mother, source of nourishment and cause of both satisfaction and frustration.

Augustine's use of hunger as a metaphor for spiritual need often leads him to analogies with the passive state of infancy. Thus he observes that "the Word was made flesh, that by thy wisdom, by which thou creates all things, he might suckle our infancy" (7.18). And again, he writes: "What am I even at the best but an infant sucking thy milk, and feeding upon thee, food which is incorruptible?" (5.1).[1] Augustine's description of his infancy in the early books of the autobiography is meant as a description of the sins of infancy: these are greed—and the infantile emotions derived from greed—anger (when hunger is not satisfied) and envy (at the satisfaction of another's hunger) (1.7). When as a youth he arrives in Carthage, it is the raging of this inner hunger that causes him to be ensnared by his own lustful appetite. Sexual hunger is accompanied by intellectual hunger: his description of his

69

interest in Manichaeism is replete with references to hunger, food, and nourishment. Later in life he observes that he is "still possessed with a greediness
of enjoying things present . . . " (6.11). It is Augustine the author, looking
back on his youth, who realizes that this is a hunger that is misdirected and
thus can never be satisfied. For the restlessness of the soul is a hunger
diverted onto lower things—a hunger that achieves satisfaction only when
the soul returns its love to its source, to God.

Throughout the *Confessions* the end of the quest is perceived as a haven
after a storm; as rest, peace, and, most important, as assuagement of the
inchoate yearnings of the heart. The autobiography ends as it begins: "our
heart is restless til it rests in thee" (1.1) and "Thou . . . are at rest always,
because that rest thou art thyself" (13.38).[2] Jung described as a major attrib-
ute of the mother archetype "the love that means homecoming, shelter, and
the long silence from which everything begins and in which everything
ends."[3] He might have been describing the Heavenly City, which Augustine
rhapsodizes over as an abode of peace—"Jerusalem my country, Jerusalem
my mother" (12.16). The theme of rest and refuge introduced in the first
paragraph of the *Confessions* is a refrain that is repeated throughout the
book: Augustine describes himself as capable "neither of rest nor counsel,"
directs us to "rest yourselves in him and ye shall rest safely," observes that
"there is no rest to be found where you seek it," and elsewhere remarks, "Let
us now at last, O Lord, return, that we do not turn aside . . . for in thee only
the soul can rest" (4.7; 4.12; 4.16; 6.16). It is true that all these references to
"rest" and "refuge" are to God, and not to the Church of the Heavenly
Jerusalem. But Augustine's idea of God, in part derived from classical epic
and philosophy, in its Christianized form is inevitably bound up in the idea of
the Heavenly City, "Jerusalem my Mother." Mother-Church and Father-God
are the archetypal divine parents: the Christian community, as "my fellow-
citizens in that eternal Jerusalem," is "subject to thee, our Father, in our
Catholic Mother" (9.13). Augustine's "fraternal" model of the spiritual family is derivative of the overarching importance for him of the mother archetype. For it is the maternal City of God that is the "home" of the collectivity
of Christian souls.

It is the archetypal mother who is the dominant figure in Augustine's
religious imagination—an archetype symbolizing both the goal of our redemptive longings and also the hunger that drives us in search of that goal.
Jung formulates the archetypal feminine duality as *"mater spiritualis"* and
"mater natura."[4] Monica functions in both roles of natural and spiritual
mother, as Augustine observes over and over during the course of his autobiography. Early in book 1, when a childhood illness brings him near death,
he writes that "the mother of my flesh . . . most lovingly travailed in birth of
my eternal salvation" (1.11); and at the end of the personal confession, he
commemorates his mother for bringing him to birth "both in her flesh, that I

might be born again to this temporal light, and in her heart too, that I might be born again to the eternal light" (9.8).

For Jung the mother archetype signifies "the son's relation to the real mother, to her imago, and to the woman who is to become a mother for him": she is thus both "the solace for all the bitterness of life" and "the seductress who draws him into life."[5] In their representation of the archetypal mother as fundamentally ambivalent, Jungian archetypal theory and biblical symbolism come together. For example, there is the duality of Eve and Mary—mother as temptress and mother as consolation. Just as Christ is a perfected type of the Old Testament Adam, so is Virgin Mary a perfected type of the Old Testament Eve. Another version of the dual nature of the feminine archetype is to be found in the wisdom literature of the Old Testament, where the feminine appears as spouse rather than as mother. The conflict between wisdom and temptation, both personified as women, is an ancient tradition and was certainly familiar to Augustine. In the book of Proverbs, *sapientia* is a female figure admonishing Man away from "the strange woman" or "the evil woman," the *meretrix* who leads Man into the path of sin and death: "Wisdom crieth without; she uttereth her voice in the streets . . . to deliver thee from the strange woman . . ." (Prov. 1:20 and 2:16).[6] Indeed, Augustine refers to his youthful sins with reference to the lures of the Old Testament *meretrix*: "I changed upon that bold woman, who knoweth nothing, that subtlety in Solomon . . . She seduced me, because she found my soul out-of-doors, dwelling in the eye of my flesh . . ." (*Conf.* 3.6). If the *meretrix* is an "adulteress" (Prov. 6:26), *sapientia* is "the wife of thy youth" (Prov. 5:18). And furthermore, the designation "wife of thy youth" is amplified in *sapientia*'s archaic origins, for she exists alongside of God before the creation of the world: "The Lord possessed me in the beginning of his way, before his works of old" (Prov. 8:22). Augustine's Heavenly Jerusalem, the maternal and intellectual mind of God whom he presents in book 12:15 (*"mens rationalis et intellectualis castae civitatis tuae, matris nostrae"*), is based on his Old Testament idea of wisdom, a feminine personification prior to and formative in the Creation.[7] So also Augustine's portrayal of Monica, who throughout the *Confessions* rebukes him with tears and lamentations for his wandering ways, can be seen as parallel to the feminine figure of *sapientia*, whose role is to admonish Man against wasting himself among the things of this world.

Thus it might seem that Augustine's own life provides characters that conform to those two great archetypes: Monica to the spiritual mother, or *sapientia*, and the concubine in whose embrace he so long postponed his conversion to the natural mother, or the *meretrix*. Just as the two women are literally antagonists and rivals—for it is Monica who finally forces Augustine to dismiss his concubine—so also in his allegorical reworking of his experience they stand for opposed forces. As allegorical personae, Monica comes to represent the voice of divine love, while the concubine represents carnal love. And yet, as I shall show, Augustine's autobiography "lives" for us precisely because the characters in his life are not so rigidly characterized. Monica is not simply the "spiritual mother." Her characterization is a very complicated one, and includes both variants of the archetypal feminine. Her positive nature is apotheosized mother in the Heavenly Jerusalem we have observed; the negative side emerges in Augustine's description of the role she played in trying to prevent him from going to Rome. His description of the incident is a vivid one: Monica weeps bitterly to see him go and follows him to the water's edge, clinging to him with all her strength in the hope that he will either return home or take her with him. To get away he must tell her a lie. He then persuades her to spend the night in a shrine and sails away in secret. Her oversolicitous concern he calls carnal affection (*"carnale deside-rium"*), for by her weeping and lamenting, he writes, she was "proving herself by those tortures to be guilty of what Eve left behind her; with sorrow seeking, what she had brought forth in sorrow" (5.8). Later on, in his Epistles, he will tell another young man oppressed with such a mother: "Whether it is in a wife or a mother, it is still Eve (the temptress) that we must beware of in any woman."[8]

Augustine's moral allegorizing here works as psychological insight, for it is an analytic axiom that the clinging, possessive, over-nuturant mother, which Monica surely was, is a type of the erotic mother. So we see why Augustine's early life seems an inverted pattern of quest where he is trying to escape his mother, whether into fraternal society, or the arms of a mistress, or the intellectual embrace of Manichaeism. He is trying to be born. But in fact Augustine's spiritual journey is one that is from the mother to the mother. What actually happens in the rebirth of conversion is a reentry into the world of the mother, only this time it is the realm of the spiritual mother, the *Catholica*.

Thus in Augustine's quest from the Earthly to the Heavenly City, Monica as spiritual mother beckons him on while Monica as natural and erotic mother holds him back. It is Monica and not the concubine who figures as Dido, left weeping on the shores of Africa as the hero pursues his divinely ordained task.[9] The *Aeneid* deploys these ambivalences in the feminine archetypes with fullness and subtlety. The loving and terrible mothers appear as Venus and Juno, the goddesses who assist and oppose the hero's quest. Even these polar types tend to overlap and blend, for the wrathful and persecuting Juno presides over Aeneas's union with Dido as the "queen of marriages," while Venus, the great patroness of Aeneas's future in Rome, cooperates to delay it in Carthage—in fact, it is she who first inspires love in Dido.

Dido the temptress and Venus the divine mother seem as opposed as their cities, Carthage and Rome. In this perspective Dido suggests Augustine's concubine: both women are seen, first, as a kind of haven from the troubles of the hero's world; second, as obstacles to his achieving his goal; and third, as victims of his abandonment. As Aeneas finds a false refuge in the embrace of Dido, so Augustine finds a false repose in the sensual pleasure his concubine symbolizes. Later Christian allegorizations of classical epic treated the "temptress" (Dido, Circe, Calypso) as a figure of the fleshly appetites. Thus an allegorical reading of the *Aeneid* along these lines would treat Aeneas's abandonment of Dido as a heroic turning away from his own lustful feelings, and his escape from burning Carthage as a resolute departure from the Earthly City of his fleshly nature in pursuit of the Heavenly City. It is certainly possible that Augustine was aware of this way of handling pagan epic. Indeed, his treatment of his concubine in the *Confessions* is carried out along very similar lines: she is presented more as a symbolic figure than a real person. We are told practically nothing about her, not even her name, although she bore Augustine's child and lived with him for some fourteen years. It is as if her personality and character are absorbed in the process of allegorization so that she becomes simply a type of the lusts of the flesh that divert Augustine from his true quest, rather than a real woman he loved and abandoned. Perhaps, too, the exaggerated emphasis in the autobiography on his affection and grief for his mother derives from a certain amount of displaced emotion—displaced from the concubine from whom he so resolutely turns.

As such a displacement suggests, the archetypes of "temptress" and "mother" are interlocking as well as alternative figures: the careful and deliberate shading of one into the other, whereby aspects of the erotic cling to the mother and qualities of the maternal enhance the mistress, is as evident in the *Aeneid* as in the *Confessions*.[10] For Vergil like Augustine links the mother (Venus) and the paramour (Dido) in the image of the cherishing mother. In book 1 Venus carried off Ascanius, Aeneas's son, and replaces him with Cupid, her own divine child. And this suggestive picture of the mother-goddess embracing and caressing Ascanius and lulling him to sleep in her sacred shrine is followed immediately by a similar one of Dido at her feast, fondling Cupid (whom she thinks is Ascanius) upon her lap. The image is rich in erotic ambivalence. Mythically, it is an action whereby the boy-god is enabled to inspire love in Dido; psychologically, it represents a maternal feeling for the child that blends into sexual desire for the father, Aeneas. It is significant that this happens while Aeneas is telling Dido the painful story of the fall of Troy. Dido is here clearly the erotic mother, cradling and comforting Aeneas in the person of Ascanius-Eros, while at the same time falling in love with him. When he has finished his story, and all the guests are gone, Dido returns to the darkened hall and relives the incident:

> she sees, she hears
> the absent one [Aeneas] or draws Ascanius,
> his son and counterfeit, into her arms,
> as if his shape might cheat her untellable love.[11]

Even the flames of sexual desire that rage so fiercely in Dido later on do not burn away all trace of her maternal feeling: when her lover announces his departure, she laments that she has not conceived his son—a "tiny Aeneas" whose face might still remind her of him. And there is some justice to her reproach that his mother cannot have been the goddess of beauty and love: Aeneas partially renounces Venus in renouncing her. Like Augustine, in leaving Carthage, Aeneas leaves one aspect of his mother behind.

Monica and the concubine can be thought of as the opposite sides of the same archetype, an archetype whose poetic ambiguity figures in the characters of Venus and Dido. To compare Dido to Monica and the concubine, to talk of the "erotic mother," to discuss the Heavenly City in terms of an apotheosized mother—all this is to allude to the great dualism of the archetypal feminine, that of carnal versus divine love. In the *Confessions* the relationship between carnal and divine love is expressed in Augustine's sublimation of his sexual love for his concubine and his filial love for his mother into a love of God, imaged as repose in the great maternal city—the Heavenly Jerusalem. The desires of the flesh are here allied with the archetype of the earthly mother, and both together are transmuted into divine love. For Augustine's relation to the apotheosized mother is as child and as transmuted spouse: while he is child to "Jerusalem my Mother," he is mystically espoused by his incorporation within the body of the Church.

The relation of the "*mater natura*" and "*mater spiritualis*" to each other can here be seen as developmental. Perhaps, then, Augustine's journey from the Earthly City to the Heavenly City is not so much a turning away from the one to the other as a transformation out of the order of nature and into the order of grace. In the words of colloquial Catholic theology, "grace builds on nature." And this is the key to Augustine's dualism. The dualism of the Manichaeans, and to some extent of the Platonists too, pits the natural world against the spiritual realm. Augustine, however, refines this concept by perceiving the spiritual as developing out of the natural.

The pattern of his life demonstrates precisely this development. There are two major instances of this in the *Confessions*. The first is when Augustine arrives at Carthage, the city of Dido (and of Venus) and finds himself in the midst of a "hissing cauldron of lust." He describes his progress as one where he begins by seeking out a suitable recipient of his love. "*Quaerebam quid amarem, amans amare*": the impulse to love is there; it is the object that is yet to be determined. Furthermore, he writes that to love and to have his love returned was what he most wanted and that it would be all the sweeter if he could also carnally enjoy his beloved. Finally, "love was returned and I was with much joy shackled in the bonds if its consummation . . ." (3.1). But before long the powerful energy of sensual love is converted into the love of wisdom when he reads Cicero's *Hortensius*. His description of this mini-conversion closely parallels that of his initial yearnings for love: "with an incredible heat of spirit I desired (*concupiscebam*) the immortality of wisdom. . . . How did I burn then, my God, how did I burn to fly from earthly delights towards thee. . . . That love of wisdom is in Greek called Philosophy, with which that book inflamed me." What he admires most about the book is Cicero's advice "to love, seek, and obtain and hold, and embrace wisdom itself, whatever it was." It is due to Cicero's words that he is "stirred up and enkindled, and inflamed . . . in such a heat of zeal" (3.4).

The second instance where Augustine transforms the sensual into the spiritual occurs during his conversion to Christianity. He writes that when on the verge of conversion, he sees the "chaste dignity of Continence" beckoning to him in an undeniably maternal metaphor, "stretching forth those devout hands of hers . . . both to receive and to embrace me" (8.11). On the other side of his crisis of choice is the voice of his sensuality—the vanities of this world ("*nugae nugarum et vanitates vanitatum*"), the chain of sin, which is habit ("*consuetudo violenta*"), the "unclean members" of concupiscence (8.11). It is significant that Augustine is here converted not to the beauty of *sapientia*, a venerable object of devotion for the Hellenic and Hebraic mind alike, but to the beauty of *continentia*.

Peter Brown observes that "relationship between mother and son that weaves in and out of the *Confessions*, forms the thread for which the book is justly famous."[12] It seems impossible to overstate the significance of this relationship.[13] Even Augustine's conversion to Christianity is finally presented as the double conversion of mother and son: "For so thou convertedst me unto thyself. . . . Thus didst thou convert her [Monica's] mourning into rejoicing" (8.12). If conversion represents the death of the natural man with his earthly ties and the rebirth of the spiritual man with heavenly ties, then the relationship between mother and son must undergo the same process. So in the early part of the autobiography, Monica is the mother grieving over her dead son, the *mater dolorosa* from whose tears and lamentations springs the resurrected son: "out of the blood of my mother's heart, through her tears night and day poured out, hadst thou made a sacrifice for me . . ." (5.7). Yet if her tears are those of mourning, they are purposive too: Augustine observes that his mother did not simply bewail him "as one dead, but as if there were good hopes of his reviving." And he continues with a strikingly appropriate biblical allusion: "Laying me forth upon the bier before thee that thou mightest say unto the son of the widow, Young man, I say unto thee, arise; and he should sit up, and begin to speak, and thou shouldst deliver him to his mother" (6.1).

In some sense Augustine has indeed defined himself in his autobiography as "the son of the widow," always perceiving his life in the larger context of his widowed mother's hopes and fears for him. His knowledge of the Christian God is, quite literally, mediated by Monica. For he perceives her as God's messenger: "And whose but thine were those words, which by my mother, thy faithful one, thou sangest in my ears?" (2.3). And furthermore, God speaks to Monica in visions—visions that foretell future events in her son's life. The greatest of these is that of the rule of faith, which Augustine believes to have foretold his conversion to Christianity:

> For she saw, in her sleep, herself standing upon a wooden rule, and a very beautiful young man coming toward her, with a cheerful countenance and smiling upon her, herself being grieved and far gone with sorrowfulness. Which young man when he had demanded of her the causes of her sadness and daily weepings . . . and she had answered that it was my perdition that she bewailed; he bade her rest contented, and wished her to observe diligently and behold, that where she herself was, there was I also. When she looked aside, she saw me standing by her upon the same rule. (3.11)

Looking back on his conversion in the garden, Augustine sees it as the fulfillment of his mother's dream: "For so thou convertedst me unto thyself . . . standing thus upon the same rule of faith, in which thou hadst shewed me unto her in a vision, so many years before" (8.12).

Not only does Augustine refer to Monica's earlier vision in his account of his conversion, but he even supplies a maternal figure out of his own imagination to match the youth figure of her dream. For the "very beautiful young man coming toward her, with a cheerful countenance and smiling upon her," who appears to Monica in her sleep, is a transposed figure of Augustine himself, transformed by the dream mechanism of wish-fulfillment. And Augustine's response to this dream-person is Continence, that "fruitful mother of children," whom he imaginatively conjures up just before describing his conversion: "cheerful was she, but not dissolutely pleasant, virtuously alluring me to come to her and hesitate no longer" (8.11). That this is a variant of the mother archetype goes without saying. That Continence is a transposed figure of Monica herself is suggested by Augustine's careful discrimination between a demeanor that is cheerful but not wanton, beckoning but not seductive.

Furthermore, the embrace of Continence is yet another way of imagining entry into the City of God. For, like the Heavenly Jerusalem, Continence is the spouse of God: to embrace Continence is to "cast thyself upon Him" (8.11). Thus does Augustine leave the embrace of his mistresses and enter unto the embrace of "thy Church, the mother of us all" (1.11). The foundations of the spiritual mother, the Church, are to be found in Monica: "But thou hadst already begun thy temple in my mother's breast, and laid the foundations of thine own holy habitation" (2.3). Just as grace builds on nature, and the spiritual develops out of the earthly, so does the apotheosis of the maternal principle, "Jerusalem my country, Jerusalem my mother," to which God is "Enlightener, Father, Guardian, Spouse, Delight and Joy" (12.16), have its origins in the "temple" of Monica's heart.

In the figure of Monica, both as individual and as archetype of spiritual love, all polarities meet: Neoplatonic and Pauline, Vergilian and Christian. It is strangely appropriate that the autobiographical section of the *Confessions* should conclude not with Augustine's *crisis* conversion of book 8—his own spiritual death and rebirth—but with his account of the death of Monica and the accompanying biographical elegy to her. Monica dies in Ostia, midway between Milan and Africa. For Augustine it appears as a triumph of her faith that, whereas she had always hoped that her body would be buried next to her husband's, she should remark, on her deathbed, "Lay this body anywhere . . . this only I request that you should remember me at the altar of the Lord, wherever you are" (9.11). Just as her concern with what happens to her body after death has been replaced by her belief in the resurrection of the soul, so also is the dead husband replaced by the living son in her last wishes.

The *Confessions* is itself meant to be this "altar of the Lord" of Monica's deathbed request—a fulfillment of her dying wish and a sacramental tribute to her memory. Thus Augustine concludes his personal autobiography: "inspire, O Lord my God, inspire thy servants, my brethren . . . that those of them who read this book may at thy Altar remember Monica thy handmaid, together with Patricius her sometime husband . . ." (9.13). The story of Augustine's conversion is the gradual weaning of the soul from the love of that which cannot last, such as friends and mothers, toward the love of that which is incorruptible and eternal. But the kind of love that he is writing about is, in both cases, libidinal in source and sensual in expression: it is rooted in the desire to see, touch, have, and possess—whether the love-object be human or divine. [14]

What Augustine finally achieves, in this narrative response to the death of his mother, is a kind of affirmation of the love of "that which cannot last." His description of his grief is worth attending to in detail, for it parallels his account in book 8 of the celebrated conversion in the garden. Though he feels "a great sorrow flowing into [his] heart," he holds back his tears, checking even the wailing of his son, Adeodatus, "For we did not think it fitting to mark the death with lamentations, tears, and moanings, because this is the accustomed way to lament those that die miserably or who are thought of as utterly perished" (9.12). He continues to maintain a countenance that does not betray the violence of his sorrow, but blames himself nonetheless for the tenderness of his passion: "I grieved for mine own grief with a new grieving (*dolore dolebam dolorem meum*)" (9.12). Restraining his tears throughout the burial, he begs God in prayer to heal him of his sorrow but the prayer is not granted. He goes to the baths, remembering that the Greek root of the Latin *balneum* meant "that which drives anxiety out of the mind." But the attempt to cure himself is ineffective, as he confesses to God, here addressed as "*pater orphanorum*." Finally he is able to sleep, and wakes up to the memory of some verses written by Ambrose—verses that celebrate God as the healer of physical and mental pain. This event is an inversion of that other "awakening" in the garden to the chanting voice of the child. The *tolle, lege* refrain in book 8 causes him to repress the "violent torrent of tears"; the verses from Ambrose in book 9 cause him to give way to his tears "so that they flowed as much as they desired." He goes on to describe himself as "making of them a pillow for my heart, and it rested upon them (*requievat in eis*)," which recalls that first reference to the *cor irrequietum* at the very beginning of the *Confessions*. Thus Augustine's description of his mourning achieves a paradoxical affirmation of *eros*—of the love of that which cannot last—within a context of *agape*. And so he urges readers, at the close of book 9, not to deride him for his tears, but rather to express charity in sorrowing with him: "let him not deride me; but if he be a man of any great charity, let him rather weep for my sins unto thee, the Father of all the brethren of thy Christ" (9.12).

For Augustine, the *Confessions* is a sacramental offering of contrition and thanksgiving made within the "large and infinite inner spaciousness" of his own memory (10.8). As a prayer to God it embodies a longing "to touch thee, whence thou mayst be touched; and to cling fast to three, whence one may cling to thee (*volens te attingere, unde attingi potes, et inhaerere tibi . . .*)" (10.17). Consistently he uses the verb *attingere*, which means both "to touch" and "to attain to," in referring to the yearning to "touch" God. The rhetoric of quest throughout the *Confessions* reflects this poignant yearning, for it is the notion of enjoying God (*ad fruendum Dei*), a variant on the Plotinian spiritual embrace (the *amplexis*) between God and the soul, which is the true object of that quest.[15] Thus for Augustine the essence of man is identified with the faculties of desiring, and concomitantly he is defined by men and judged by God in terms of the object of his desire. It follows then that the quest of the hero of the *Confessions*, and thence of the archetypal soul, is to fulfill that desire by finding the right object for his love. And the "right object" is defined simply as that which can satisfy this love: in Augustine's words, that to which one can say, "It is enough, it is good (*sat est et bene est*)" (7.7). The object of this love is, of course, God—but it is not an intellectual idea of deity. It is therefore appropriate that Augustine should end his personal confession with an appeal to charity in his impassioned story of the life and death of Monica. For when he is able to affirm his grief over her death, he is able finally to affirm his great, even too great love for her—that "*carnalis affectus*"—and thus achieve a final unity between *eros* and *agape*.

THE PATERNAL ETHOS: *SENEX* AND CHILD

In the preceding section I tried to show how the transcendent ideas of the City of God, Mother Church, and the Heavenly Jerusalem have their bases in Augustine's transvaluation of his own mother; similarly, Augustine's idea of God is shaped in part by his attitude toward his natural father, Patricius. Moreoever, just as the maternal archetype manifests itself in the dualities of "natural" and "spiritual," or temptation and redemption, or hunger and satisfaction, the paternal turns on the dualities of false and true.

Throughout the *Confessions* Patricius is negatively represented. And Monica actively perpetuates this attitude. Thus Augustine writes that his mother "by all means endeavoured, that thou, my God, shouldst be my father, rather than Patricius" (1.11). Augustine's father is mentioned only a few times in the *Confessions*; in each instance the narrative is tinged with criticism. For example, Patricius is represented as immoderately proud of his son. He is praised by his neighbors for sending his son to Carthage to further his education, but Augustine's response is only to blame him for attending to the wrong things: "But yet this father of mine never troubled himself with any thought of how I might improve myself toward thee, or how chaste I were . . ." (2.3). Indeed, Patricius is not at all concerned over his son's chastity, or lack of it. Augustine recollects a scene in the baths where Patricius is delighted to see "how the signs of manhood began to bud in me" (2.3). Augustine sums up his father as having "but vain conceits of me" (2.3). Patricius dies when Augustine is seventeen: he mentions this fact only in passing and with no show of grief whatsoever, whereas he will soon experience the depths of sorrow in mourning the death of a friend (3.4; 4.4).

The natural fathers of both Augustine and Aeneas are unsatisfactory, although in opposite ways. Patricius typifies the weak or absent father, leaving Augustine to search for the "true" father in one inadequate substitute after another. Anchises, whom Aeneas must carry on his back away from burning Troy, typifies the burden of the strong father who repeatedly misdirects the hero on a quest that cannot reach its goal until the old man dies. Yet if Anchises fails as a *senex* in life, he succeeds in death, where he functions as a kind of spiritual counselor in the episode in the underworld. Furthermore, there are resemblances between the depiction of the divine father in the two narratives. Zeus is a remote and transcendent deity in the *Aeneid*; he never descends to earth, as do Juno and Venus, but always works through his messenger, Mercury. So also is Augustine's God remote and transcendent; communicating to Augustine either through Monica or through the various *senex* figures in Augustine's life. The providential plan of Zeus, whereby it is Aeneas's destiny to found the city of Rome, is not unlike the providential plan of God for Augustine, which is revealed to Monica in her dream of the rule of faith.

Thus for Augustine the paternal archetype is organized around the two extremes of an imperfect but present father and a God who is perfect but transcendent. In his youth, Augustine will repeatedly seek out surrogate fathers to bridge this distance between the natural and the "ideal" father— *senes* who either hinder or assist him in his quest for God, the ultimate father.

Jung equates the archetype of the father-figure with the "wise old man," the *senex*, and identifies both as psychic manifestations of the phenomenon called "spirit." This archetypal figure, Jung observes, is one who emerges in situations where insight and purposiveness are needed but lacking in the hero: "The old man always appears when the hero is in a hopeless and desperate situation from which only profound reflection or a lucky idea—in other words, a spiritual function or an endopsychic automatism of some kind—can extricate him."[16] This relationship between *senex* and hero, moreover, is one that is both ancient and common. For example, in poetry and myth the archetype of the father figure emerges as the wise counselor: thus Teiresias functions as an archetypal *senex* to Odysseus and Anchises as a *senex* to Aeneas. Similarly, in philosophy Plato uses the figure of Socrates to validate his own role as philosophic teacher and guide.

Throughout the autobiography Augustine presents himself as an avid seeker after wisdom. He goes about this search in the conventional way, by seeking the right master. And indeed the many *senex* figures in Augustine's life can be seen as representatives of his maturing ideas of wisdom. They include teachers, bishops, a magician, and a doctor, and occur in pairs, as type and antitype of the *senex* archetype. The first pair of surrogate fathers are chosen for him and are childhood manifestations of the *senex*. These are his early schoolmasters, who function as antitypes of the *senex* archetype, or false *senes*. Augustine remembers them bitterly as unjust disciplinarians. As the unjust schoolmaster is an antitype of the true *senex*, the Christian bishop whom Monica tries to coerce into instructing Augustine is a type of the true *senex*. But the bishop refuses, saying that Augustine is "yet unripe for instruction." Monica persists, and the bishop finally exclaims, in one of the most portentous passages in the *Confessions*, "Go thy ways . . . and God bless thee, for it is not possible that the son of these tears should be lost" (3.12). It is an aborted *senex* relationship, but it prefigures Augustine's future relationships with the bishops Ambrose and Simplicianus.

Augustine encounters the next pair of *senes* in the course of a poetry contest. Their vocations are those of magician and doctor, and they represent the adolescence of his spiritual quest. The "false counselor" appears in the person of a sorcerer, who offers to ensure with his magic that Augustine win the contest. Augustine rejects his advances—an action that prefigures his later rejection of Faustus. The role of true *senex* is filled by Vindicianus, who awards him the prize for the poetry contest. Vindicianus, an astrologer turned physician, is characterized as "*vir sagax*," a physician of the soul who "courteously and fatherly" advises Augustine to throw away his books on astrology and waste no further care "upon that vain study" (4.3).

The final and most important pair of *senex* figures in the *Confessions* are both chosen by Augustine and represent the maturity of his spiritual quest. Both are admired exponents of opposing religious doctrines. The false *senex* is Faustus, high priest in the Manichaean hierarchy. The Christian bishops Ambrose and Simplicianus, on the other hand, function as a composite image of the true *senex*. In fact, Faustus might be said to represent the "spirit" or *genius loci* of the entire Carthage experience, and Ambrose the "spirit" of the Milan experience. The two cities and the two men are polar opposites: Faustus and Carthage represent the false and earthly vision, whereas Ambrose and Milan represent the true and spiritual vision. Augustine meets Faustus when he is twenty-nine years old. He has been waiting for him some nine years, fully expecting that Faustus will be the wise tutor who can lead him to total, undoubting belief. But Augustine is disappointed. What happens is a rather surprising reversal of roles whereby Augustine becomes the teacher and Faustus the student. For Faustus, Augustine discovers, appears to be "ignorant of those arts in which I thought he excelled." But if Faustus is unable to resolve Augustine's questions about Manichaean doctrines, Augustine is able to help Faustus in his enthusiasm for literature: "I began upon a course of study with him . . . in that kind of learning, in which at that time being a rhetoric reader in Carthage, I instructed young students; and I began to read with him, either what he himself desired to hear, or such books as I judged fit for his abilities" (5.7). The episode is for Augustine the author an expression of God's providential intervention. Disenchanted with Faustus, Augustine loses interest in the sect and accepts a position in Rome.

When Augustine finally arrives in Milan and finds Ambrose, he feels that he has at last found the ideal *senex*, the wise counselor who will be worthy of his own great gifts. But Augustine's advances are rejected, for he finds that the great Ambrose is too busy to talk to him. That Augustine was hurt by this rebuff is evidenced in his attempt to excuse Ambrose, suggesting that he had not fully understood the severity of Augustine's condition: "As little . . . knew he of my private heats, nor of the pit of my danger" (6.3). Thus all the conditions of an ideal *senex* relationship are there—Augustine is the Jungian hero-figure "in a hopeless and desperate situation" and Ambrose, he feels, holds the keys to the understanding that will release him. But what he hopes for does not happen: "Ofttimes when we were present . . . we still saw him reading to himself, and never otherwise: so that having long sat in silence (for who dared be so bold as to interrupt him, so intent in his study?) we were fain to depart" (6.3). Augustine must be content to join the multitudes and absorb the wisdom of Ambrose through listening to his sermons. During this entire time he sees himself as tending inevitably toward conversion, yet "hanging in suspense" (6.4).

Rebuffed by Ambrose, Augustine turns to the aged bishop Simplicianus, who is Ambrose's own spiritual father. Simplicianus tells Augustine the story of Victorinus, a parable intended to direct Augustine's attention away from his mentors and back onto himself. Victorinus was a very learned man who accounted himself a Christian (Augustine is by now a catechumen), but who, out of fear and pride, refused to join the Church. When he finally did so, he rejected the possibility of making a private profession of faith and publicly professed himself before multitudes (8.2). The effect of the parable is, as Simplicianus surely intended, that Augustine is "all on fire" to imitate Victorinus (8.5). But Simplicianus has a deeper motive in telling Augustine this story. He sees through Augustine's pride, and "the better to exhort [him] to Christ's humility (hidden from the wise, and revealed to little ones)" tells the story of the eminent rhetorician and translator of Plotinus who "blushed not to become the child of Christ, and an infant at the font, submitting his neck to the yoke of humility . . ." (8.2).[17]

It is the lesson of humility taught to him by Simplicianus, to "become the child of Christ and an infant at the font," that provides the most important link to Augustine's conversion. For the last of Augustine's *senex* figures is not an old man but a child. When he hears the child's words, "*tolle lege, tolle lege*," interprets them as a divine command, and reads the Pauline passage from Romans, the verses prove to be a revelation—the final self-knowledge toward which the series of *senex* figures and the parables of Simplicianus and Ponticianus have been leading.

The *senex* archetype achieves its persuasive, guiding function in the archetype of the child. Jung is here again relevant, for he observes that the psychic manifestations of the "spiritual helper" can be either the *senex* or the child: "Greybeard and boy belong together."[18] The child archetype is a symbol of the fully and newly realized self and thus a representation of the potential future; as Jung writes, the appearance of the child archetype "paves the way for a future change of personality."[19] Jung distinguishes between the "retarding ideal," which is "always more primitive, more natural . . . and more 'moral' in that it keeps faith with law and tradition" and the "progressive ideal," which is "always more abstract, more unnatural, and less 'moral' in that it demands disloyalty to tradition."[20] The child archetype, although it might at first appear to be a regressive configuration, is in fact a manifestation of the "progressive ideal." Augustine's painstaking attempts to acquire wisdom and his studies of philosophies and systems are examples of the working of the "retarding ideal"—a kind of "progress enforced by the will," in accord with tradition, and "natural" to a man of his intellectual gifts. As such, the retarding ideal is manifested in Augustine's various *senex* figures. It is only when he abandons his will, "becomes as a little child," and turns his back on the traditional approach to attaining wisdom that he can embrace the progressive ideal. And the symbol of this is the child. His final ability, in the garden, to hear and obey the voice of the child marks a reflexive turning to his own inner capacities for renewal. And these capacities are released through the act of relinquishing his own will (Law, the "old man") and accepting the will of God (Grace, the "new man"). In such a way does the *senex* archetype give way to the *puer aeternus*. That Augustine can respond in this way, a response embodied in the child archetype, provides the final link to his conversion and effects a reconstitution and a redemption of the earthly family within the divine family: Monica and Patricius, Augustine and his sibling friends are transformed into Jerusalem the Mother, God the Father, and the children of the City of God.

NOTES

*This essay first appeared as the chapter, "St. Augustine: Archetypes of Family," in Anne Hunsaker Hawkins, *Archetypes of Conversion* (Bucknell University Press, 1985) 56–72. Reprinted by permission. The original essay had to be retyped, which was graciously done by Jessica Champlin Appleby, Teri MacGill, and Consuelo Bennett.

1. O'Connell discusses this theme at length in his chapter, *"Fovisti Caput Nescientis,"* in *St. Augustine's Early Theory of Man* (Cambridge: Harvard University Press, 1968).

2. George P. Lawless points out that the theme of "rest" is structurally represented in the *Confessions* in three crucially placed passages: *"donec requiescat in te"* (1.1), *"et tu solus requies"* (6.16), and *"requiescamus in te"* (12.36). "These three passages," he writes, "point to the artistic and theological unity of the *Confessions*. Present time is contrasted with future time in terms of work and rest" ("Interior Peace in the *Confessions* of St. Augustine," *Revue des Études Augustiniennes* 26 [1980] 59).

3. Jung, "Psychological Aspects of the Mother Archetype," in *Archetypes and the Collective Unconscious*, p. 92.

4. Ibid.

5. Jung, "The Syzygy: Anima and Animus," in *Aion, Collected Works*, trans. R. F. C. Hull, Bollingen Series 20, vol. 9, pt. 2 (Princeton, N.J.: Princeton University Press, 1959), pp. 11, 13.

6. See also Proverbs 5:3–8 on "the strange woman." *Sapientia* and *meretrix* are vividly described in Proverbs 7:7–27 and Proverbs 8 in their parallel roles as crying out to Man for his allegiance. Also see Ferrari, who observes that *meretrix* for Augustine was allegorized as *superstitiones* and thus an appropriate opposition to *sapientia* ("The Theme of the Prodigal Son," p. 113).

7. Note the imagery in Proverbs 8:30: "Then I [Wisdom] was by him, as one brought up with him" and "I was daily his delight, rejoicing always before him . . ." Compare this with the imagery in *Confessions* 12:16: "Jerusalem my country, Jerusalem my mother; and thyself that ruleth over it, the Enlightener, the Father, the Guardian, the Husband, the chaste and strong Delight, the solid joy of it . . ." Note also Wisdom of Solomon (Apoc.) 8:2–3: "I loved her [Wisdom], and sought her out from my youth, I desired to make her my spouse, and I was a lover of her beauty. In that she is conversant with God, she magnifieth her nobility: yea, the Lord of all things himself loved her."

8. *Ep.* 243; in Brown, *Augustine of Hippo*, p. 63.

9. Kligerman sees Augustine as preoccupied with the story of Dido and Aeneas, which he had had to memorize as a child, because it "contains the nuclear conflict of Augustine's infantile neurosis and played a most decisive role in his subsequent career" (p. 472). Here, he remarks, is the infantile sexuality that had been omitted from the narrative of his early years. Augustine identifies himself with Aeneas and his mother with Dido, and "the bitter tears he shed in childhood for poor slain Dido were the tears of rage, frustration and guilt he felt toward his mother" ("A Psychoanalytic Study," p. 479).

10. It is no accident that Venus first appears to her son as a beautiful maiden, garbed like a huntress, as Dido will be in the cave episode. Aeneas mistakes his mother for Diana—ironically, considering her present purpose—and it is to Diana that Vergil compares Dido at her first appearance later in the same book. But Dido is not just an alluring temptress for Aeneas; she is also a motherly figure for him. The widowed queen who offers Aeneas welcome and safety, who feasts and pities him, seems as maternally protective as Venus herself.

11. Vergil, *The Aeneid*, trans. Allen Mandelbaum (New York: Bantam, 1971), bk. 4 109–112, p. 84.

12. Brown, *Augustine of Hippo*, p. 29.

13. It may be impossible to overstate this point, but it is certainly possible to distort it. Not surprisingly, Augustine's representation of his mother in the *Confessions* has served as the basis for a number of psychoanalytic interpretations of a Freudian persuasion. As L. J. Daly observes in an article on Augustine's conversion, "Psychohistory and St. Augustine's Conversion Process," *Augustiniana* 28 (1978) 231–254, which is itself a superb critique of psychoanalytic and historical methods alike, "The deleterious impact of Monica on Augustine's personality from nursery through episcopacy is the idée fixe of psychoanalytic interpretations of his conversion process" (p. 245). Though psychoanalytic studies of the *Confessions* may contribute valuable insights, they are often severely limited by the tendency to see Augustine's life and thought as governed by an unresolved Oedipal situation and by the unquestioned (and unfounded) assumption that religious phenomena can simply be reduced to the category of the sexual. For Kligerman, Augustine's conversion is the result of "an identification with the mother and a passive feminine attitude to the father displaced to God" ("A Psychoanalytic Study," p. 483), and for Dittes, Augustine's conversion represents a simultaneous surrender to his mother and abandonment of masculine sexuality ("Continuities," p. 139). What these interpretations fail to recognize is that Augustine's abandonment of sexuality is both functional and teleological in the religious framework within which it is grounded. By failing to acknowledge the reality, at least to Augustine, of this religious framework, such interpretations inevitably distort both the autobiography and the experience upon which it is based. And even the vocabulary is wrong: August neither "repressed" nor "suppressed" his sexuality; he renounced it, and moreover did so in order to get something that he believed would offer him deeper pleasure and more complete satisfaction.

It would seem that the archetypal approach is here superior to the Freudian; first, because it assumes an underlying dualism of natural (sexual) and spiritual realities rather than a monism that reduces the spiritual to the sexual; and second, because its quasi-allegorical method is closer to Augustine's own system of thought.

14. Thus Augustine writes of the quest for wisdom, awakened in him by Cicero's *Hortensius*, as a desire that left him free "to love, and seek, and obtain, and hold, and embrace wisdom itself . . ." (3.4). These words will be echoed in Augustine's several visionary apprehensions of God, who is identified with wisdom later on in the book (9.10).

15. O'Connell, *Early Theory*, chap. 8, "Vision"; Teselle, *Augustine the Theologian*, p. 67.

16. Jung, "The Phenomenology of the Spirit in Fairytales," in *Archetypes and the Collective Unconscious*, pp. 217–218. Jung writes that "the psychic manifestations of the spirit indicate at once that they are of an archetypal nature—in other words, the phenomenon we call spirit depends on the existence of an autonomous primordial image which is universally present in the preconscious makeup of the human psyche. . . . It struck me that a certain kind of father-complex has a 'spiritual' character. . . . Mostly, therefore, it is the figure of a 'wise old man' who symbolizes the spiritual factor" (pp. 214–215).

17. The fact that Augustine remembers himself to have been so deeply affected by this story that it serves as a link in his own conversion (a narrative link, at least, for it is at the beginning of the same chapter in which he describes his conversion) may well indicate a wish rather than a reality—an autobiographical emendation of actual events to make them conform to what he wished had happened. On the basis of works written just after his conversion, it has been pointed out by many that there is a discrepancy between the way Augustine "really" professed his Christianity and the description he gives in the *Confessions*. And indeed, there is some ambiguity as to the way in which Augustine made known his newly acquired Christianity. In several of the works written after his conversion he indicates that he resigned his post as teacher

of rhetoric because of a *dolor pectoris* and with the intention of pursuing the study of philosophy; in the *Confessions*, very little is made of the *dolor pectoris* and nothing of the intent to study philosophy. About this B. R. Rees, "The Conversion of St. Augustine," *Trivium* 14 (1979) 1–17, observed: "He consciously glossed over this, the true reason for his resignation, in order to throw into greater prominence the transformation brought about by his religious conversion" (p. 6). Rees is probably right, though there is no indication that this was a "conscious" distortion of the truth, as Rees implies. Again, it is not the literal truth of Augustine's description of these events that is here important; what does matter is the way in which he revises and edits this part of his life to present a truth that is paradigmatic, rather than literally real.

18. Jung, "The Phenomenology of the Spirit in Fairy-Tales," in *The Archetypes and the Collective Unconscious*, p. 215.

19. Carl Jung and Carl Kerényi, "The Psychology of the Child Archetype," in *Essays in a Science of Mythology*, trans. R. F. C. Hull, Bollingen Series 22, 2nd ed. (Princeton, N.J.: Princeton University Press, 1969), p. 83.

20. Ibid., p. 82.

Chapter Five

Between Two Worlds

Morton T. Kelsey

If any one man stands between this era [late Antiquity] and the modern world, it is Augustine. There is good reason for his influence, not only on Western Catholicism but perhaps even more on Luther, Calvin, and the entire Protestant world. Within his own experience, Augustine was able to stand between several pairs of worlds, particularly the spiritual and the worldly. His youth was spent carelessly, or sometimes almost carefully, doing what he should not and absorbing Gnostic Manicheism. At the same time he became an excellent teacher of rhetoric and so came to Milan, where Ambrose was bishop. Here he was touched by Neo-Platonism, and turning toward Christianity, he sought out personal contact with Ambrose.

It was then he had his great religious experience, which brought him to baptism. And in the next half century Augustine went on, almost single-handedly, to prepare the intellectual foundation for Western Christian thinking for another thousand years. Until Aquinas became accepted, Augustine was *the* Western theologian.

Not only do we find in him a deeply religious, a mystical longing and experience, but here was one of the most inquiring minds of the time. His philosophical ability and the penetrating psychological insight his studies show would make him important entirely apart from his Christian connections. The study of dreams is for him a significant tool in understanding both the psychology of man and his relations with God and the spiritual world.

Augustine's psychology and epistemology were based upon a sophisticated psychophysical dualism in which he saw two essentially different kinds of reality—the purely corporeal or physical, and the non-corporeal or "mental," which is spiritual in nature. This is essentially the theory that Lovejoy supports in his classical study of modern epistemology, *The Revolt against Dualism* [London: Allen and Unwin, 1930]. It is again essentially the theory of

87

the objective psyche proposed by Dr. C. G. Jung and his followers to explain the experiences of their medical and psychological practice.

Augustine's study of perception was as sophisticated as any in the ancient world. He saw reality as consisting of outer physical objects to which we react with our bodies and then of the impressions of this sense experience, impressions that are "mental" in nature. We then have the inner perception of this sense experience, and finally the mental species in its remembered form. It is the action of the ego (called the will by Augustine) that unites these perceptions to the object. In one place he calls the faculty of imagination the bridge that mediates the object to consciousness, thus presenting almost the same thinking as that worked out by Synesius of Cyrene. Augustine saw man as possessing an outward eye that receives and mediates sense impressions and an inward eye that observes and deals with these collected and stored "mental" realities that are called memory.

In addition to the realities that come from outer perception and from inner perception of "memories," autonomous spiritual realities (angels and demons) can present themselves directly to the inner eye. These are of the same nature as the stored "mental" or psychic realities that are perceived inwardly. Augustine writes that men in sleep or trance can experience contents that come from memory "or by some other hidden force through certain spiritual commixtures of a similarly spiritual substance."[1] These autonomous realities are non-physical; yet they can either assume a corporeal appearance and be experienced through the outward eye or be presented directly to consciousness through the inner eye in dreams, visions, and trances. Thus through dreams man is presented with a storehouse of unconscious memories and spontaneous contents; he is given access to a world that the fathers called the realm of the spirit, which Jung has seen as the "objective psyche." Man has no control over this world; the contents of a dream or vision are as objective, as much "given" to the inner eye as sense experience is to the outer eye.[2]

Augustine admitted that it was easier to describe what the angels and demons do than to explain what they are. In discussing the dreams people have of the dead, he stated that it is not the dead person himself who appears (just as one doesn't expect the living person to know when one dreams of him), but "by angelical operations, then, I should think it is effected, whether permitted from above, or commanded, that they seem in dreams to say something. . . ."[3] Just as angels have direct contact with man's psyche and present their messages before the inner eye, so also do demons.

> They persuade [men], however, in marvelous and unseen ways,
> entering by means of that subtlety of their own bodies into the bodies
> of men who are unaware, and through certain imaginary visions mingling
> themselves with men's thoughts whether they are awake or asleep.[4]

Augustine, as we can see, considered these experiences equally important whether they came in a waking vision or a dream.

When asked by his lifelong friend, the bishop Evodius, how man can have such strange experiences of telepathy and clairvoyance, or precognition, Augustine replied that ordinary experience is strange and difficult enough to explain, and such things as this happen, but they are beyond man's power to explain. It should also be noted that, although Augustine believed that these visionary experiences are important sources of knowledge, the highest experience of God transcends even these means. Dreams and visions do not reveal the nature of God, but they are given by him. They are examples of his providential care, his gifts. Referring to a dream that had brought conviction about life after death, he wrote of this vision: "By whom was he taught this but by the merciful, providential care of God?" It is also clear that Augustine found the operation of the inner eye and its lack of dependence upon the physical body to be excellent grounds for belief in the persistence of man's psyche after death.[5]

In addition to presenting a theory of dreams and visions, Augustine also discussed many examples of providential dreams in the course of his writings. One of the most important of them was the famous dream of his mother Monica, in which she saw herself standing on a measuring device while a young man whose face shone with a smile approached her. She was crying, and when he asked why, she told of her sorrow that her son turned away from Christ. He told her to look, and suddenly she saw Augustine standing on the same rule with her and she was comforted. Realizing the significance of the symbolism, she was able to go on praying for him with patience and hope; her dreams and visions are also mentioned in several other places in *The Confessions.*[6]

Fascinating stories of a number of parapsychological dreams, as well as stories and discussions of other influential dreams, are found in various places in Augustine's writings. Particularly in the correspondence with Evodius there are accounts of dream experiences as uncanny as any in the modern literature on psychical research, or even in the Bible. Some of this material is included in the appendix, and there are other references in a letter to Alypius and in *The City of God*,[7] as well as in material already referred to. It is no wonder Augustine was led to study these experiences so thoroughly and with such faith in his Christian calling.

NOTES

* This essay originally appeared in Morton T. Kelsey, *God, Dreams, and Revelation: A Christian Interpretation of Dreams* (Minneapolis: Augsburg Publishing House, 1974) 148–151. Reprinted by permission. Any additions are in square brackets. We have not changed any wording (e.g., as to gender inclusive language).

1. St. Augustine, *On the Trinity*, XI.4.7.

2. The reference to Augustine's psychology of perception and parapsychological experience are scattered throughout his writings. Most important theoretically are his discussions on the nature of man in his book *On the Trinity*, where he sees in man's inner diversity and unity an archetype of the nature of God. Discussions are found in this work in Book II, 5.9, 6.11, 13.23, and 18.34; Book III, 1.4 through 11.26; Book IV, 17.22, 21.30ff.; Book VIII, 7.11; Book XI, 4.7, 5.8f., 8.13 through 11.18; Book XII, 12.21f., 13.22. In addition in Book III of Augustine's *Literal Commentary on Genesis* he presents a complete discussion of his psychology, together with his theory of angels, and in Book XII he discusses ideas about different kinds of visions in relation to modes or revelation. (*De Genesi ad Litteram*, J.-P. Migne, *Patrologiae Latinae*, Paris, 1887, Vol. 34.) Shorter discussions are found in Letter IX, To Nebridius, and Letter CLIX, To Evodius. There is even one reference to the relation between dreams and providence in his earliest Christian work, *The Soliloquies*, II.10ff. This belief is found from the earliest to the latest of his works, and it is essential to his teaching.

3. *On Care to Be Had for the Dead*, 12.

4. *The Divination of Demons*, V. 9, New York, Fathers of the Church, Inc., 1955, Vol. 27, p. 430. [Square brackets in original.]

5. Letter CLIX, To Evodius, 2ff.; *The City of God*, XI.2.

6. *The Confessions*, III.19, V.17, VI.23, VIII.30.

7. Letters IX and CLIX; Letter CCXXVII; *The City of God*, IV.26 and XXII.23.

Chapter Six

Augustine among the Ancient Therapists

Paul R. Kolbet

CLASSICAL THERAPY

Augustine's psychological acuity is widely known and plainly evident to any reader of his *Confessions*.[1] Not a few commentators have seen Augustine's exploration of the "feelings, conflicts, and anguish of the individual . . . as the earliest forerunner of psychoanalysis."[2] However tempted we may be to see in Augustine anticipations (or confirmations) of contemporary psychological insights, we should not lose sight of the great distance between his time and ours. To the extent that modern psychology is a formal discipline that extends the methods of the natural sciences originating in the 17th century to the human psyche, it has little in common with what Augustine would have understood by the term. That being said, when Augustine theorized about the human psyche, its desires, internal conflicts, pains, and satisfactions, he believed he was analyzing the same realities we experience. Greek, Roman, and biblical traditions—each with its own distinctive insights—informed his understanding of the soul's ailments and cures. Situating Augustine firmly in the past as one ancient therapist among many enables us both to understand the psychology that people of another era found helpful and to become more aware of our own presuppositions about the self that they did not share.[3]

Augustine assumed with his pagan contemporaries that the study (*logos*) of the soul (*psyche*) was already in his time an ancient injunction reflected in the inscription at Delphi enjoining, "Know thyself." While we might interpret the inscription as bidding us to pay attention to the inner dynamics of one's own particular psychic history, Augustine understood it to mean that the mind should reflect upon itself (*se cogitet*) and live according to its nature (*secundum naturam suam*). He explained that this entails desiring to abide in the peculiarly human psychic space governed by the God we are under while morally exercising our agency over what we govern. According to this type of thinking, human problems arise largely from a self-forgetfulness that manifests itself in the desire to be what we are not.[4] The fundamental human questions are ultimately about *who* we are, or to put it crassly, *what* we are. In his own time, Augustine's interpretation was entirely conventional. In fact, he largely reproduced Cicero on these points. In one of Cicero's dialogues that Augustine knew well, he had the great Roman hero, Cato, explain that the command to "know thyself" could not be fully grasped "without a knowledge of physics." Only by understanding oneself within the "whole system of nature" (*omni ratione naturae*) can one form relations with human beings characterized by justice and show the proper amount of gratitude to the gods.[5] Knowing oneself requires understanding one's capacities and limits within an order of things that both preceded our first moment of awareness and will continue relatively unchanged when our short lives are over.

Psychology, therefore, is necessarily an aspect of the broad form of inquiry they called philosophy. Self-knowledge required thinking through one's situation from the widest possible purview. Acquiring a more accurate appraisal of our own lives and societies required mentally climbing above our narrowly drawn self-regard and the hearsay we have believed. It involved the effort to conform oneself to the world as it is and let it have value apart from one's own right to assign parts of it value and not others. Its worth is determined by the gods quite apart from the interests of individuals and collectives. Cicero illustrates the general outlines of this therapeutic approach in his fable of Scipio Africanus's grandson's dream of his illustrious grandfather, the conqueror of Carthage. In the dream the elder Scipio responded to his grandson's aspiration to attain the glory of his celebrated grandfather by exhorting him to study the heavens.[6] While peering upward, the younger Scipio perceived that the earth is but a small part of a vast whole. As he became accustomed at looking at the heavens, he turned to see that despite its great name, the Roman Empire was just a small island (*parva insula*) on the earth. He then was led to ponder how momentary the present time on that island was within the long succession of human generations. By acquiring such a perspective, the younger man is called upon to realize "how little value is your fame among men!" The glory to be sought, then, is not found in reputation, but in virtue, that is, in being a particularly good human being. According to the elder Scipio, this involved learning how to care for what was best in himself, his mind instead of his body. Rather than a speech of despair after his death, the grandfather's instruction communicates how the paragon of Roman virtue kept perspective in the epic struggle between Rome and Carthage with an untrammeled equanimity and no fear of death.

Ancient Greek and Roman writers were keenly aware of our experience encompassing the discontinuity of being creatures who both attain a godlike understanding of eternal laws and still die like beasts of the field. The human being as commonly defined by them as a "mortal rational animal" occupies a confusing, bewildering, halfway house between gods and beasts.[7] Sophocles' tragic play *Oedipus Rex* vividly captures this existential quandary in a narrative of a man who saves Thebes by brilliantly outwitting the sphinx while struggling with his utter inability to know himself and make decisions when so much about his life was determined by forces beyond his control.[8] It is in this tradition that Cicero contends it is only by understanding what is mortal and eternal in the universe that one can begin to sift through what is transient and permanent in oneself. By means of this knowledge the mind can begin to see "that it is not shut in by [narrow] walls as a resident of some fixed spot, but is a citizen of the whole universe (*civem totius mundi*), as it were of a single city (*unius urbis*)—then in the midst of this universal grandeur . . . how well it will know itself, according to the precept of the Pythian Apollo!"[9]

The sophistication, diversity, and genuine insight of the philosophical traditions Augustine inherited has become increasingly evident in recent years.[10] Greek and Roman writers knew that extracting oneself from one's naïve certainties and gaining cognitive purchase upon reality "as it is," is exceedingly difficult (if possible at all). It is for this reason that the traditions following Socrates had skeptical tendencies and associated the search for self-knowledge not with a conclusive vision of a set thing but rather with a disciplined questioning that continually exposes our pretension and reminds us of our nature.[11] Philosophy is the realm of merely human reasoning in time. It is the examined human life. Sophia itself is reserved for the gods. The language of "the gods" that pervades the classical tradition is not so much evidence of an uncritical, pre-scientific worldview, as it is a means of criticism that is in no way incidental to their therapeutic regimes. Augustine's famous statement of only wanting to know God and the soul is not particularly innovative but was the definition of wisdom itself.[12]

In a Greek text from the fourth century BCE, the character Socrates explains to a promising young man how impossible it is for individuals to acquire self-understanding by themselves. He likens this vain effort to turning the eye backward. It cannot do it. Exploration within the isolated self provides no escape from ignorance and solipsism. With the eyes we have that face outward, we must, therefore, look for reflective surfaces to acquire a glimpse of ourselves. Socrates reasons that the best mirror is what most approximates ourselves. In this case, that is the eyes of another human being, looking, as it were, soul to soul.[13] Throughout the Hellenistic era, there was a powerful cultural ideal extolling the philosophical guide who cures the soul with words in the same manner that a physician cures the body by gradually leading those less mature to perceive wisdom for themselves. Such a guide had to be wise and not only know all the possible psychic states and the various forms of human rhetoric but also how to adapt speech so that it will be persuasive on specific occasions.[14] Through such personal conversations with a philosophical guide one was initiated into philosophy, experienced its transforming effects, and sought to bring oneself into harmony with the universe. While learning words could not be equated with understanding "the way things are," they were a means of engaging the mind, strengthening its perception, and helping it attend to what it needed to. With the right expertise, spoken words themselves could form a reflective surface allowing one to gain a glimpse of oneself and even provide some order to the tumultuous world of inner instinct.

Augustine agreed with the common sentiment of his time that underneath the to and fro of human striving, people universally desire to live the happy life (*de beata vita*).[15] Although there were vying schools of thought about what constituted happiness, people realized that there were a host of factors largely beyond our control that affect our well-being. The evils of sickness, war, famine, blindness, slavery, crushing poverty, or early death could intrude at any time. It would seem therefore that human happiness was largely a matter of chance—one more item determined by fate. The philosophically inclined reasoned that the best strategy in such a situation would be to learn to distinguish what we can control from what we cannot and locate happiness in the realm of our own decision making. Once again, this reasoning required one to know oneself, that is, to strive to flourish *as a human being* (rather than acting like god or beast). The Hellenistic philosophical schools were often skeptical about how much one could really know about the vagaries of human history but were sure that it was a mistake to base one's happiness on one's ability to determine external circumstances. Instead, they placed great emphasis upon preserving the integrity of one's own internal volition. Thus, Epictetus, in a Stoic version of this tradition, emphasized that one must, above all, learn "to discriminate between what is your own and what is not your own." We should value what is properly ours by nature and in no way base our happiness on anything not determined by our own choice, that is, on things that are not ours.[16] If misery arises from willing what is not ours, then happiness derives from desiring what is ours by nature. Epictetus advises, "Do not seek to have everything that happens happen as you wish, but wish for everything to happen as it actually does happen, and your life will be serene."[17] Unlike the unhappy life of tyrants who isolate themselves by their efforts to control the whole, the wise, by living within the bounds of their own willing, discover their connection to the rational whole.

Psychological health and personal happiness, then, primarily had to do with one's ability to will and act "according to nature." The intervening centuries have made it difficult for us to grasp what they meant by "nature."[18] In addition to being a word for "those aspects of ourselves that we cannot change but must work with," it carried within it "ethical content" as "the correct way of developing the given aspects of ourselves."[19] Understanding what is properly ours and seeking a corresponding happiness, is therefore not primarily about measuring a particular psychic state that we identify as "happy." It has more to do with engaging in activities that promote the optimal functioning of one's natural capacities. For any organism, "happiness" is the word for the condition where it is using its natural faculties as they are meant to be used and realizing, thereby, its potential. There was a long-running debate about whether or not one could be "happy" while starving or being tortured. Those who answered in the affirmative did so because, like Socrates, they believed evil not to be something we suffer but to be something we do.[20] Having done the hard work of coming to know themselves, the wise are armed by philosophy against the blows of fate and are thereby free to choose their natural moral purpose in any number of circumstances. It is this choice that is properly their own and the object of their desire. They experience the kind of invulnerability that comes only to those who are in control of their own happiness. They would flourish by their own achievements of moral character rather than be vulnerable to the whims of fortune.

The success of classical therapy depended to a large extent on the personal involvement of those seeking to be cured. They were often told that psychic health was similar to physical health. It had to be acquired and maintained through exercise and discipline. Cure of soul required that they understand themselves as athletes in training. Philosophers developed increasingly elaborate "spiritual exercises" that were to be practiced daily to allow philosophy to "form and fashion the soul."[21] It was not enough to learn about philosophy or to master arguments rather than oneself. Philosophy was an art of living which strove for complete harmony between words and deeds. Although ancient therapists differed in their understanding of the ultimate goal of this training, they employed many of the same therapeutic methods. Even as these traditions thrived in largely non-democratic political systems, they insisted that the constraints that bind most tightly are found within.

Classical models assumed that human beings live as rational agents. Their therapeutic methods were, as a consequence, highly intellectual, emphasizing the internal workings of the mind. Even the Epicurean cultivation of the life of pleasure required daily intellectual exercises. Philosophical guides employed their methods with a great deal of flexibility. The sources preserving ancient therapeutic conversations indicate common strategies. Those seeking philosophical guidance were often verbally led to anticipate adverse circumstances (loss of loved ones or wealth, exile, etc.) and analyze their reactions to them. Their strong reactions revealed their excessive attachments to things that were not in keeping with the nature of the objects valued. Seneca's chiding of a father who was felled by grief over the death of his son sounds harsh, but Seneca's point was that the father loved the child as if he were immortal. According to Seneca, it was this misplaced judgment that was the real source of the pain. The father would have been a healthier human being if he would have loved his son for who he really was, a mortal that would die.[22] That the father's emotions were not in keeping with the world that he actually lived in was, according to Seneca, the common human plight. We overvalue what is indifferent to happiness (health, reputation, wealth) and fail to value what really matters (virtue) because we have passively accepted unexamined judgments from the societies in which we live. We are too ready to assume that our feelings come upon us rather than arise from our own prior intellectual commitments. These mistaken beliefs distort emotional responses and are the real diseases of the soul.[23]

Stoics such as Seneca had a highly evolved cognitive psychology that focused especially on the internal beliefs present in the mind.[24] Seneca's letters of spiritual direction to the young Lucillius approximate the conversation he would have in person if it were possible. In them, like other philosophers of his time, he frequently invokes compact phrases (*sententiae*) that directly oppose common errors of judgment. Phrases such as "death is nothing" or "virtue is the only good" are invoked repeatedly to insinuate themselves into the mind. Such phrases were themselves intellectual judgments. They were meant to expose and dislodge the defective maxims that were fueling the emotional responses of the student. Although students may not have been aware that they believed that their humanity was categorically better than that of their slaves, their actions and emotions revealed this flawed internal reasoning.[25] It is important to realize that these therapeutic conversations had as their basis a fictional division in the soul between what can be called "a core self" and its deformed modes of presentation. The point of the therapy was not to create a lifelong dependency upon the philosophical guide. The conversation was to influence the shape of the dialogue within. In adverse circumstances the core rational self was to replicate the conversation within, having learned to root out false beliefs moment by moment and invoke good judgments. As the student made progress, the soul was to become more and more thoroughly identified with its rational core. Whatever impressions the senses may bring, and whatever desires may erupt within, the mature person's educated mind entirely determines the course of action. The soul that was being cured had internalized this peculiar conversation and given it the power to order its emotions.

In addition to strengthening the mind's critical capacities, classical therapists found that they needed to instill a positive vision of living—that is, a way of life forming citizens who value what is of value, honor what is to be honored, and pursue what is to be pursued. As a consequence, there was a great deal of reflection on the optimal way to exhort souls to aspire to what is best for them. Those seeking advice needed to be persuaded on a case by case basis. As in all other things, such exhortations had to be adapted to the psychic state of the hearers, their motives, abilities, and levels of maturity. Philosophers adopted different practices about how much they were willing to shift their own presentation in order to become persuasive to those they were guiding. If students were ill prepared for the truth, the guide's adaptation could in some cases become so pronounced as to resemble lies artfully constructed to be a therapy for those believing them. The fictional world of the poets was used to great effect by philosophers as fragile filaments extending, as it were, down into the cave of the mind. The interpretation of myth could engage the minds of hearers who had no taste for the syllogisms of philosophy. Fictions, carefully manipulated, could become in some cases the only avenue to the truth. For example, Cicero attempted to lead his readers not to think of basic drives such as hunger and lust as being reined in by a disinterested referee called reason. Instead, we should grasp that reason itself is an appetite. It dominates because, as the preeminent human faculty, it is natural for it to lead. The mind's hunger to understand, sufficiently cultivated, naturally overwhelms weaker passions. Knowing that the pleasures of the mind are not always convincing, Cicero asked what exactly Odysseus found to be so tempting in the song of the sirens that he had to chain himself to the mast of his ship. Was it the beauty of the singing? Cicero claimed that such a reading lacked plausibility. What would so seduce Odysseus amid the arbitrary waves of suffering and time that he would be willing to give up the journey to his homeland? According to Cicero, it could be nothing other than the promise of a knowledge that would explain his plight. The reader who truly understands the epic poem understands that reason has its own pleasures. It is an appetite that yearns for satisfaction.[26]

No matter how effective the methods of philosophy were for the individual, the Greek and Roman traditions recognized that human happiness, since we are social by nature, is something that is shared with others. To varying degrees philosophy was imagined as an activity engaged in with others associated with any given philosophical school and the cities in which they lived. The wise understood that the self and society were not opposed but flourished together.[27] They were, however, well aware of the difficulties involved in continuing to participate in the flawed social conditions that largely brought about the problems afflicting the soul in the first place. The wise would thus need to carry out their duties to society while remaining true to the philosophical norms they had internalized. Stoics would thus continually remind themselves that they were citizens of two cities, one local and governed by custom, and another universal and governed by nature. Health could only be safeguarded to the extent that one continued to pay attention to oneself, maintained one's spiritual exercises, and continually reminded oneself who one truly was. This balancing act was not always possible given the realities of political life. Philosophy had its share of martyrs after Socrates, who, like him, died assuring themselves that death was not to be feared as long as one persevered in virtue.

THE USEFULNESS AND LIMITATIONS OF COGNITIVE INTERVENTIONS

While Augustine was not a professional philosopher, his learning was certainly impressive. He studied throughout his life and mastered in varying degrees a wide swath of Latin literature, especially Cicero's philosophical works, the writings of Platonists that he found in translation, Christian literature, and the Bible. His real gift, nevertheless, by all accounts, was his rhetorical skill. He was a professional orator and teacher of rhetoric before he was ever a Christian writer and bishop. As an orator Augustine was paid to construct speeches that were adapted to each particular audience in such a way that they were persuaded of whatever his patron wanted them to be. Augustine the bishop lamented the fact that he had ever sold his talents in such a way and considered his former self to have been little more than a professional liar.[28] Augustine's conversion brought about many changes in his life, but none were more significant than his resolution to use his rhetorical gifts only for good. His life would continue to be one where he made use of his eloquence, but now he would attempt to write and speak in such a way that his words would lead people to see the truth for themselves. If beautiful words could make lies seem true, could they not also lead people to delight in the truth itself?

Augustine's first writings resemble Cicero's philosophical dialogues. Like Cicero, Augustine invited his readers into a literary conversation that was intended to be so captivating that they would eventually replicate it within. One of his early dialogues is an exploration of the broader order of the universe where the reader discovers that the primary obstacle to knowledge of the whole is a lack of self-knowledge.[29] As a remedy, Augustine advocated practices of self-attention that were to free readers of the opinions they had absorbed about everything, correct these opinions through learning, and eventually enable them to conform themselves to the true order they had come to perceive. The strategies associated with the cognitive therapy of the Hellenistic philosophical schools can be discerned not only in his early philosophical dialogues and his written treatises on points of Christian doctrine but also in the huge body of sermons preserved from his thirty-nine years of ordained ministry. To read Augustine is to find oneself entangled in something of a maze of competing propositions that vie for ascendancy both in his text and in the mind of the reader. This dialogic process is responsible for the circuitous quality of many of Augustine's writings. He is rarely content simply to assert normative propositions without context. As an author or speaker, Augustine continually made efforts to solicit the personal involvement of his readers and to use their investment in the process as a means for them to make his ideas their own. Augustine is so clever at this game that it is easy to think that his writings are more straightforward than they are and lose track of their rhetorical and therapeutic artifice. There are times when the reader thinks Augustine is truly making declarations about the way things are, when, in fact, he is playing with the reader to develop certain habits of mind. This is nowhere more manifest than in his nearly constant discussion of God. Rather than condensing divinity to a definition, his words about God are intended to lead one to becoming the kind of person who could have an experience of God. Whatever one thinks about Augustine, his reader (or hearer) is compelled by him to ask, "What do I believe?" and eventually, "Who am I?"[30]

While accepting the mainstream classical therapeutic framework, Augustine argued that Christianity possessed unparalleled resources to overcome ignorance of self and promote human flourishing. The Christian way of life constituted a more comprehensive program than its pagan antecedents. There was a coherence and a power to its spiritual exercises as they were experienced in the Church's liturgy, sacraments, scriptural reading, preaching, and ascetic practices. Their effectiveness, moreover, extended well beyond the small demographic of elite citizens. This was a therapy for all, rhetorically adapted to all psychic states with the resources to liberate both the learned and the unlearned from their false beliefs and lead them by steps gradually along the same path toward a wisdom which is undiminished by being possessed by all.[31]

The mature Augustine instructed his congregation to realize that the Christian scripture has so "many medicines" that they should think of it as a pharmacy.[32] In Augustine's hands, it was a wellspring of powerful *sententiae* embedded in a persuasive narrative. It was thought superior to pagan epic, mainly because it was simultaneously beguiling and historically true. It was a history that enfranchises its interpreters into the way things are because God had providentially orchestrated it for this purpose. Augustine considered the whole inherited dogmatics of the Christian tradition necessary for healing the mind. When internalized these beliefs become the guiding maxims of the soul's emotions rather than others. In this sense, Christian beliefs were taken by him to be judgments about the kind of things believed about the world by people who flourish. In the many places where Augustine argues against pagan beliefs or the doctrines of competing forms of Christianity, he contends that such doctrines in fact inhibit the soul's flourishing. The dogmatics were not only false (that is they were not a true account of the way things are) but were psychologically stultifying for their adherents. He believed that for

specific reasons Stoic materialism, Manichaean dualism, Pelagian perfec-
tionism, and Donatist purity all, in different ways, inhibit psychic maturity.
They fail as therapies for the soul because of their flawed theological reasoning.[33]

It would be a mistake, however, to see the continuity between classical
practices and Augustine's appropriation of them in too simple of terms. It
was common for Augustine to promote a human cultural project (such as
philosophy, music, law, political order), describe the genuine beauty of whatever finite instrument it is, and then severely criticize it. Rather than a rejection of human striving, one should understand his criticism as arising from a
concern that the goodness of human art will be betrayed by its success. In
other words, Augustine worried that we will overextend our this-worldly
projects because their very beauty has become a pretext for self-satisfaction.
Augustine often likened human beings to people who set out on a journey
home and never arrive because of the delights they find on the way.[34] It was
because of this conviction that he frequently warned his readers not even to
absolutize his own words by treating them as an end to inquiry rather than as
a beginning. Instead of giving him divine authority, they should *use* his
words to have their own experiences and become whoever God wants them
to be. This pattern of reasoning applies entirely to his reception of classical
therapy. He made maximal use of classical therapy throughout his life without allowing its effectiveness to blind him to its limits. Augustine thought
that certain other Christians of his time (such as Pelagius) were insufficiently
critical of their cultural inheritance and had come as a consequence to see the
goal of their religion to be little different than the equivalent of pagan virtue.

Augustine determined that the classical traditions he inherited not only
insufficiently accounted for interpsychic conflicts but also failed to remedy
them. Knowledge of the centuries of Roman history after Cicero and of his
own human experience were enough to convince Augustine that something
more is needed than the eloquent speech of the wise. Augustine created a
strikingly original account to explain the failures of human wisdom. He came
to insist first of all that human virtue is entirely determined by the manner in
which one loves.[35] Character, therefore, is largely determined by what object
each of us desires. It is what we love that most gives form to our becoming in
time.[36] Our self-determining will, no matter how free we believe it to be,
ultimately comes under the sway of our own intellectual judgments about
what we regard as desirable and good.[37] Augustine states starkly, "Whether
he will or no, a man is necessarily a slave to the things by means of which he
seeks to be happy."[38]

We can only will wholeheartedly when we will and love the good. When
we will and love what is not good, it results in an internal splitting. This is the
case because we can never will to become wholly evil. Our created goodness
remains even if it is only preserved in our bare existence. When we will what

we are not, that history of willing remains a part of us and draws strength from habit. The self is henceforth fragmented from within. The emergence of new wills chasing new objects of desire does not eliminate or solve prior splits. Augustine explains, "They tear the mind apart by the mutual incompatibility of the wills—four or more according to the number of objects desired."[39] This internal splitting has a weakening effect upon our own agency. It is a kind of diminishment that Augustine likens to the effects of civil war. We find ourselves not with a singular "strong and whole" presence in the world, but a "turning and twisting first this way, then that, of a will half-wounded, struggling with one part rising up and the other part falling down."[40] Since reason is never completely free of the will's motion, reason's functioning is retarded as it is pulled in different directions and burdened by successive experiences. Rather than a war between our rational and irrational faculties, the self has within it competing rationalities whose ends are incompatible with one another.

The primary consequence of the fragmentation of the will, according to Augustine, is that each will becomes, to varying degrees, disassociative. Its narrowly defined interest, its stunted growth, peels away from the fullness of reality. With each part of the self clamoring for its respective objects, the induced desperation subtly justifies treating the objects of love as end points. Externals, thus, become the means to realize one's own autonomous goals. Regardless of what part of the self is leading in any given moment, in such a situation who we think we are is not who we are. The disassociation brought about by our multiplicity is not something readily accessible to reason's gaze because there is no way to stand outside ourselves to see ourselves. Our own descriptions of experience are not what is really happening to us. According to Augustine, this condition would constitute a kind of insanity or mental illness if it were not so universal that it is socially enforced. Augustine often contended that we naturalize a host of evils that are, in fact, unnatural. We assure ourselves that the suffering of infants and the premature death of our most dear loved ones is natural and normal and seek theologies that give death legitimacy and create therapies to destroy our natural repulsion from what should not be.[41] This is to say nothing of constant warfare and seeing the truth as something to be extracted by means of torture.[42] When such strategies receive the approval of the state and are supported by coercive power, how can the individual resist such social pressures? How can there be a therapy that by means of human words single-handedly unburdens all the parts of the self, heals the will, and helps it discover a single integrating desire that associates it with the real and enables it to experience the world as it is? As much as Augustine admired the wisdom of Cicero and Seneca, he believed that classical therapy lacked the means to overcome the ignorance and difficulty universally afflicting the human race.

Augustine also strongly suspected that even if a therapy existed that reduced all our inner "parts" to a singular experience of the hegemony of our own rational capacity, it would be bad for us, or even dehumanizing. Although he made use of the methods associated with Stoic cognitive therapy, he harshly criticized its goals. If we become invulnerable to the intrusions of fortune because we have become entirely identified with a rationality that cannot be taken from us, how then do we become vulnerable to a God who transcends rationality? How is the sage to be lured by love outside the constructions of his own well-fortified mind? The attempt to achieve self-sufficiency, or be, as it were, "grounded in oneself" was for Augustine not psychic health but a proud and "perverse kind of exaltation."[43] Augustine concluded that instead of idealizing the rational determination of the Stoic sage, or merely feeling vicariously what is determined by cultural norms, we should aspire to have authentic responses to the real world. The best human life is one filled with desire, gladness, fear, pain, and grief all flowing in the right way.[44] According to Augustine, such was the life of Jesus of Nazareth, a man of undivided subjectivity, yet who was still capable of shedding tears over Jerusalem which in no way diminished his human flourishing. Here was a man whose "weakness resulted from his power."[45] Autonomy and self-sufficiency are, therefore, the kind of substitute satisfactions which the soul is unable to become free of as long as it suspects that the love it most fundamentally seeks will not be forthcoming.

No less than the Greek and Roman traditions he inherited, Augustine believed that there was a reciprocity between the self and society. He stated, "For the source of a city's happiness (*beata*) is no different from that of one man, since a city is simply a united multitude of individuals."[46] Readers of the *Confessions* learn how miserable the infant is because it depends on others for what it needs. Augustine is taught from a young age to acquire skills that would not only make him self-sufficient but also perhaps bring him glory. The worldly city's commitment in the *City of God* to a security understood as autonomy requires it to be constantly at war. These two great books of Augustine mirror each other in their telling explication of the individual and social dimensions of the tragic human quest for a happiness that is secure because it is in our control. The young Augustine and the Empire both become images of the very therapy that was meant to cure them of the ills afflicting them. Philosophy's cognitive interventions are woven into the story in both books.[47] Again and again, the human search for wisdom is not so much rejected as it is pressed to its limits by a Good that itself subverts our misguided quest for autonomy and gives rise to a self and a city that transcends our own psychological and technological achievements.

DIVINE LOVE AND HUMAN VULNERABILITY

The mature Augustine saw human problems arising less from losses of self-control or failures of reason to impose its order upon unruly emotions, than from misguided attempts to impose a rational order of our own making. This worry about the human mind becoming self-satisfied and captivated by its own point of view is underscored in one of Augustine's last books: "To attain happiness our mind ought not to be satisfied with itself but rather should subordinate itself to God."[48] Decades earlier he had argued that worship was not to be directed toward the "perfect and wise rational soul" because "rational life does not owe its excellence to itself, but to the truth it willingly obeys."[49] The mind's independence simply is not in keeping with its nature. By rejecting the ends of Stoic intellectual cultivation, Augustine reintroduces the problem the Stoic strategy solved. One could easily imagine a Stoic interlocutor pressing Augustine on the repercussions of locating our happiness outside the sphere of our rational control. If human flourishing does not depend upon us, is it not then a matter of chance and Augustine's psychology ends in fatalism?

Augustine's exhorted the Christians of Carthage that even though "[w]e all want to have such well-defended hearts" invulnerable to intruders, realistically there is no such security in this life. Human fulfillment depends entirely on God's promises.[50] Rather than his theological commitments issuing in fatalism, Augustine's argued in numerous ways that faith in the Christian God was the missing element in the classical tradition. Without this faith, classicism (Stoic psychology as one example among many) not only fails to bring its best insights to bear in the real world but also inevitably contorts around its shortcomings. No matter how wise, talented, and attractive classical therapists were, they never could point to an object that was so persuasive that the very desire of it could unify the fractured "parts" of the soul. Augustine believed it made all the difference that his speech drew the attention of his hearers not to the ethereal truths of philosophy but to the divine rhetoric that in the flesh of Jesus Christ adapted itself to every psychic state. Augustine explained that in Christ Wisdom acted as a doctor healing "wounds in minds" (*vulnera in cordibus*) by means of the "scars in his body." Christ's flesh present to the five senses becomes the path to the truth about the whole: "a man being touched, God being understood; flesh being touched, wisdom being understood; weakness being touched, power being understood. The whole of it true and real."[51]

Augustine never wavered in his conviction that the love that has the power to heal, integrate, and lead to the truth is not our own. It is not constructed. It does not arise from heroic acts of will. It is not earned or deserved. Augustine often quoted Paul's assertion that "God proves his love for us in that while we were still sinners Christ died for us" (Rom 5:8). With great psychological discernment, Augustine interpreted this verse to mean that we only come to love rightly in response to being loved first. Thus Augustine insists that we love God not with our own independently generated love but with the love God gives us.[52] According to Augustine, this dynamic was nowhere more evident than in Christ's crucifixion. He asked, "To what kind of eyes would Christ appear beautiful?" Why would one be drawn to such a gruesome spectacle? Is it the meat of his torn limbs? The blood flowing from his lacerated side? No, it is his love. "Charity falls in love with charity! He loved us in order to win our answering love, and to empower us to love him in return he came to us in his Holy Spirit."[53] Healing does not occur because one part of the interiorly fractured, deeply divided, self gains the upper hand, wins the civil war, and imposes its will on the other wills. The histories of shameful desires that have been split off are not finally forgotten in favor of a new and better present will.[54] Instead, they each are completely known and loved. The experience of Christ is one of divine love seeping into the whole conflicted history of desires. Augustine's customary word for the effects of divine love is grace (*gratia*).

The thrust of Augustine's positive proposal then does not impel reason to engage in a cartography of wounds that only becomes, in the end, a sort of morbid circling of the sources of pain. For Augustine, chiefly, our growth requires contact with what is uncomfortably beyond the self's carefully constructed boundaries. His contention is that only a faith in what is beyond ourselves is inwardly liberating although it may well amount at first to nothing more than the belief that we are ultimately believed in. Such faith frees the self from the narrow confines of its own willing even when it knows that it lacks the ability to control circumstances. Our own fragmented parts, even when not understood by us, can feed on divine love and grow. Psychic growth is, therefore, a stretching of trust, love, and understanding in imitation of the Love we love and are loved by. Health is the perfecting of a kind of vulnerability. The core self has, therefore, a certain passive quality before God. It is loved and valued. The reason why it is remains inexplicable to the core self. Its experience of itself as divinely created, therefore, is one of wonder and gratitude rather than of certainty.

Augustine's narrative of his life in the *Confessions* is thoroughly informed by this theological understanding of it. For example, the sexual renunciation that is the fruit of his conversion in Book Eight is not the solution to his history of habitually misdirected sexual desire (*consuetudo carnalis*). If it were, the moment of conversion would be yet one more proud self-enclosure.[55] According to his own telling, he was being pulled between different inner voices during the moments preceding his conversion, an argument he describes as "in my heart between myself and myself."[56] The part of himself associated with his old habitual desires questioned whether or not he would even be a man without those desires and habits.[57] Another voice,

Continence, chides him, "Why do you stand on yourself and so not be able to stand at all? Cast yourself upon him, do not be afraid."[58] Still another voice, this time a child's voice intrudes *from the outside*, exhorting him to "pick up and read" which Augustine understood as a call to read the Bible. In scripture he heard yet another external voice, Paul, who agrees with the inner voice of Continence by assuring him that his core identity is not found in drinking parties, eroticism, indecencies, and career ambition, but will be sustained by "putting on the Lord Jesus Christ" (Rom 13:13-14). With surprisingly little explanation, Augustine informs his readers that suddenly it was "as if the light of security shone" into his "whole heart" (*cordi meo omnes*) and not only upon some parts and not others.[59] What changed in that moment was not that he learned something new from a text that he had read many times since childhood. Augustine wants his readers to see how the fractured, competing, alienated, "parts" within himself, representing competing objects of desire, became reconfigured. They did not need to be afraid because none of them would suffer defeat by losing the inner civil war. With this assurance, the ossified histories of desire within Augustine responded to love from outside and began themselves to desire the one who desired them, Jesus Christ. This shared desire became the basis of peace between the parts and was profoundly integrating. Their growth would no longer be stunted by having been split off from reality.[60] Augustine's celibacy is one aspect of this larger healing process. It was made possible because the needy, searching, erotic aspect of himself was not banished but was finally loved as it needed to be. He exchanged an unnatural dependency upon sexual experience as constitutive of personhood for a natural dependency upon divine love which is, in fact, the core of the human self.

In recounting his story in the way he did, Augustine was not telling us that once we come to desire God we cease desiring anything that is not God. We continue to desire ourselves and other things, but we do so in a manner that does not come at the expense of our other desires or set them in conflict. This is possible because things are loved for what they are within the ordered whole, rather than isolating them and clinging to them as a means of resolving our unhappiness. To love objects and especially human flesh in any other way is to love without knowledge. In the particularly Augustinian version of the Delphic command, this disordered, nearsighted love of self or others is a species of ignorance. It is a love that is incompatible with self-knowledge. According to Augustine's account, the scarcity that is experienced by the wills' competition with one another is superseded by an experience of abundance. All proximate desires flow into the ultimate desire of God, and this makes it possible that "all of us who enjoy him should also enjoy one another in him."[61]

It would be a mistake to see Augustine's therapy as ultimately "affective" rather than "intellectual." Feelings continue to involve intellectual judgments as much as intellectual judgments affect how we feel. Love, for Augustine, is chiefly an intellectual virtue. Because of our propensity to become captivated by our own lives and societies, it takes continual intellectual work to culti- vate an ongoing openness to divine love.[62] Thus, as one might expect of Augustine, he qualifies his own proposal and wards off any psychological triumphalism. Some readers of the *Confessions* are disappointed to discover that the converted Augustine is never fully converted. When the writer as- sesses his present state in Book 10, he confesses that he can make no confi- dent declarations to have mastered even his five senses.[63] What he has learned is that "dependence on grace produces awareness of one's own weak- ness."[64] For all his theological and psychological awareness, he laments, "I [still] find my own self hard to grasp."[65] Augustine never comes to an ex- haustive account of God or the self. There is no scaling of the summit of inner being to rise to the peak above the cloud. There is no perfecting of one's rational self-consciousness to arrive at a steady serenity. The "self" is never discovered as a destination that yields an experience of peace.[66] Any semblance of this is at best an illusion and at worst an idol. No part of the self (not even the mind) can become a cornerstone upon which to build anything. Augustine certainly describes experiences of integration, of greater under- standing, and of growing compassion for oneself and others, but this does not mean that the psychic "parts" are entirely unified in this life. Even God is not, moreover, known as a datum which can become the basis of our own selfhood and quest for fulfillment. Life's meaning is inextricably found in faith rather than certainty. In a particularly revealing passage, Augustine describes the effects of time relentlessly tearing apart his body and soul as he leans into divine love as the only means of sustenance and hope.[67]

Our abiding weakness, ongoing neediness, and receptivity, nevertheless, become sources of compassion for others and their plight. It is crucial to understand that for Augustine divine love is mediated to us in countless ways when we are receptive to it. Augustine gives special priority to divine love coming to us from Christ by means of his body that extends through time in the form of the Church. This community spread throughout the world is especially charged to open itself up continually to being loved by God so that its sacraments become concrete experiences of grace. While Augustine cer- tainly believed in private experiences of inner illumination, the overriding emphasis in his works is upon the ordinary means of grace experienced in community. Psychic health in this life for Augustine had less to do with binding up our wounds and rising above our imperfect condition than with perfecting in love the vulnerability of creaturely finitude. Having whittled away our psychic defenses, Augustine, thus, offers no protection from the blows of fate. Instead of rationally walling off the human soul, Augustine encourages us to believe in love's resiliency.[68] Of his own life, he prayed to God, "Amid all these temptations and in dangers and toils of this kind, you see my heart trembling. I have not ceased to experience such wounds, but continually they are being healed by you."[69] Faced with all the unpredictable horrors that this life can bring, Augustine was convinced that there were good reasons to entrust oneself to love's renewing spirit rather than to reason's protective strategies.

CONCLUSION: FREEING THE MIND FROM ITS SELF-ENCLOSURE

Early Greek and Roman philosophers understood the psychic tension inherent in their experience of living amid the ruins of prior civilizations while contemplating ageless realities in thought. They realized that if mortal rational animals are going to flourish they will have to learn to care for each of the apparently conflicting aspects of their nature. The writings of theirs that have survived the millennia, nevertheless, show that they believed that this insight was easier stated than lived. Psychology, as an aspect of philosophy, was deemed necessary because human beings had an exceedingly difficult time acquiring self-knowledge. As their literary tragedies repeatedly demonstrate, without understanding the possibilities and limits of human nature within the ordered whole, people are doomed to fail in their care of both body and soul. The art of living called philosophy was thought by them to liberate its adherents from such destructive illusions. The practical reasoning of philosophy supplied its initiates with the means to live according to human nature in the world as it was. However one judges the traditions of reasoning about the human person they constructed, the dilemma posed by their books remains. In the living succession of forgetful human history, the universe, in a sense, is discovered again and again. The struggle to learn who one *is* is a task that every individual must accomplish anew.

More centuries separate us from Augustine than separated him from the founding of philosophy in classical Athens. Perhaps, then, it is hardly surprising that the presuppositions of his highly Christian psychology have far more in common with his pagan contemporaries than with most strands of modern thought. Augustine the Catholic Bishop and the Roman philosophers all knew how hard it was to speak about truths that were, as it were, above the human mind. They each constructed elaborate spiritual exercises to train the emotions and composed linguistic ladders to raise the mind above its prejudices. Although they disagreed about the gods, their philosophical systems never assumed that human intelligence established much of anything on its own. Given this assumption, one can hardly blame them for understanding psychological health as conforming oneself to prior truths that one did not make. Indeed, it is a logical consequence of their theological reasoning to conclude that the purpose of human life is to be the kind of thing one was designed to be and grow in understanding of the whole.

From a modern vantage point, Augustine's critique of pagan virtue appears to be a fight within a family. Rather than an overturning of his classical inheritance, Augustine's psychology is in important ways its flowering. One would be hard pressed to find his equal in the ability to use words to heal the soul, that is, to reorder the inner scaffolding upholding the self. Much as the Roman Stoics argued that the best citizens understood that their higher cosmopolitan loyalties made them better citizens of the local city, so Augustine's Christians were taught that the City of God did not bring about Rome's destruction, but was its salvation. Augustine wrote against any flat-footed identification of the capital city of the empire as the city that perfected our social nature. Everyone, however, continued to agree that the inner drives of the individual human heart were perfected in the life of the city.[70] They did not imagine that the needs of civilization necessarily come at the expense of the psychological health of the individual.[71]

However hard it may be to countenance, Augustine thought that although we can make no small amount of progress by means of good philosophically informed psychology, ultimately there was no way of evading theological questions. Augustine's psychology is relentlessly theological by design. Any attempt to distill his psychological insights from his theological beliefs will make them both into something that would be unrecognizable to him. He was a man that believed that the largest threat to human life would always arise from the human will's effort to be self-determining. According to Augustine, the primordial fall in Genesis was not about good and evil as such. It was about human beings taking upon themselves the *right to determine* what was good and what was evil for them.[72] Instead of knowing themselves as they were created to be in the divine image, they would remake themselves and the world in their new image. In the rise and fall of human empires, in the violence, degradation, and enslavement of human flesh, Augustine saw only ignorance, psychological fragmentation, and, above all, pride.

Given his realistic assessment of the destructiveness of human collective power, Augustine believed that a forceful psychological iconoclasm was a necessary feature of any redemptive therapy. The transcendent God alone undoes all human pretensions and can never be remade by the human will. Augustine found great consolation in his belief that the more pretentious and dangerous human ambition became, the more it would collapse because of its opposition to the divine order. It was this same divine order that ensured that all technologies of self-improvement, no matter how highly evolved, would never yield what people ultimately desire. The writer of the *Confessions* discovered that while his past self thought he was unhappy because he did not get what he willed, he came to see that all along he was struggling against God's love in him. It was preventing him from becoming satisfied with objects of desire less than were in accord with his God-given dignity. According to Augustine, if cognitive interventions fail to calm the human heart, it may well be that the restlessness of the heart is there because it is quite rightly resisting a "healing" that boxes it into an immanent frame of reference. Its disquiet is a sign of its healthy longing for what outstrips its mental capacity and technical abilities.

Since Augustine and his fellow ancient therapists assumed that psychology and physics were logically connected, they would have misgivings about the prospects of therapy in a purposeless universe without gods.[73] A modern student of Augustine, Hannah Arendt, inquiring into what kinds of effects the impressive scientific advances of the twentieth century had on our notions of human nature, took the astronaut as the paradigm for an emerging form of human consciousness. She writes, "The astronaut, shot into outer space and imprisoned in his instrument-ridden capsule where each actual physical encounter with his surroundings would spell immediate death . . . will be the less likely [than] ever to meet anything but himself and man-made things the more ardently he wishes to eliminate all anthropocentric consideration from his encounter with the non-human world around him." He no longer encounters "anything in the world around him that is not manmade and hence is not, in the last analysis, he himself in a different disguise."[74] If Augustine accused the Stoics of becoming trapped in the citadel of their own rational processes, would he not worry with Arendt about what is left to lead the mind out of its own self-satisfaction and world construction? If he characterized the Stoic project not so much as good philosophy but as a means they used to protect themselves from a world that was not in their control, would he not see many of our cultural projects as yet another species of psychic defensiveness and control? If he found the one dehumanizing in its eschewal of vulnerability, it is hard to conclude that he would not have similar worries about the other.

Augustine's modern readers may remain unconvinced that cosmic reason or divine love and all the corollaries drawn from them can be a plausible basis for human psychology. After all, pre-modern psychologies claim to know things about us without studying us in a way that is scientifically recognizable. It is true that they all were quite innocent of the physical structures that hide from the unaided eye but are the causes of undeniable physical effects and so many modern technical achievements. This may be grounds for dismissing their psychological conclusions, especially since the same technologies that allow us to peer out into space are enabling us to peer into the human brain. It is, nonetheless, true that much of what we know about political freedom, law, rhetoric, love, and beauty come to us from prescientific times. It would seem that if we still look to the ancients for inspiration about the virtues of democratic freedoms and just societies, why not also for the other needs of the human heart? It may well be that in the comparatively unimpressive villages that most ancient authors spent their entire lives—their material space and imaginations not overshadowed by industrial civilization—they were able to see some things that we no longer can. Even if the material surface of our planet has changed a great deal in the last 3,000 years, the human heart has not.

NOTES

1. See, for example, Ellen T. Charry, "Augustine of Hippo: Father of Christian Psychology," *Anglican Theological Review* 88 (2006) 575–89; Donald Capps and James E. Dittes, eds., *The Hunger of the Heart: Reflections on the Confessions of Augustine* (West Lafayette, IN: Society for the Scientific Study of Religion, 1990); and how convincingly Charles Taylor is able to give an account of modern identity by telling the story of Augustinian "inwardness" giving birth both to any number of forms of Christian spirituality and secularized methods of "self-exploration" in the West, in his *The Sources of the Self: The Making of the Modern Identity* (Cambridge: Harvard University Press, 1989).

2. Franz G. Alexander and Sheldon T. Selesnick, *The History of Psychiatry: An Evaluation of Psychiatric Thought and Practice from Prehistoric Times to the Present* (New York: Harper & Row, 1966) 59.

3. In psychology, as in other matters, it is best to assume that Augustine is revising a legacy of classical antique wisdom that he largely accepts rather than attributing to him unprecedented notions. Augustine is not usually as *sui generis* as he is often credited with being. In order not to multiply instances, see, for example, James Wetzel's discussion of the many problems involved in the idea that Augustine invented the modern notion of the will: J. Wetzel, "Will and Interiority in Augustine: Travels in an Unlikely Place," *Augustinian Studies* 33 (2002) 139–60.

4. Augustine, *De trinitate* 10.7 (CCL 50: 320.1–6). Augustine finds the precept in the Bible in, among other places, Song of Songs 1:7. For a history of the Delphic maxim (that includes an extensive discussion of Augustine), see Pierre Paul Courcelle, *Connais-toi toi-même: de Socrate à saint Bernard*, 2 vols. (Paris: Études augustiniennes, 1974–1975) and also Wayne J. Hankey, "'Knowing as We are Known' in *Confessions* 10 and Other Philosophical, Augustinian and Christian Obedience to the Delphic *Gnothi Seauton* from Socrates to Modernity," *Augustinian Studies* 34 (2003) 23–48.

5. Cicero, *De finibus bonorum et malorum* 3.22.73 (trans. H. Rackham; Loeb Classical Library [LCL] 40 [Cambridge, MA: Harvard University Press, 1914], 292); see also 5.16.44 (LCL 40: 442–44).

6. Cicero, *De Re Publica* 6.9–26 (trans. C. W. Keyes; LCL 213: 260–82). For an analysis of Cicero on these terms, see Stephen A. White, "Cicero and the Therapists," in *Cicero the Philosopher: Twelve Papers*, ed. by J. G. F Powell (Oxford: Oxford University Press, 1995) 219–46.

7. See, for example, Cicero, *Academica* 2.21 (trans. H. Rackham; LCL 268: 494); compare Augustine, *De Ordine* 2.31; *De magistro* 8.23–24; and the long exploration of the theme in *De animae quantitate*.

8. Sophocles, *Oedipus* (trans. Hugh Lloyd-Jones; LCL 20).

9. Cicero, *De Legibus*, 1.23.61 (LCL 213: 364–66).

10. See Pierre Hadot, *What is Ancient Philosophy?*, trans. by Michael Chase (Cambridge: Harvard University Press, 2002); Robert A. Kaster, *Emotion, Restraint, and Community in Ancient Rome* (New York: Oxford University Press, 2005); Martha C. Nussbaum, *The Therapy of Desire: Theory and Practice in Hellenistic Ethics* (Princeton: Princeton University Press, 1994); Richard Sorabji, *Emotion and Peace of Mind: From Stoic Agitation to Christian Temptation* (Oxford: Oxford University Press, 2000).

11. This theme is brought out well by Rowan Williams, "'Know Thyself': What Kind of an Injunction?" in *Philosophy, Religion and the Spiritual Life*, ed. by Michael McGhee (Cambridge: Cambridge University Press, 1992) 211–27.

12. Augustine, *Soliloquiorum* 1.2.7; cf. Cicero, *De officiis* 2.2.5 (trans. W. Miller; LCL 30: 172); *Tusculanae disputationes* 4.26.57 (trans. J. E. King; LCL 141: 392): "Wisdom (*sapientia*) is the knowledge (*scientia*) of things divine and human and acquaintance with the cause of each of them, with the result that wisdom copies what is divine, while it regards all human concerns as lower than virtue."

13. Plato, *Alcibiades* 132d–133c, in *Plato: Complete Works*, ed. John M. Cooper (Indianapolis: Hackett Publishing, 1997) 591–92.

14. These criteria are articulated in Plato's *Phaedrus* 271c–277c, trans. Cooper, *Plato*, 548–54. For the ideal, more generally, see Ilsetraut Hadot, "The Spiritual Guide," in *Classical Mediterranean Spirituality: Egyptian, Greek, and Roman*, ed. by A. H. Armstrong (New York: Crossroad, 1986) 436–59 and my *Augustine and the Cure of Souls: Revising a Classical Ideal* (Notre Dame: University of Notre Dame Press, 2010) esp. 19–61.

15. Augustine encountered this argument as early as his reading of Cicero's *Hortensius* (quoted in Augustine's *De trinitate* 13.4.7–5.8). See also Augustine, *De beata uita* and William S. Babcock, "*Cupiditas* and *Caritas*: The Early Augustine on Love and Human Fulfillment," in *The Ethics of St. Augustine*, ed. William S. Babcock (Atlanta, Ga.: Scholars Press, 1991) 39–66.

16. Epictetus, *Dissertationes* 1.1; 4.1.81–85 (trans. W. A. Oldfather; LCL 131: 7–14, 218: 270–72). Compare Cicero, *Tusculanae disputationes* 5.10.28–31 (LCL 141: 454–56) and Seneca, *Epistulae* 9.15 (trans. R. M. Gummere; LCL 75: 50).

17. Epictetus, *Enchiridion* 8 (LCL 218: 490); compare Seneca, "[T]hat man is a weakling and a degenerate who struggles and maligns the order of the universe and would rather reform the gods than reform himself" (*Epistulae* 107.12 [LCL 77: 228]).

18. For shifts in the perception and meaning of nature, see Pierre Hadot, *The Veil of Isis: An Essay on the History of the Idea of Nature*, trans. by Michael Chase (Cambridge, Mass.: Belknap Press of Harvard University Press, 2006).

19. Julia Annas, *The Morality of Happiness* (New York: Oxford University Press, 1993) 135–220, 214.

20. See Plato, Apologia 30c, *Gorgias* 474b–476a; compare Cicero, *Tusculanae disputationes* 5.19.56 (LCL 141: 482); Seneca, *Epistulae* 66:12 (LCL 76: 10): "[J]oy and a brave unyielding endurance of torture are equal goods; for in both is the same greatness of soul."

21. Seneca, *Epistulae* 16.3 (my translation; LCL 75: 104).

22. Seneca, *Epistulae* 99 (LCL 77: 128–48).

23. See Seneca's statement, "we suffer more often from opinions than from reality" (*Epistulae* 13.4); Seneca defines disease of soul as "a persistent perversion of judgment" (*iudicium in prauo pertinax*) (*Epistulae* 75.11 [LCL 76: 142]).

24. See Robert J. Newman, "*Cotidie Meditare*: Theory and Practice of the *meditatio* in Imperial Stoicism," *Aufstieg und Niedergang der römischen Welt*, 2.36.3 (1989) 1473–1517.

25. Seneca, *Epistulae* 47; *On Mercy* 1.18; Epictetus, *Dissertationes* 1.13.4–5.

26. Cicero, *De finibus* 5.48–50 (LCL 40: 448–52) commenting on Homer, *Odyssey* 12.184–191. This style of reading was quite common among philosophers, see Robert Lamberton, *Homer the Theologian: Neoplatonist Allegorical Reading and the Growth of the Epic Tradition* (Berkeley: University of California Press, 1986).

27. See Seneca, *Epistulae* 66.10 (LCL 76: 8): "The advantage of the state and that of the individual are yoked together."

28. Augustine, *Confessions* 6.6.9; 9.2.2 (trans. H. Chadwick, *Confessions* [Oxford: Oxford University Press, 1991]).

29. Augustine, *De Ordine* 1.1.3 (CCL 29: 90.50): *Cuius erroris maxima causa est, quod homo sibi ipse est incognitos.*

30. The reader who perseveres to the last book of his massive *De trinitate* (15.45–49) is told that although he has failed to capture God in words, perhaps he has exercised his readers sufficiently so that they might have become the kind of people able to experience what they believe.

31. This is Augustine's argument in *De uera religione* (trans. John H. S. Burleigh, *Augustine: Earlier Writings*, Library of Christian Classics [Philadelphia: Westminster Press, 1953] 222–83).

32. Augustine, *Sermones* 32.1 (CCL 41: 398.1–6); trans. Edmund Hill, *Sermons, The Works of St. Augustine: A Translation for the 21st Century* [WSA], ed. John E. Rotelle, Part 3/1–3/11 (Hyde Park, N.Y.: New City Press, 1990–1997) 137. For an extended discussion of Augustine's therapeutic reasoning with scripture, see my *Augustine and the Cure of Souls*, 139–209.

33. Contemporary readers should keep in mind that leading representatives of each of these groups in late antiquity did not accept Augustine's characterization of them.

34. See the entire first book of *De doctrina christiana* (trans. Edmund Hill, *Teaching Christianity*, WSA 1/11, 106–26).

35. See how Augustine defines the four classical virtues as species of love in *De moribus ecclesiae catholicae* 1.15.25; trans. Donald A. Gallagher and Idella J. Gallagher, *The Catholic and Manichaean Ways of Life*, Fathers of the Church (Washington, D.C.: Catholic University of America Press, 1966) 22–23.

36. As Augustine states, "Hold fast, rather, to the love of God, that, as God is eternal, so also you may abide in eternity; for each person is such as is his love is. Do you love the earth? You will be earth. Do you love God? What shall I say? Will you be a god? I dare not say this on my own. Let us hear Scripture: 'I have said, 'You are gods and sons of the Most High, all of you'" (Ps. 81.6) (*In epistulam Iohannis* 2.14.5; trans. John W. Rettig, *St. Augustine: Tractates on the Gospel of John*, 5 vols., The Fathers of the Church [Washington, D.C.: Catholic University of America Press, 1988–1995] 5.158).

37. Note how Augustine's *uoluntas* only approximately translates as "will," see John Rist, "Faith and Reason," in *The Cambridge Companion to Augustine*, ed. Eleonore Stump and Norman Kretzmann (Cambridge: Cambridge University Press, 2001) 26–39 at 32–37. In James Wetzel's words, "There is no faculty of will, distinct from desire, which we use to determine our actions" (*Augustine and the Limits of Virtue* [Cambridge: Cambridge University Press, 1992] 8). See also David C. Schindler, "Freedom Beyond Our Choosing: Augustine on the Will and Its Objects," in *Augustine and Politics*, ed. John Doody, Kevin L. Hughes, Kim Paffenroth (Lanham, MD: Lexington Books, 2005) 67–96.

38. Augustine, *De uera religione* 38.69 (CCL 32: 233.14–15); trans. Burleigh, 260. See also Augustine's assertion that "we necessarily act in accordance with what delights us more" (*Expositio epistulae ad Galatas* 49; Latin text and English translation in Eric Plumer, *Augustine's Commentary on Galatians: Introduction, Text, Translation, and Notes* (Oxford: Oxford University Press, 2006) 214–15.

39. Augustine, *Confessions* 8.10.24 (CCL 27: 128.51–53); trans. Chadwick, 150. For the sake of presentation and in keeping with Paul's narrative of Romans 7, Augustine limits the discussion in his own case to a conflict between two wills, but according to his theory there could be more.

40. Augustine, *Confessions* 8.8.19 (CCL 27: 126.27–30); trans. (altered) Chadwick, 147.

41. Augustine, *C. Jul. op. imp.* 3.187; trans. Roland J. Teske, *Answer to the Pelagians, III: Unfinished Work in Answer to Julian* (Hyde Park, NY: New City Press, 1999) 373–74.

42. Augustine, *De ciuitate dei* 4.4, 19.6–7; trans. Henry Bettenson, *Concerning the City of God against the Pagans* (Harmondsworth, Middlesex: Penguin Books, 1984).

43. Augustine, *De ciuitate dei* 14.6–13 at 14.13 (CCL 48.434.5–8; 48.435.58–61). See also *Sermones* 150, 198.36, 348.

44. Augustine, *De ciuitate dei* 14.9 (CCL 48.426.4–8, 429.142–143). See also John Cavadini, "Feeling Right: Augustine on the Passions and Sexual Desire," *Augustinian Studies* 36 (2005) 195–217.

45. Augustine, *De ciuitate dei* 14.9 (CCL 48.428.83); cf. 14.9 (CCL 48.427.66–68): "For human emotion was not illusory in him who had a truly human body and truly human mind."

46. Augustine, *De ciuitate dei* 1.15 (CCL 47: 17.47–48); trans. (altered) Bettenson, 25.

47. See particularly Augustine's encounters with Cicero and the Platonists in *Confessions* 3 and 7 and the discussion of the limits of pagan virtue throughout the *City of God.*

48. Augustine, *Retractationum* 1.1.2 (CCL 57: 8.49–51); trans. (altered) Mary Inez Bogan, *The Retractations*, The Fathers of the Church (Washington, D.C.: Catholic University of America Press, 1968) 8.

49. Augustine, *De uera religione* 55.110 (CCL 32: 257.49–56); trans. Burleigh, 280.

50. Augustine, *Enarrationes in Psalmos* 99.11 (CCL 39: 1400.20–28); trans. Maria Boulding, *Expositions of the Psalms*, WSA 3/15–20, 5.22.

51. Augustine, *Sermones* 237.3, 264.6 (PL 38: 1124, 1218); trans. Hill, 53, 232.

52. Augustine, *Enchiridion* 76; *De trinitate* 4.2.

53. Augustine, *Enarrationes in Psalmos* 127.8 (CCL 40: 1872.22–34); trans. Boulding, 6.104–105.

54. See not only Augustine's remembering of his own history in his *Confessions*, but also his conjecture that in the Heavenly City just as the bodies of the martyrs have painless scars, so also the soul "will remember even its past evils as far as intellectual knowledge is concerned; but it will utterly forget them as far as sense experience is concerned" (*De ciuitate dei* 22.19, 30).

55. See James Wetzel, "Body Double: Saint Augustine and the Sexualized Will," in *Weakness of Will from Plato to the Present*, ed. Tobias Hoffmann (Washington, D.C.: Catholic University of America Press, 2008) 58–81, esp. 75.

56. Augustine, *Confessions* 8.27 (CCL 27: 130.48–49); trans. (altered) Chadwick, 152.

57. Augustine, *Confessions* 8.26 (CCL 27: 130.30).

58. Augustine, *Confessions* 8.27 (CCL 27: 130.42–43); trans. (altered) Chadwick, 151.

59. Augustine, *Confessions* 8.29 (CCL 27: 131.36–38); trans. (altered) Chadwick, 153. Note that the command to make no provision for the *concupiscence* of the flesh is not a command to leave flesh behind but to desire to be clothed with another kind of flesh, the flesh of Jesus Christ.

60. As Augustine states elsewhere: "We pray for help and a cure . . . from the one who is able to heal all infirmities, not by removing from us a foreign substance, but by repairing our own nature within us" (*De continentia*, 7.18 [CSEL 41: 162.20–23]); trans. Ray Kearney, *Marriage and Virginity*, ed. David G. Hunter, WSA 1/9, 204.

61. *De doctrina christiana* 1.32.35 (CCL 32: 26.17–19). Augustine's early distinction articulated in *De doctrina christiana* between use (*uti*) and enjoyment (*frui*) is a means of apportioning desire to nature. He is interested in experiences of attachment and supplies a vocabulary to differentiate affective experiences and their effects.

62. For more on the daily training of the affections, see William S. Babcock, "Augustine and the Spirituality of Desire," *Augustinian Studies* 25 (1994) 179–99.

63. Augustine, *Confessions* 10.42–70.

64. Augustine, *Confessions* 10.4 (CCL 27: 156.19–21); trans. Chadwick, 180.

65. Augustine, *Confessions* 10.25 (CCL 27: 167.18–19); trans. Chadwick, 193. Cf. 10.15 (CCL 27: 162.60–61): "I myself cannot grasp the totality of what I am."

66. For this reason, John Cavadini has pointed out that our language about the "self" tends to give it a solidity that it never had for Augustine: J. Cavadini, "The Darkest Enigma: Reconsidering the Self in Augustine's Thought," *Augustinian Studies* 38 (2007) 119–32.

67. Augustine, *Confessions* 11.39.

68. See Augustine's call to enter the world naked like David with only faith rather than placing one's trust in armor (Saul) or in one's own strength (Goliath) (*Sermones* 32).

69. Augustine, *Confessions* 10.64 (CCL 27: 190.8–10); trans. Chadwick, 217.

70. Augustine, *De ciuitate dei* 19.5 (CCL 48: 669.1–2): "The philosophers hold the view that the life of the wise man should be social; and in this we support them much more heartily."

71. The argument most famously made by Sigmund Freud, *Civilization and Its Discontents*, trans. James Strachey (New York: W. W. Norton, 1989). Freud's rejection of the classical analogy between the self and the polis (not necessary his analysis of the shape of the conflict) has been commonplace since Rousseau.

72. Augustine, *De Genesi ad litteram libri duodecim* 8.29–31, 11.39.

73. As Sigmund Freud presupposes, "The question of the purpose of human life has been raised countless times. . . . It looks . . . as though one had a right to dismiss the question. . . . One can hardly be wrong in concluding that the idea of life having a purpose stands and falls with the religious system" (*Civilization and Its Discontents*, 24–25).

74. Hannah Arendt, *Between Past and Future: Eight Exercises in Political Thought* (New York: Penguin, 1993) 277. Arendt wrote her dissertation at Heidelberg on Augustine's concept

of love (*Love and Saint Augustine*, ed. J. V. Scott and J. C. Stark [Chicago: University of Chicago Press, 1996]).

Chapter Seven

Augustine and Freud

The Secularization of Self-Deception

Margaret R. Miles

I have met many people who wanted to deceive,
but no one who wanted to be deceived.
—Augustine, *Confessions* 10.23

The concept of self-deception, in which the same person "is both the doer and the sufferer," has played many roles in Western thinkers' analysis of the human condition.[1] What is self-deception, and why does it occur? Or, more accurately, why do we do it, for philosopher Herbert Fingarette insists that self-deception is an activity, "not something that 'happens' to the ego but something the ego does."[2] He describes how self-deception works: I "take account of my situation and detect a condition which is relevant to my interests, but which would gravely disrupt my mental equilibrium if my attention were to focus on it. [So I] avoid turning my attention in that direction."[3] Self-deception is "as ordinary and familiar a kind of mental activity as one can imagine"; it is woven into the deepest layers of habitual behavior.[4] Simultaneously a "peculiarly human" and "peculiarly demoralizing" strategy, self-deception "turns upon the personal identity one accepts rather than the beliefs one has."[5] According to Fingarette, it is a spiritual failure, "involving spiritual cowardice and inner warfare."[6]

I will examine the phenomenon of self-deception as it is described in the thought of two "founders of [Western] discursivities,"[7] Augustine of Hippo (d. 430 C. E.) and Sigmund Freud (d. 1939 C. E.). Because this agenda appears to assume that ideas are ahistorical, I must quickly explain what I do *not* intend to argue in this essay.

First, I do not propose to compare ideas that have verbal similarity. Michel Foucault, Arnold Davidson, and others have pointed out that ideas are always and necessarily historically situated and conceptually perspectival.

> It is this automatic and immediate application of concepts, as though concepts have no temporality, that allows, and often requires, us to draw misleading analogies and inferences that derive from a historically inappropriate and conceptually untenable perspective. [8]

"Lexical continuity" can hide "radical conceptual discontinuity," Davidson writes.[9] For example, an idea may be a central tenet of one author and quite peripheral in another. Is it, then, the "same idea" in both authors? Our answer must be no. But what if a concept can be shown to address a similar central question or concern in two authors? As I will shortly describe in more detail, Augustine and Freud each discuss self-deception as both cause and effect of human unhappiness. Perhaps we are on somewhat firmer ground, then, for noticing similarities and differences in the function of the concept in these authors.

Furthermore, I do not discuss Augustine's and Freud's analysis of self-deception in order to exhibit the greater complexity or beauty of one author at the expense of the other. Both authors introduced perspectives and generated conversations not formerly in existence. However, what my discussion does assume is an unwieldy and largely indefinable shared cultural repertoire of knowledge, sensibilities, and values in Western European societies. Inheriting some assumptions from Augustine's religious view of self-deception, Freud secularized the language, method, and goal of the process of alleviating self-deception. An unanticipated benefit of examining Freud's prescription for addressing self-deception is that it enables a re-reading of Augustine's conversion that notices the long-term, patient work leading up to and following his dramatic conversion experience.

I.

Augustine, Christian bishop of Hippo in North Africa at the end of the fourth century, described his pre-conversion unhappiness and self-deception in particularly graphic language. He pictured himself as "scratching the itching scab of concupiscence with poisoned nails," leading to "feverish swellings, abscesses, and running sores."[10] He relates that while he was in this state, walking about the streets of Milan,

> I noticed a poor beggar; he was fairly drunk, I suppose, and was laughing and enjoying himself. It was a sight which depressed me. . . . I thought of how I was toiling away, spurred on by my desires and dragging after me the load of

my unhappiness and making it all the heavier by dragging it, and it seemed to me that the goal . . . was simply to reach a state of happiness that was free from care; the beggar had reached this state before us, and we, perhaps, might never reach it at all. [11]

Happiness is, Augustine recognized, the state that everyone—every single person—desires. Yet, he asked, how can we desire it if we lack knowledge of what it looks and feels like? Is happiness in one's memory? It must be, for it can be no place else, but in what form? Is it in the memory of joyful moments? Joy cannot be remembered by any bodily sense, but it is experienced in the mind and can be re-collected by the mind. And, for the purpose of reconstructing the memory of happiness, *any old joys will do*: "For even base and disgraceful things have filled me with joy . . . and at other times I have had joy in good and worthy things." Thus, "joy is something that no one can say he has no experience of; he finds it in his memory and recognizes it when he hears the words: 'the happy life.'" [12]

It may be that any old joys will do when one tries to remember the *feeling* of happiness, but Augustine had nonnegotiable requirements for happiness, requirements that only his God could meet. To be worthy of the name, Augustine said, happiness must be permanent and unchanging: "This is the happy life—to rejoice in you [God] and to you and because of you. This is the happy life; there is no other." [13] Augustine says that happiness *should* be quite simple; two commandments teach how it is to be achieved, namely, "'Thou shalt love the Lord thy God with all thy heart, and with all thy soul, and with all thy mind,' and 'Thou shalt love thy neighbor as thyself.'" [14]

Why, then, are people unhappy? Augustine's analysis, described in *The Spirit and the Letter*, is both complex and practical: we do not have the knowledge necessary for choosing what is good for us, and we do not delight in the good: "The extent of a [person's] knowledge is not in his own power, and . . . it does not follow that he will pursue what he knows to be worth pursuing, unless he delight in it." Pondering this frustrating human helplessness, Augustine invoked the scriptural text he quoted more often than any other throughout his writings: "For we see now through a glass darkly; then, however, face to face" (I Corinthians 13:12). [15] Augustine's prescription for the cure of unhappiness similarly lies beyond human control. It is conversion. He described his conversion as a process of being taken "from behind my own back, which was where I had put myself during the time when I did not want to be observed by myself." [16] Before discussing Augustine's model of conversion further, however, let us consider Freud's understanding of self-deception, its cause and its effects.

II.

As is well known, Freud described the structure of mental processes as realms, regions, or provinces designated as superego, ego, and id. He described the goal of psychoanalysis as strengthening the ego, making it more independent of the demanding and judgmental superego, widening its field of perception, and enlarging its organization, so that the ego can balance the demands of the superego and disorderly and aggressive id.

Augustine was one of the primary creators of the Western European Christian civilization against which Freud proposed an alternative "religion" of psychoanalysis, a "secular cure of souls."[17] There is no evidence but every possibility that Freud read Augustine. In any case, many of Augustine's ideas were available to him in late nineteenth-century Western European culture. Moreover, Freud had multiple points of acquaintance, both domestic and social, with the dominant religion of his society, Roman Catholicism. A nursemaid to whom the young Freud was deeply attached, and whom he regarded as a second mother, "was a devoted Catholic and introduced Freud to the area churches and teachings about heaven and damnation."[18] Freud received a classical *gymnasium* education where, as "top boy" for seven years, he excelled in study of the classical (Greek and Latin) and Christian roots of eighteenth-century values. Moreover, several of the adult Freud's closest friends and colleagues were deeply versed in Christianity—Oskar Pfister, Carl Jung, and Ludwig Binswanger, to name only the most obvious.

According to Freud's biographer, Ernest Jones, Freud was more interested in religion than in any other topic except sexuality.[19] But he was interested solely in what he called the "common man's religion." "The deeper, more sophisticated views championed by theologians like Soren Kierkegaard . . . and mystics like Meister Eckhart simply fell outside of what the 'common man' understood by his religion—'*the only religion* [Freud wrote] *that ought to bear that name.*'"[20] He described his impatience with intellectually sophisticated philosophical religion. And he confessed himself to be tone-deaf to religious mysticism.

Freud's highly esteemed friend Romain Rolland argued that mysticism is "the true subterranean source of *religious energy* which . . . has been collected, canalized, and *dried up by the Churches* to the extent that one could say that it is inside the churches (whichever they may be) that true 'religious' sentiment is least available."[21] But Freud insisted that the origin of mysticism lay in the infant's primary narcissism, or oceanic feeling, his inability to differentiate himself from the universe. He wrote *The Future of an Illusion*, published in 1927, against the simplified and caricatured version of Christianity he preferred to tilt against. He followed up on this book and Rolland's letter when he wrote *Civilization and Its Discontents*, in which he commented:

In my *Future of an Illusion* I was concerned much less with the deepest sources of the religious feeling than with what the common man understands by his religion—with the system of doctrines and promises which on the one hand explains to him the riddles of the world with enviable completeness, and, on the other, assures him that a careful Providence will watch over his life and will compensate him in a future existence for any frustrations he suffers here. . . . The whole thing is so patently infantile, so foreign to reality, that to anyone with a friendly attitude to humanity it is painful to think that the great majority of mortals will never be able to rise above this view of life.[22]

But Freud had another concern about religion that was much more specific and self-serving than the pain of someone "with a friendly attitude to humanity." Understanding his life project as the "institution of psychoanalytic knowledge," he sought an intellectual and social space in which psychoanalysis could thrive.[23] When he failed to establish psychoanalysis as a university discipline, he identified the niche presently occupied by religion as the most appropriate cultural space for psychoanalysis. So he set about to discredit religion in order to appropriate its social and psychological niche. Before psychoanalysis, people with "personal problems" sought counsel from their priest, minister, or rabbi. Sarah Winter has demonstrated the extent to which the establishment of psychoanalysis involved replacing religious counselors with analysts—"secular pastoral workers."[24] In short, in order to establish psychoanalysis, Freud needed to de-legitimize religion.[25]

He did this, as already mentioned, by interpreting religious feeling as a "shrunken residue" of the infant's "oceanic feeling," a feeling rooted in the infant's simple inability to distinguish himself from his surroundings:

An infant at the breast does not as yet distinguish his ego from the external world as the source of the sensations flowing in upon him. He gradually learns to do so, in response to various promptings. . . .[o]riginally the ego includes everything, later it separates off an external world from itself.[26]

Freud said that in the adult, the vestiges of the infant's "limitless narcissism" are codified in religious systems in which it is prolonged and extended. He proposed that these childish longings for love, protection, and security should be addressed, not by religion but by psychoanalysis. The narcissism of the oceanic feeling, he wrote, should not be mistaken for "Reality."[27] Neiman suggests that, although Freud knew that "pointing out the origins of a belief is never an argument against it," his reduction of religion to infantile fantasy may be stronger than a legitimate argument because it has the effect of making us ashamed of, and embarrassed by, religion.[28]

Like Augustine, Freud believed that all people seek to be happy. In *Civilization and Its Discontents*, published in 1930, Freud addressed the essentially religious question, "What is the purpose of human life?" His short answer was that people "strive after happiness; they want to become happy and to remain so. . . . [W]hat decides the purpose of life is simply the programme of the pleasure principle."[29] William Parsons summarizes:

> The question is how, given the tendencies, capacities, and limits of man's nature, we can best fulfill the program of the pleasure principle. Freud eventually argued for a general position that stressed the value of work, being loved, and loving others.[30]

Yet Freud acknowledged that "our very constitution" prevents anything more durable than the momentary gratification of our desires. He concludes bluntly, "The programme of becoming happy, which the pleasure principle imposes on us, cannot be fulfilled."[31] His discussion of the pursuit of happiness in *Civilization and Its Discontents* is interrupted by lengthy considerations of *un*happiness. He analyzes at length the sources of human unhappiness and the most common responses to it. One such response is the reduction of one's demand for happiness, settling for escaping the more dramatic forms of unhappiness. Another response is use of the various forms of intoxication that temporarily enhance pleasure and suppress pain. (Recall Augustine's drunken beggar.) A select few, he granted, can even obtain pleasure from intellectual work. Freud reiterated his belief that "we cannot dispense with palliative remedies. . . . Something of the kind is indispensable."[32]

Religion is also a common strategy for managing unhappiness. According to Freud, religion, the "mass-delusion," attracts adherents by promising happiness, but it fails to deliver. It also fails the social projects of adapting people to civilization and controlling their morality.[33] In *Civilization and Its Discontents,* he gives religion short shrift:

> If the believer finally sees himself obliged to speak of God's "inscrutable decrees," he is admitting that all that is left to him as a last possible consolation and source of pleasure in his suffering is an unconditional submission. And if he is prepared for that, he could probably have spared himself the *détour* he has made.[34]

III.

> The falsification of memory—the adjustment, abbreviation, invention, even *omission* of experience—is common to us all, it is the business of psychic life.[35]

Because unhappiness is common, so is self-deception. For Freud, as for Augustine, self-deception occurs as a virtually automatic response to unhappiness. At the core of Freud's understanding of self-deception is what he calls the "subjective illusion" that conscious choices govern the individual's psychic life and behavior. In fact, unconscious wishes and mental processes shape the individual.[36] As Fingarette writes, "rather than taking explicit consciousness for granted, we must come to take its absence for granted."[37]

Both Augustine and Freud observed and interpreted common behavior. Recall Fingarette: self-deception is "as ordinary and familiar a kind of mental activity as one can imagine," it is woven into the deepest layers of habitual behavior.[38] In short, self-deception, for most of us, most of the time, goes unnoticed. Self-deception begins in infancy and has, by the time a person reaches adulthood, become habitual. Both Augustine and Freud sought the origins of what Augustine called "sin," and Freud called "repression," in infant behavior.[39] They share a bleak and disrespectful view of children.[40] "Freud's child is a humiliated creature, driven by discomfort, dread, and shame."[41] He is anxious, grasping, ignorant, and insecure, cravenly seeking protection, reassurance, and love. These infant insecurities have not disappeared in the adult; they are merely concealed and/or given other expressions.

Augustine's child is greedy, disobedient, lying, lazy, jealous, and unhappy. Augustine is notorious for his description of the sinful infant at his mother's breast, envious of another baby who is fed at the same breast. Adults smile at infantile omnipotence, Augustine wrote, but "infants are harmless because of physical weakness, not because of any innocence of mind."[42] He describes the condition more fully:

> And when people did not do what I wanted, either because I could not make myself understood or because what I wanted was bad for me, then I would become angry with my elders for not being subservient to me, and with responsible people for not acting as though they were my slaves; and I would avenge myself on them by bursting into tears. . . . Who can recall to me the sin I did in my infancy?[43]

Augustine saw in the infant's behavior the source and paradigm of lifelong aggression and acquisitiveness: "For it is just these same sins which, as the years pass by, become related no longer to tutors, schoolmasters, footballs, nuts, and pet sparrows, but magistrates and kings, gold, estates, and slaves."[44] In middle age he recalled his childhood beatings with horror: "Is there anyone who, faced with the choice between death and a second childhood, would not shrink in dread from the latter prospect and choose to die?"[45]—a dramatic exaggeration, or an accurate description of his memory of boyhood?[46] Yet punishment was apparently preferable to the boredom and difficulty of studying: "Yet still we sinned by doing less than was demanded of us in writing or reading or studying literature."[47]

He referred to the Manichaeans (with whom he was affiliated for nine years as a young adult) as "deceived deceivers" (*deceptos deceptores*),[48] but he also recognized that self-deception is not merely intellectual and psychological. Behavior can also be self-deceiving. While he thought he was merely playing, he wrote, he was in fact undermining the preparation for adulthood promised by his education. He commented on the behavior of the "subverters," students who disrupted classrooms: "When they took pleasure in mocking and deceiving others, there were hidden within themselves deceiving spirits, laughing at them and leading them astray."[49]

Augustine did, very briefly, discuss his childhood virtues, recognizing his delight in truth and that "I hated to be deceived."[50] And it is striking that, despite his negative view of children, Augustine nevertheless characterized his own helplessness and trust in God as that of a child. "I am only a little child," he wrote, "but my Father lives forever."[51] He pictured himself as a nursing infant: "What am I at my best, except suckling the milk you give and feeding upon you, the food that is imperishable?"[52] However, neither Augustine nor Freud emphasized the child's wonder, her relentless curiosity and search for sense, or her spontaneous love for those around her.

In Augustine's society gender roles were firmly delineated so that, although he observed an infant's behavior closely (to help him understand himself as an infant), it is very unlikely that he participated in the daily care of his son. Similarly, in late-nineteenth and early twentieth-century Vienna, Freud's household employed servants to do the work of childcare. It was not until the second half of the twentieth century that European and North American societies have seen significant changes in the role of fathers. Until then, fathers were expected to fulfill the roles of provider and protector, while women bore and raised children. I suggest that Augustine's and Freud's bleak views of infants and children emerged from their lack of close acquaintance with them. Indeed, it is entirely possible that they noticed a child primarily when he was angry and loudly demanding, namely, in his least attractive state.

IV.

Is the self-deceiver the helpless victim of a mental breakdown leading to a loss of self-control? Or is she, a moral agent, responsible for creating the deception? If one views the self-deceiver as helpless, one is likely to be sympathetic to the suffering involved. But recall Fingarette's insistence that self-deception is "something we *do*," not something that we suffer passively. If this view is taken to be the case, one is likely to be judgmental. It is striking, however, that both Augustine and Freud saw the self-deceiver primarily as sufferer and understood that *the appropriate reaction to suffering is sympathy*. This observation challenges the common criticism that Augustine's view of sin is harsh.[53] After discussing the child's aggressive possessiveness (for "footballs, nuts, and pet sparrows"), as continuous with the adults' efforts to acquire and control "gold, magistrates, and slaves," Augustine insisted that the only appropriate and adequate response by the observer is compassion. He deplored the fact that "no one is sorry for the children; no one is sorry for the older people; no one is sorry for both of them."[54] Freud was also sympathetically aware of the suffering involved in human life: "Life as we find it is too hard for us; it brings us too many pains, disappointments, and impossible tasks. In order to bear it, we cannot dispense with palliative measures."[55]

Pain drove Augustine to conversion. He described himself as "sick and in torture,"[56] as simultaneously lethargic and frenzied,[57] as "drowned and sightless."[58] From the perspective of conversion Augustine can see "how unhappy I was then! . . . I was eaten up with anxieties . . . I was unhappy indeed, and you [God] really made me see my unhappiness."[59] He came to be grateful for his unhappiness; had he been a bit happier, he would not have been driven to seek change. Indeed, *recognition* that one is unhappy is crucial to finding a solution. As long as one is happy *enough*, or can, through self-deception, resist awareness of unhappiness, no cure is possible.[60] Augustine and his friends endeavored to conceal unhappiness from themselves with sex, coliseum spectacles, and professional success. And no one seeks the long, painful, and expensive process of psycho-analysis who has not been driven to it by symptoms too persistent and painful to ignore.

Is self-deception gendered? While one cannot generalize about all men and all women, gender socialization can be examined for common assumptions about women's and men's forms of self-deception. Both internalizing and resisting these roles create struggle that often entails self-deception. The early feminist work of Valerie Saiving described women's "temptations" as different from men's. While men are socialized to aggressive and self-aggrandizing behavior (and must be reminded to be "mindful of the needs of others"), she suggested, women's socialization has (until recently for a few, and still for many) prohibited "male" behavior, leading women to a lack of focus, initiative, and intentional, self-chosen direction.[61] These tendencies vary enormously according to individuals, of course, but the urge to shelter in socially prescribed attitudes and behavior is common to women and men, no matter how the details differ. Self-deception is associated with failure to take responsibility for one's actions, and socialization is a major, often implicit, rationalization for lack of responsibility. Augustine condemned the "hellish river of [human] custom" ("*flumen tartareum*") as misleading and corrupt,[62] and psychoanalysis sought to alleviate the pain of "civilization and its discontents."

Are self-deceivers responsible? The answer must be yes, and no. No, in that according to both Augustine and Freud, people are driven by pain and trauma to self-deception. Yes, in that according to both, something can be done to address and alleviate self-deception. In the following section I discuss the prescriptions they offer.

V.

How does change occur in an individual? How can a person *get closer to happiness*? Both Augustine and Freud diagnosed and prescribed according to the cure to which they were committed. Augustine advocated conversion; Freud replaced conversion with the "talking cure." Perhaps a simple analogy can illuminate the difference between Augustine's prescription and Freud's. Hindus have long argued about whether divine assistance is best described as the "cat-carrying method" or the "monkey-carrying method." The kitten collapses and its mother seizes it by the scruff of its neck; it dangles limply from the mother's mouth. The baby monkey, on the other hand, climbs onto the mother's back and holds on for dear life as she carries him. Augustine's prescription most closely resembles the cat-carrying method; he repeatedly, throughout his writings, pictures himself as utterly helpless to effect his own conversion, entirely dependent on God "turning his head" (*"fovisti caput"*).[63]

Augustine described self-deception as detectable only from the perspective of conversion. Conversion *is*, in fact, a radical adjustment of perspective:

> But you, Lord, were turning me around so that I could see myself; you took me from behind my own back, which was where I had put myself during the time when I did not want to be observed by myself, and you set me in front of my own face so that I could see how foul a sight I was—crooked, filthy, spotted, and ulcerous. I saw and I was horrified, and I had nowhere to go to escape from myself. . . . You were setting me in front of myself, so that I might see my sin and hate it. I did know it, but I pretended that I did not. I had been pushing the whole idea away from me and forgetting it.[64]   *P.7*

Augustine's conversion, as he describes it, was not his prerogative. He, for his part, had been actively avoiding the honest and profound assessment of himself that might have led to change.

Freud's prescription resembles the monkey-carrying method: the talking cure assumes the painstaking, committed work of analysis. Replacing Augustine's model in which one agent [God] does something to another agent [Augustine], Freud proposes that the talking cure is something two agents [analyst and analysand] do *together*. The hard *work* of analysis is recovering to consciousness and re-experiencing the patient's memory of trauma—or as the later Freud came to think, the patient's fantasy—and working it through in analytic sessions.

Like Freud, Fingarette proposes that alleviating self-deception involves developing consciousness. Consciousness does not occur automatically with being/having a body; it is, rather, a skill that is *learned.* Fingarette's proposed method for achieving consciousness is "spelling out one's engagement in the world."[65] However, he acknowledges that intentions, even rigorously scrutinized, may still offer no trustworthy understanding of a person's engagement in the world. Nor does awareness of one's own intentions provide a basis on which to understand others' motives and actions: "a generalization from one's own case may be both logically too feeble and explanatorily too narrow in its scope to account for the full range and robustness of . . . human nature."[66]

Moreover, one's intentions are only part of one's engagement in the world; the discernible and foreseeable *effects* of behavior, and the attempt to predict the effects of certain behaviors, are also highly important. Of course, the deliberate and delicate effort of discernment is at best fragile and flawed, yet it is a necessary exercise.

VI.

The two thinkers we have considered—one religious, one secular—gave the concept of self-deception a central place in their thought. Both understood self-deception as cause and effect of unhappiness. Both understood change as dependent on recognition and acknowledgment of unhappiness. But their prescriptions differ. For Augustine, conversion effectively altered the "weight" and operation of the psyche, from anxious grasping in the fear that something will be missed, to love. At the end of his *Confessions* he made the (astonishing, if true) statement "My weight is my love; by it I am carried wherever I am carried."[67] Freud's goal, though modestly stated, was no less ambitious: namely, to remove obstructions to a person's capacity to love and work.

In conclusion, I want to examine more closely a foundational assumption made by Augustine and Freud, as well as by the more contemporary theorist of self-deception, Fingarette.[68] Each assumes that self-deception is necessarily, and by definition, destructive. Indeed, if anything positive were found to be associated with it, this positive something would need to be renamed. Yet, although the concept of self-deception has been useful to religious leaders, philosophers, and psychologists for centuries, the concept is imprecise, unwieldy and potentially dangerous.[69] For example, the boundary between self-deception and optimism is faint and movable; there are occasions and areas in which self-deception and optimism are impossible to distinguish.

Moreover, the notoriously perspectival concept of "reality," on which the diagnosis of self-deception rests, renders diagnosis problematic. Doesn't the concept of self-deception assume that we know what is real, what is really going on, and that we choose to disavow it? But one of the most poignant

features of human being, as Augustine pointed out, is our limitation of perspective, due to our lack of knowledge and lack of delight. Do we ever know
ourselves and others—really? Can we ever identify with precision "masks,
disguises, rationalizations, and superficialities?"[70]

Depressed people sometimes insist that they possess the only accurate
perspective on reality, namely, their almost constant awareness of the mean-
inglessness of life and the inevitability of pain and death. This awareness,
they claim, is the opposite of the self-deception that optimists routinely practice. But is suffering and death, because of its inevitability, the irreducible
"really real"? I suggest that depression can be seen as itself a form of self-
deception in that it refuses to notice the given day, full of possibility for life,
beauty, and pleasure.

Then are happiness, beauty, and pleasure the "real"? This, despite his
"press," was Augustine's proposal. His goal, and the goal of all humans, he
said, is the happy life—a life that that can be achieved only in loving God.
Augustine had several definitions of God. He, like Plotinus, called God the
"great beauty" that forms and informs every visible beauty.[71] And in *On
Christian Doctrine* he wrote that "anyone who thinks of God as anything
other than 'life itself' has an absurd notion of God.[72] When commenting on 1
John 4:16 he said that "God is love," and he added, that this is all you need to
know about God.[73]

Perhaps the only useful way to understand the concept of self-deception is
to acknowledge its imprecision and to develop criteria that limit its uses.
Self-deception, *defined* as a spiritual disorder that inevitably damages and
undermines life, tends to be an accusation of self or others rather than a
morally neutral diagnosis. But if, as Augustine thought and taught, conversion is not at the prerogative of the self-deceiver, but is entirely in God's
control (the cat-carrying method), one can only

> confess one's finitude, and, if the conflict is predominantly moral, one's
> sin; . . . to lay oneself open, vulnerable, as a radically divided nature, and to
> hope for the grace of some healing movement which is not at the moment
> entirely within one's own personal powers to effect or even to foresee.[74]

If the flexibility of the concept is acknowledged, however, it can immediately be seen that a certain level of what could be called self-deception is
extraordinarily fruitful, even necessary. Ignoring the reality and inevitability
of pain and death may encourage the *discipline* of living in the present,
enjoying the present moment in gratitude for the gift of life.

On the other hand, a positive and fruitful awareness of one's own death is
possible. The recognition that I will one day die *can* be used, not to trivialize
a present pleasure, but to enhance and augment it. In ancient Rome, a victori-
ous general, returning from a conquest, paraded the streets of Rome to tumul-

tuous acclaim, accompanied on his left by a slave who continuously murmured in his ear, "*memoria mortis Caesar*." This practice has usually been interpreted as preventing the Caesar's *hubris* with the reminder that he is mortal. I think, however, that this interpretation is far from evident. I suggest that it was intended to augment the general's pleasure in the moment of victory. To consciously and purposefully *place* one's vivid immediate pleasure *in the face of* one's own death does not etiolate but strengthens pleasure.

In short, room needs to be made in our use of the concept of self-deception for its positive interpretation. The question is, then, what criteria can be developed for identifying when self-deception is productive and when it is not? At this point Freud's criterion is useful: blockages to one's ability to love and work indicate that debilitating self-deception is operative.[75] But once we acknowledge that such blockages exist, shall we accept Augustine's or Freud's solution?

Let us examine Augustine's proposal more carefully. His description of his conversion dramatizes what his *Confessions* narrates as a long and ardent search for intellectual and emotional resolution. The few moments in the garden at Milan that he and most of his interpreters pinpoint as his conversion were, in fact, only a foreshortened version of a long process that led to, and continued beyond, those moments. The high drama of tears, voices, and flailing limbs described in book 8 have effectively masked for readers his years-long passionate search.[76]

Augustine's conversion—the short version—became a model of conversion throughout the subsequent history of Christianity. According to this model, conversion is granted by God, with the convert playing no role (the cat-carrying method); conversion changes everything instantly, resolving all hesitancy and overcoming all barriers; and conversion is permanent.[77] But this is not what Augustine painstakingly describes in the *Confessions*. His *whole* discussion contradicts his—and his readers'—focus on his "conversion." The *Confessions* is all about the gradual and cumulative shift in his intellectual, emotional, and erotic attractions. And the work went on, as he narrates in detail, long after the climactic moments in the garden at Milan.

Freud's proposal, namely, that slow, patient work must be done over a rather long time period, insists that the analysand must participate in the process of change. She must be both committed to, and vigorously engaged in, her healing (the monkey-carrying method). The work will be long and difficult, but it will not be done alone. A highly trained analyst, one who has herself been analyzed, will accompany and facilitate the process.

In fact, Freud's prescription suggests a different reading of Augustine's conversion. It redirects attention away from the few vivid moments of conversion to his long *process* of conversion, described at length and in detail—now that we notice it—throughout his *Confessions*. Indeed, Freud corrects the conversion model assumed throughout Western Christianity. The long process, passionately pursued, *is*, for most people, the way grace operates in their lives.[78] Even if a dramatic moment of conversion does occur, the patient, daily work of *becoming* a Christian, as demonstrated by Augustine's memoirs, is the way grace works.

NOTES

Epigram is from Edward Bulwer-Lytton, quoted by Herbert Fingarette, *Self-Deception* (Berkeley: University of California Press, 1969, 2000) 2.

1. Edward Bulwer-Lytton, quoted by Herbert Fingarette, *Self-Deception* (Berkeley: University of California Press, 1969, 2000) 1.

2. Ibid., 129.

3. Ibid., 169.

4. Ibid., 162.

5. Ibid., 66.

6. Ibid., 138.

7. Michel Foucault's term for authors whose new ways of seeing and describing phenomena attract conversations that could not previously have been conducted.

8. Arnold Davidson, *The Emergence of Sexuality: Historical Epistemology and the Formation of Concepts* (Cambridge, MA: Harvard, 2001) 41.

9. Ibid., 139.

10. Augustine, *Confessions* 3.2; see also 9.1; trans. Rex Warner (New York: Mentor-Omega, 1963).

11. Augustine, *Confessions* 6. 6.

12. Ibid., 10. 20–21.

13. Ibid., 10. 22.

14. Matt. 22:37 and 39, as quoted in Augustine, *The Spirit and the Letter* 64.36, in *Augustine: Later Works*, trans. John Burnaby (Philadelphia: The Westminster Press, 1965).

15. Augustine, *The Spirit and the Letter*, 63.35–64.36.

16. *Confessions* 8.7.

17. I will make clear as this essay progresses why psychoanalysis can be thought of as a "religion" with its own doctrines and practices.

18. William Parsons, *The Enigma of the Oceanic Feeling* (New York: Oxford University Press, 1999) 26.

19. Ibid., 3; citing Ernest Jones, *The Life and Work of Sigmund Freud* (New York: Basic Books, 1953) 3:349.

20. Ibid., 43. Emphasis added.

21. Letter to Sigmund Freud, December 5, 1927, reproduced in Parsons, *Oceanic Feeling*, 174, emphasis in the original.

22. Freud, *Civlization and Its Discontents* (1930); *Standard Edition of the Complete Works of Sigmund Freud*, ed. J. Strachey, Vol. 21 (London: Hogarth Press, 1968) 74.

23. Sarah Winter, *Freud and the Institution of Psychoanalytic Knowledge* (Stanford, CA: Stanford University Press, 1999) 8.

24. Ibid., 173.

25. See also Freud's *New Introductory Lectures on Psychoanalysis* (1933); *S.E.* 22, 167–168:

> the pronouncements of religion promising men protection and happiness if they would only fulfill certain ethical requirements had also shown themselves unworthy of belief. It seems not to be the case that there is a Power in the universe, which watches over the well-being of individuals with parental care and brings all their affairs to a happy ending.

. . .psycho-analysis, [showed] how religion originated from the helplessness of children and [traced] its contents to the survival into maturity of the wishes and needs of childhood.

. . .our view is that the question of the truth of religious beliefs may be left altogether on one side.

26. Freud, *Civilization and Its Discontents* (1930); *S. E. 21*, 66–67 and 68.

27. Ibid.

28. Susan Neiman, *Evil in Modern Thought* (Princeton, NJ: Princeton University Press, 2002) 319.

29. Freud, *Civilization; S.E.* 21, 75–76.

30. Parsons, *Oceanic Feeling*, 84.

31. Freud, *Civilization; S.E.* 21, 83.

32. Ibid., 75.

33. Ibid., 84–85.

34. Freud, *Civilization; S.E.* 21, 85, emphasis in original.

35. Patrick McGrath, *Trauma* (New York: Alfred Knopf, 2008) 46.

36. *New Introductory Lectures on Psychoanalysis; S.E.* 22. Similarly, Iris Murdoch, "Against Dryness," in *Existentialists and Mystics: Writings on Philosophy and Literature*, ed. Peter Conradi (New York: Penguin Books, 1997) 293: "We are not isolated free choosers, monarchs of all we survey, but benighted creatures sunk in a reality whose nature we are constantly and overwhelmingly tempted to deform by fantasy."

37. Fingarette, *Self-Deception,* 41.

38. Ibid., 162.

39. In *On Narcissism* (1914), Freud said that repression "is the cornerstone on which the whole theory of psychoanalysis rests." However, Alan Bass has shown that in his later years, Freud "began to rethink the centrality of repression in favor of a theory based on disavowal and splitting"; *Difference and Disavowal: The Trauma of Eros* (Stanford, CA: Stanford University Press, 2000) 7.

40. Similarly Lacan disparaged infants and their abilities; see Maxine Sheets-Johnstone, *The Roots of Power: Animate Form and Gendered Bodies* (Chicago: Open Court, 1994) 161–162.

41. Neiman, *Evil in Modern Thought*, 320.

42. Augustine, *Confessions*, 1.7.

43. Ibid., 1.6–7.

44. Ibid., 1.19.

45. Augustine, *City of God* 21.14; trans. Henry Bettenson (New York: Penguin Books, 1972).

46. See also *Confessions* 1.9, in which Augustine compares his boyhood dread of beatings with people's dread of "racks and hooks and different forms of torture."

47. Ibid. Later Augustine mused, "How is it that what we learn with toil we forget with ease?" *City of God* 22.22.

48. Augustine, *Confessions* 7.2.

49. Ibid., 3.3.

50. Ibid., 1.20.

51. Ibid., 10.4.

52. Ibid., 4.1. In most translations, the passage is rendered: ". . .except an infant suckling the milk you give. . ." The Latin, however, makes no mention of an infant, picturing Augustine, presumably an adult, "*sugens lac tuum*" (sucking on your milk).

53. Ibid., 1. 12; "I, so small a boy and so great a sinner."

54. Ibid., 1.9.

55. Freud, *Civilization; S.E.* 21, 75.

56. Augustine, *Confessions* 8.11.

57. Ibid., 8.5.

58. Ibid., 6.16.

59. Ibid., 6.6.

60. In a society such as ours in which unhappiness can be masked by consumerism, entertainment, and addictions, incentives for recognizing and acknowledging unhappiness are minimal.

61. "The Human Situation: A Feminine View," in *Womanspirit Rising: A Feminist Reader in Religion*, ed. Carol P. Christ and Judith Plaskow (San Francisco: Harper & Row, 1979) 37.

62. Augustine, *Confessions* 1.16.

63. Robert J. O'Connell, *Augustine's Early Theory of Man, 386–391* (Cambridge MA: Harvard University Press, 1968) 66.

64. Augustine, *Confessions* 8.7.

65. Fingarette, *Self-Deception*, 40.

66. Ibid., 165–166.

67. Augustine, *Confessions* 13.9.

68. Fingarette, *Self-Deception*; Fingarette acknowledges that "I am frankly delineating large areas whose boundaries are ill-defined" (39), although his purpose, stated early in the book, is "to present the texture of our experience, not just coherently, but with the patterns more visible and their significance more clearly displayed than before" (7).

69. The seventeenth-century English author, Thomas Traherne, said that the problem with misunderstanding a concept is that "what we misapprehend, we cannot *use*"; see *Centuries of Meditation* (London: Dobell, 1948).

70. Fingarette, *Self-Deception*, 49.

71. Augustine, *Confessions* 10.27.

72. *On Christian Doctrine* 1.8; trans. D. W. Robertson, Jr. (New York: Bobbs-Merrill, 1958).

73. Augustine, *Homilies on 1 John*, 9th homily, 10; in *Augustine: Later Works*, trans. John Burnaby (Philadelphia: The Westminster Press, 1955) 336.

74. Fingarette, *Self-Deception*, 137.

75. Similarly, fourth-century desert ascetics' criteria for knowing when one's psychic life needed work was when it interfered with prayer.

76. Like Augustine, Martin Luther described his conversion as a single moment of startling insight. In fact, his realization that "the just shall live by faith," occurred after years of monastic practice, spiritual direction, and teaching. The mantra given him years earlier by his spiritual director, Johann von Staupitz, vicar general of the Augustinian friars, was "I am yours; save me" (Psalm 119. 94). This verse carries virtually the same meaning as his later insight, namely, the centrality of faith and trust to conversion.

77. This point has been contested, however, most directly at the 1614 Council of Dort in which Arminians and Calvinists argued over whether salvation, once given, could be lost.

78. Powerful models are misleading, omitting or ignoring many people's experience. There are occasional dramatic conversions, but this is not the experience of most Christians, and some who have not had that kind of conversion, feel disenfranchised because of the model.

Chapter Eight

Augustine and Dopamine

Daniel B. Morehead

INTRODUCTION: AUGUSTINE AND COGNITIVE SCIENCE

Near the end of his stimulating and thoroughly post-modern biography of Augustine, James O'Donnell offers a few somber reflections on Augustine and contemporary thought. Augustine's influence on psychology, it seems, hangs by a fraying thread. Augustine, after all, centered his psychology around beliefs about the "soul." Therefore, "whatever becomes of 'soul' will determine what becomes of Augustine" (O'Donnell, 326). And since "soul," quite evidently, has no place in contemporary cognitive thought, things are not looking very good for Augustine. O'Donnell is too gentlemanly to say it explicitly, but he notes that contemporary cognitive science brings into question even the substantial existence of a unitary "person" or "mind" which might be an equivalent to soul. And so, "If his view of the human person and his narrative account of the inner life is supplanted by better science, then all that he has been to centuries of devout and not so devout heirs could crumble very quickly into irrelevance" (O'Donnell, 327). O'Donnell's is the self-consciously "unauthorized" biography of Augustine and can appear by turns playful, provocative and cynical. It is difficult to tell how seriously he himself takes much of it. But his thoughts on Augustine and psychology are, though brief, very much to the point. If contemporary psychology finds itself increasingly wedded to brain science, and if brain science calls into question the very fundamentals of Augustine's intensely psychological style of thought, then of what use is Augustine to psychology?

I suspect that most admirers of Augustine's *Confessions* (not to mention his other writings) would feel intuitively that there is something incomplete in O'Donnell's speculations, and in this chapter I will attempt to provide some explicit content to that intuition. I will argue, without reference to "soul," that Augustine's psychological thought is quite congenial to a neuro-biological perspective. I will do so by comparing one aspect of Augustine's thought, on desire (*libido, concupiscentia, cupiditas*), with one aspect of the neurobiology of human behavior, the dopamine system. I hope to show that a detailed, though limited, treatment of this intersection will do more than correlate and confirm Augustine's self-observations and self-analysis. It will also demonstrate that Augustine's thought can help us utilize neurobiological knowledge to advance toward a more generally valid psychology of religion.

THE DOPAMINE SYSTEM: A SUMMARY

Readers more familiar with religious thought than neuroscience should bear in mind that neurobiology, like theology, is filled with specialized, obscure, and often redundant multi-syllabic terms. I will reference these, but the discussion will not rely on the reader's prior knowledge of these terms.

Dopamine is an important neurotransmitter which appears to have a specific purpose or role in mammalian brain systems: overall, the dopamine system appears to activate the organism toward obtaining positive goals. It can readily be contrasted with the norepinephrine system, famously critical to the "fight or flight" response. The norepinephrine system activates the organism to deal with potential negative or threatening events, while dopamine activates the organism to deal with possible positive or rewarding events. Simplistically put, dopamine is the carrot of the human nervous system, norepinephrine the stick.

A few details will help fill out this general description of dopamine's role. First, throughout the brain, dopamine stimulates wakefulness and alertness. Stimulants such as amphetamines used to promote wakefulness act primarily to stimulate dopamine activity. Second, in the midbrain, dopamine has a well-known role in biasing the organism toward physical movement. Dopaminergic neurons from the substantia nigra suffer damage in Parkinson's disease, leading to progressive difficulty initiating movements. This renders patients with Parkinson's nearly paralyzed as the disease progresses. The condition is partially corrected by l-dopa, which is converted to dopamine in the brain, helping patients to initiate movements more easily. Third, dopamine has a role in emotion as well: dopamine in the nucleus accumbens (located centrally near to base of the brain's two hemispheres) is central to reward and desire. Dopamine released here acts to create emotional desire and motivation to pursue positive goals. Finally, dopamine has a cognitive function: in the frontal lobes (associated with conscious awareness and logical thought), dopamine is important for focus and sustained attention. Stimulants such as Ritalin (methylphenidate) improve concentration for those with ADHD (attention-deficit hyperactivity disorder) by increasing dopamine activity in the frontal lobes (Stahl, 233–234, 272–279, 490–496, 816–821, 871–873, 945–946).

Dopamaine, then, has cognitive, emotional, and physical effects. But all of these combine to arouse the organism to focus upon and move in the direction of positive goals: dopamine creates wakeful alertness, physical readiness for action, emotional desire and motivation, and cognitive focus for this purpose. These positive goals include food, water and sex. They also include almost all other positive motivations common to human beings: social success and dominance (Morgan et al., 169ff.), acquiring money or other possessions (Knutson et al., 1ff.), gambling (Grosset et al., 2206), hunting and gathering, and various amusements. For instance, even sports cars have been shown to increase dopamine release for many men (Erk et al., 2499). So have videogames (Koepp et al., 266), a finding which strongly correlates with their nearly addictive qualities. Being in love is associated with strong dopamine activity (Aron et al., 327). Finally, all drugs of abuse and addiction trigger dopamine release, whether directly or indirectly (Nestler and Self, 888–889).

There is broad agreement among neuroscientists about the nature of the dopamine system. It has been variously associated with foraging, exploration, curiosity, interest, sensation seeking, thrill-seeking, craving and expectancy. It has been called the "behavioral activation system," the "incentive or appetitive motivational system," and characterized as "wanting" rather than "liking," desire rather than pleasure itself (Panksepp, 145). While dopamine is associated with a pleasurable feeling, it is associated more with tantalizing desire than with feelings of satisfaction or pure physical pleasure (Kelly and Berridge, 2206ff.). Dopamine, it seems, exists to motivate and activate organisms, not to give them a feeling of satiety, satisfaction or relaxation (Nesse and Berridge, 65).

DOPAMINE AND AUGUSTINE'S DESIRES

It is not difficult to compare dopaminergic activity with Augustine's ideas about lust (*libido*) and desire (*concupiscentia, cupiditas*). (I will use these interchangeably, as Augustine often appears to do.) In *City of God*, he defines lust as a "certain appetite" which precedes pleasure and "is felt in the flesh like *a craving, as hunger and thirst and that generative appetite* which is most commonly identified with the name 'lust,' [*libido*] though this is the generic word for all desires [*cupiditatis*]" (*City of God* 576; 14.16, italics mine). Augustine, ever the acute self-observer, is readily able to separate desire or lust from pleasure itself, just as desire and pleasure can be separated neurobiologically. He goes on to note the manifold objects of lust, including sexual desire, desire to dominate others, greed, hunger and thirst. Similar to the motivations and desires of the dopamine system, desire or lust is an indelible characteristic of human life and human nature. It may be redirected or resisted "by coercion and struggle" (*City of God* 581; 14.19) but continues to exist in the body and mind of even the most just and devout persons (*City of God* 580–581; 14.19; *On Continence* 718; sec. 6). Finally and most telling-ly, Augustine observes (contrary to some other ancient authorities, such as Plato) that desire is never a servant of the mind, but ever defies the will, sometimes even when humans will themselves to be lustful (*City of God* 577; 14.16). Desire has a mind of its own, leading us to pleasures which we do not wish to choose, and which often prove destructive. And this Augustinian observation too has its neurobiology. To this, the neurobiology of desire and will, we shall now turn.

Dopamine, the Will, and Addiction

I will begin the discussion with a neurobiological treatment of addiction as an extreme but paradigmatic example of desire's ability to defy the will. This will lead to a more general discussion of desire in the context of choice, will and habit, before we turn to Augustine's subtle treatment of these subjects.

It is indeed possible to distinguish between desire and will, and neurobiol-ogists have done so (needless to say without reference to Augustine). They have identified two overlapping systems of human motivation: motivation from "above," and motivation from "below." Motivation from below corre-sponds to the dopamine system and the many widespread brain systems associated with it. At root, the basic desires and motivations of this system are "hard wired" to link motivation to certain rewards such as food, sex, novelty and social status. Its responses are not under direct willful control, but are automatic, tend to be impulsive and (when strong) may feel obligato-ry. Whether consequential or inconsequential, urges such as eating the extra piece of chocolate, looking at online pornography, sharing juicy gossip, or spending too much on the latest big-screen television often feel "too good to resist." And in addiction, by definition, the impulses of the dopaminergic reward system become impossible to resist, overwhelming other brain sys-tems which should counterbalance such impulsive, pleasure-driven motiva-tion.

Psychiatrist Stephen Stahl has dubbed this system the "reactive reward system" and contrasted it to the "reflective reward system," or motivation from above (Stahl, 946ff.). He describes the reflective reward system as both complementary and competitive to the dopamine-driven reward system. This system consists primarily of the frontal lobes, in coordination with a variety of other nuclei and networks distributed throughout the central nervous sys-tem. In describing this system, I will again oversimplify neurobiological research and knowledge, in hopes of presenting a readily useful treatment to those wholly unfamiliar with neuroscience. But a few illustrative details appear to be in order.

First, the frontal lobes appear to serve a general function of conscious awareness of both thoughts and feelings, along with the ability to weigh, analyze and process those thoughts and feelings. Their most important function, after weighing options for planning and behavior, is to initiate that behavior through activation of lower level systems. In short, the frontal lobes are necessary for conscious decision making and execution. Secondly, there appears to be a rough anatomical division in the frontal lobes between intellectual and emotional function. The upper parts of the frontal lobes (especially the dorsolateral prefrontal cortices) seem to serve such intellectual functions as conscious, logical thinking, intellectual self-awareness and intellectual decision-making. They are necessary for planning efforts to seek and reach long-term goals, especially those not associated with immediate pleasure or direct desire. (Graduate school provides a ready example of the pursuit of a long-term goal which often involves great sacrifice of other pleasures and desires, providing relatively little short-term pleasure along the way.)

In contrast, the lower frontal lobes appear more relevant to emotional life. While emotions (including desire) do not originate in the frontal lobes, the lower sides and undersides of the frontal lobes (especially the orbitofrontal and ventromedial prefrontal cortices) appear to be vital for conscious awareness of emotions and the ability to modulate or control those emotions. Patients with damage to this area of the brain classically show a lack of awareness of their own and other's feelings. They also show a strong tendency to alternate between apathy on the one hand and explosive, impulsive, unmodulated expression of emotions on the other. They are prone to impolite, antisocial expression of their emotions, including cursing, sexually inappropriate behavior, and violent outbursts. Anger and desire (especially sexual desire) are most difficult for these unfortunate patients to control.[1] Only with an efficiently functioning inferior frontal region are human beings able to maintain awareness of their own emotions, reflect on them, inhibit them, or express them appropriately. Therefore, both the upper frontal lobes (intellectual) and lower frontal lobes (emotional) are necessary for good decision-making and self-control. Both are critical components of the reflective reward system.[2]

As Stahl relates, the reflective and reactive reward systems sometimes act in concert, but more often (it seems) in conflict. He describes this as the conflict between the "temptation" of the reactive dopamine system and the "will power" of the reflective frontal lobe system (Stahl, 954). And he, along with other neurobiologists, has characterized addiction as the reactive reward system's pathological ability to completely overwhelm other motivational systems, causing addicts to act in a way which often directly contradicts their conscious values and preferences. For instance, drug addicts may often lie to and steal from their closest family and friends in an effort to obtain drugs, in spite of deep shame and guilt about these actions, and the fervent wish not to do them.

Researcher Nora Volkow (also director of the National Institute on Drug Abuse) has gone further, describing this aspect of addiction as an erosion of "free will" (Moran, 16). Addiction, as she has described it, involves both a strengthening of the reactive dopaminergic system and a weakening of the reflective system, centered around the frontal lobes. The dopamine system becomes sensitized to the drug of addiction and desensitized to other rewards. In other words, dopamine release is increased in anticipation of the drug but decreased in regard to other rewards and tasks (Kalivas and Volkow, 1407). Clinically, this correlates with increased desire and craving for the drug and decreased interest and motivation for other rewards such as food and sex. On the other side, there is a progressive weakening and "destruction" of the frontal lobe systems which comprise the reflective reward system. The function of the frontal lobes (and related brain systems) becomes increasingly weakened and ineffective as addiction progresses, associated with a progressive loss of conscious choice and free will. The dopamine-driven system of desire simply overwhelms the weakened frontal lobes' ability to exert conscious, willful control over impulses toward drug use. Volkow asserts that, early in addiction, addicts may be able to exert some control and choice over their drug use. However, as the addiction progresses, they lose the ability to reflect upon and control their choices, becoming narrowly obsessed with obtaining and using the drug.

AUGUSTINE AND THE TWO WILLS

It does not require much imagination to see close parallels in this neurobiological description of addiction and Augustine's description of his own development in the *Confessions*. He readily describes the selfish, rebellious and pleasure-seeking acts of his childhood, including the pear-tree, his love of sensuality and "being in love," and his love of praise and fame. These he acknowledges to be ignorant but entirely willful and intentional choices. As the developmental narrative progresses, Augustine untangles himself intellectually from ignorance, but finds he is utterly unable to free himself emotionally and behaviorally. He finds that he has become a prisoner of his own willful and lustful habits, unable to pull himself away from them. Persuaded of the truth of Christianity and the virtuous, philosophical life, he cannot break free from the habits of "treasures and worldly kingdoms and . . . bodily pleasures" (*Conf.* 8.7.17). The consequences of his previous choices have now robbed him of the power to choose effectively. Two wills, he finds, struggle within him. He wills to begin his new life, but he cannot will it completely. He finds another will within him toward the pleasures of the old. This "sickness of mind" (*Conf.* 8.9.21) is one which he cannot heal, whether by rational argument, psychological self-flagellation or the support of his friends. Only a divine intervention saves him.

Even if it is not difficult to see parallels, my brief, rough sketch of this aspect of *Confessions* may seem all too convenient to the purposes of this paper. In lieu of a more detailed argument, I will cite the treatment of one of Augustine's more subtle interpreters, Peter Brown. Brown calls Augustine's *Confessions* the story of Augustine's heart, his feelings, his *affectus*. Feelings, for Augustine, were "what really counted for personal growth" (Brown, 170). But feelings, in the *Confessions*, are woven into a wider study of will and motivation. In *Confessions*, Augustine squarely faces "the central problems of the nature of human motivation" (Brown, 170). Here and elsewhere, Augustine sees will and conscious action as a "mysterious alliance of intellect and feeling" (Brown, 170), an alliance which goes terribly wrong by Book VIII of *Confessions*. There, the "problem of will leaps into focus" (Brown, 172) as Augustine realizes that he has crippled his own capacity to choose freely what he consciously wants. His previous choices have formed the "chain of habit" (Brown, 172), by which his past choices and acts have become a "second nature" (Brown, 172) which cripple and imprison him. And "the strength of this chain obsesses Augustine throughout the *Confessions*" (Brown, 172).

In both accounts, the Augustinian and the neurobiological, early choices based upon desire gradually become compulsions which overcome all ability for reason to exert self-control. In both accounts, the victims of desire become its slaves, unable to free themselves. In both, early pleasures and desires ultimately become self-destructive compulsions. And in both, pleasure and desire become paths to misery.

THE CHAIN OF HABIT

In a critical passage of Book VIII of the *Confessions*, Augustine summarizes the process of enslavement in a few vivid strokes: "In truth, lust [*libido*] is made out of a perverse will, and when lust is served, it becomes habit [*consuetudo*], and when habit is not resisted, it becomes necessity. By such links, joined one to another, as it were—for this reason, I have called it a chain—a harsh bondage held me fast" (*Conf.* 8.5.10). Augustine, like any addict, had made foolish choices in a misdirected effort to please himself (perverse will). Such choices fed ever-growing cravings for pleasure (lust). These choices initiated a chain that bound desire to compulsion, or enslavement of the will, and compulsion to deep unhappiness and misery. This process, so elegantly described by Augustine, has a neurobiology as well.

As previously described, addicts pursuing the pleasures of their drugs show an increased sensitivity and dopamine response to cues associated with drug use and a decreasing dopamine response to other rewards (such as food and sex). On the other hand, this should not be taken to mean that overall dopamine release is greater and pleasure is higher as addiction develops. On the contrary, counteradaptive changes occur in the brain with ongoing, chronic substance use. This means that the brain (like most other biological systems) tends to counterbalance ongoing changes in its internal and external milieu. Overall, the "reward threshold" becomes increasingly elevated with ongoing use—it becomes more and more difficult to trigger a high, or rewarding experience (Koob and Kreek, 1149ff.). With substance use, this nearly universal effect is known as tolerance: decreasing response to the same dose of a drug over time. In the case of cocaine, amphetamines, and other drugs which directly cause dopamine release, dopamine release and effects are decreased by a variety of counter-adjustments (Koob and Le Moal, "Drug Abuse," 52ff.). Addicts often describe themselves as "chasing that first high," as the thrill and pleasure of the substance ebbs away. In the case of natural rewards, there is an initial (though smaller) release of dopamine when cues appear that the reward is "on its way." On the other hand, once the reward becomes predictable and routine, dopamine release is nonexistent at the time the expected reward is actually obtained. Dopamine release is even lessened below baseline when the expectation of reward is disappointed (Schultz, 4). And this normal neurobiology is likely to correspond to the experience of addicted drug users over time: they do not feel much better as a result of taking the drug; they simply stop feeling worse. They find themselves on a treadmill of misery and relief, seeking and taking the drug to stop the suffering and deprivation, rather than any enjoyment or pleasure.

This transition occurs in part because pleasure steadily diminishes over time, leaving unsatisfiable desire in its wake. Desire becomes less delectable, and far more tormenting. But it also occurs because the substance use induces a vicious cycle of stress and negative feelings which inevitably follow the high. Drug use itself triggers release of stress chemicals such as CRF (corticotrophin releasing factor, the central substance coordinating the brain's stress response). CRF and other stress mediators continue to increase as addiction develops, remaining at abnormally high levels between bouts of drug use. Not only are these strongly associated with feelings of anxiety and dysphoria, but CRF itself has been shown to trigger cravings directly (Koob and Kreek, 1153–1154). Thus, a vicious cycle ensues, in which ongoing use alters the brain's baseline state: steadily decreasing pleasure with steadily increasing stress and negative feeling, which in turn triggers desperate cravings for drug use which further exacerbates the process. This process has been described as a transition for "impulsivity" (use driven by desire and pleasure) to "compulsivity" (use driven by stress and emotional pain) (Koob and Le Moal, "Addiction and the Brain," 32).

ADDICTION AND "NORMAL" SIN

For Augustine, too, this "chain of necessity" held him in a state of misery. He felt "foul," "deformed" and "defiled" (*Conf.* 8.7.16), "unhappy" (*Conf.* 8.5.12) and "filled with ever increasing anxiety" (*Conf.* 8.6.13).[3] But there is one obvious gap between Augustine's report of his own experience and the neurobiological one I have summarized above. Addiction may be compared to Augustine's experience of flesh, desire and sin, but how much does this neurobiological research apply to experiences which are *not* based on the abnormalities of drug use and substance addiction? Does any of this apply to more "normal" experiences of pleasure and desire, habit and necessity?

Oddly enough, there is much less research on the neurobiology of normal reward than on the abnormalities of addiction. Certainly, numbers of psychologists and psychiatrists have declared that addiction is possible with non-drug rewards such as sex, gambling and even the Internet (Pies, 31). While such assertions are controversial, neurobiologists have routinely agreed that addiction "hijacks" normal brain mechanisms of reward and motivation which are centered around dopamine. Much of the research on addiction appears to apply to such activities as eating and sex, which humans regularly find difficult to control (e.g., Volkow and Wise, 555). However, the more fascinating question of whether desire leads to habit, and habit to necessity and even character, remains quite open on a neurobiological level. In this way, brain science has not yet caught up to Augustine's account of himself. In order to remain within the confines of this paper, I will mention only a few observations from neuroscience and other areas of psychology which may apply to "normal" life and "normal" sin.

First, there is no question that pleasure and satisfaction are fleeting feelings and rarely enjoyed for long periods of time. There is some evidence (Schultz, 1998, cited above) that the dopamine system recalibrates itself to regular and expected rewards, correlating with the fact that few of life's rewards have ever been associated with sustained feelings of euphoria, pleasure or happiness. Predictable and routine motivated-behaviors appear to become less dependent on the dopamine reward system over time (Chambers, Taylor and Potenza, 1045; Kalivas and Volkow, 1407–1408). In positive psychology (the study of happiness), this phenomenon is known as the "hedonic treadmill" (Diener, Lucas and Scollon, 305ff.). On average, most persons rapidly adapt to changed circumstances, return to nearly the same baseline level of happiness and life satisfaction. An early and classic study in this field dramatically illustrates the principle (Brickman, Coates and Janoff-

Bulman, 917). Researchers compared two groups in their reports of life satis-faction and overall happiness: lottery winners and paraplegics permanently disabled in accidents. Although lottery winners reported initial large in-creases in life satisfaction, and disabled persons reported initial decreases, the subjects reported they were at or near their previous levels of happiness by the end of one year. Subsequent research has modified some of the origi-nal conclusions of such research—for instance, most people appear to adapt only partially to life changes such as severe disability and prolonged unem-ployment—but there is little question that people adapt rapidly and fully to most pleasurable events. As religious belief has foretold, such "goods" as new houses and cars, sex with a new and desirable partner, or an amazingly successful presentation at work quickly effervesce and disappear into the background of subjective well-being.

Why is this the case? Why are human beings not continually motivated by the same pleasures? Most psychologists agree that the dopamine system (and other neurobiological motivators) exist to move us forward in pursuit of goals, not to make us feel "fat and happy." Long-term feelings of satisfac-tion, happiness, euphoria and pleasure are more likely to be de-motivating, as the long-term experience of opiate and cocaine addicts shows (Nesse and Berridge, 65).

I suspect that the dopamine system works exactly as it is supposed to: early and relatively intense pleasurable feelings accompany rewarding expe-riences. These motivate us to obtain those rewards on a regular basis. If we are able to do so, "rewards" soon become routine expectations. They do not induce pleasure by being present, but they do induce pain and frustration when they are absent. Thus, they become motivated acts but not markedly pleasurable ones. They become automatic, assumed and habitual, even as Augustine described. We are likely to be grateful for new rewards and angri-ly demanding for old ones. Yesterdays "benefits" become tomorrow's "enti-tlements." "What have you done for me lately?"

Where has pleasure gone? I suggest that pleasure and euphoria go in search of bigger game. The quick adaptation to pleasurable experiences ef-fectively "ups the ante," demanding either more of the same or something even better for a repeated high level of pleasure. Almost everyone feels that life would be so much better with 10 percent more income, for instance, no matter what their level of income. The dopamine and opiate systems give us just enough of a "taste" of what we want to focus us on the "next big thing," or what Milan Kundera more poetically called "the golden apple of eternal desire" (Kundera, 117). Meanwhile, old rewards are unconsciously and ha-bitually obtained, escaping much conscious attention unless they are denied us.

Such a process of habit formation, shaped in part by pleasure and desire, is fundamental to human psychology. William James made habit the centerpiece of his psychology in his early classic synthesis, *Principles of Psychology*. Human beings were, from one point of view, "mere walking bundles of habits" (James, 127). Habit was the basis of character formation, rooted in the plastic nature of nervous tissue. "The hell to be endured hereafter, of which theology tells us, is no worse than the hell we make for ourselves in this world by habitually fashioning our characters in the wrong way" (James, 127). Subsequent experimental and behaviorist psychology altered James's terminology from "habit" to "learning" and "conditioning" but maintained his emphasis on the layering of learned, reinforced, repeated behaviors as the essence of psychological life. Neuroscience has as well, summarized famously in Hebbe's law: neurons that fire together, wire together (Spitzer, 40–45). That is, repeated experiences literally shape the physical development and networking of neurons, reflecting habit's "fashioning" of character. And dopamine itself is relevant to habit formation. The dopamine system functions to promote habitual reinforcement of behaviors which bring about experiences of reward. It also helps trigger learned sets of automatic thoughts and behaviors "stored" in the basal ganglia, deep brain nuclei responsible for remembering sets of well-learned behaviors. (For instance, you "never forget how to ride a bike" because these skills/memories are stored in the basal ganglia.) Through this mechanism, repeatedly rewarded skills or sets of behaviors transform themselves from willful, effortful actions driven by desire, to habits ingrained deeply in the brain and triggered automatically by circumstances (Graybiel, 733ff.).

Thus, conscious, effortful and willful acts, made in pursuit of happiness and pleasure, gradually become habits. Unconscious, recurrent habits, in turn, join the "bundles of habits" which constitute personality and character. And, as development proceeds into adulthood, personality and character become progressively more difficult to alter in any fundamental way. We become the products and prisoners of our own choices, just as Augustine recognized in himself. Ignorance of the consequences gives rein to whatever we instinctively desire, desire gives birth to habit, and habit hardens into the necessity of character. Like the early residents of the Soviet gulags, we ourselves construct our prisons. Hell is of our own making, as James put it.

SO WHAT?

Whether or not this account has been convincing in all its details, I hope I have shown that Augustine's understanding of desire and its developmental course in his life easily interweaves itself with neurobiological perspectives on human nature, especially addiction. Augustine hardly appears outmoded or irrelevant when viewed through this lens. Cognitive science has not fully undone his psychology, as O'Donnell feared.

But I want to suggest more than a mere correlational approach with such an effort. It would hardly be satisfying, or intellectually challenging, to merely assert that, "Augustine is backed up by modern brain science, so Augustine is still valid and relevant." Neuroscience may help reinforce the plausibility of some of Augustine's views, but Augustine's thought is truly relevant if it helps us advance our understanding of religious psychology. I will propose that it does so in two ways: First, Augustine asserts that his psychology of desire (and its development) is rooted in human nature. By correlating his account with neurobiology, we are in a position to develop and strengthen a religious psychology which is generally applicable precisely because it is neurobiologically grounded in a human nature discernible by brain science. Secondly, such a generally applicable religious psychology should advance our ability to understand religious experience across a variety of religious cultures and traditions. I suggest that Augustine's treatment of desire is one obvious point of intersection, not only with neuroscience but with world religions as well.

A BIOLOGICAL RELIGIOUS PSYCHOLOGY?

Augustine's perspective would be of little use if it were merely redundant with current neurobiological perspectives. On the contrary, it is useful because it contains a religious psychology which is self-consciously biological. Certainly, Augustine had no more inkling of the brain's role in psychological function than any other ancient writer. But the body, for Augustine, was no mere appendage to be one day shed by the soul, nor was it the soul's enemy. In contrast to many ancient philosophers and some of the church fathers, Augustine viewed the body as flawed but not evil. He equated it with neither flesh nor sin. He insisted that the body was to be loved and cherished, in expectation of its ultimate redemption and perfection. "It [the fleshly body] is not then itself that is our enemy: and when its faults are resisted, itself is loved . . ." (*On Continence* 728–729; sec. 19).

Furthermore, Augustine viewed desire as the product of both body and soul. Certainly, the body seemed central to such base pleasures as "fornications and drunkenness" (*On Continence* 738; sec. 28). But Augustine readily recognized that the mind's propensity toward competitiveness, pride and the like also constituted pernicious desires. Even physical pleasures and pains themselves, though felt in the body, were not simply bodily but states of the soul experienced in and from the body (*City of God* 14.15). There, in the "motion and troubled states of the soul," (*On Continence* 738; sec. 28) such sins of the flesh warred against the spirit and its desire for the delights "of things above" (*On Continence* 739; sec. 29; also 728–729; sec. 19). Thus, Augustine was no dualist in the strict sense: he did not think of the human person as complete or perfected without the body, and he did not equate the body with evil and imperfection, the soul with purity and transcendence.

Why bother to note this? Because a fully dualistic perspective vitiates the problematic nature of desire for religious life. The tendency, the longing toward self-destructive acts is no "foreign body," some disposable appendage or "other nature" which clings to one's "true self" (*Conf.* 8.10.22–24; *City of God* 14.2–5). Sin lurks in the mind, the soul as well, in ignorance and pride, in desire and hatred (*On Continence* 737–738; sec. 28; *City of God* 14.3, 5). For Augustine, desire and sin cannot be consigned to something other than ourselves. And this too is congenial with modern cognitive science, rooted as it is in a non-dualistic perspective. Here, mind and brain are viewed as two sides of the same coin, the same object seen from two perspectives (Kendler, 434). Desires experienced as physical are, by definition, as much a part of mind/brain as the "highest" intellectual interests.

In a (perhaps) unexpected way, Augustine's spirituality is rooted in his anthropology, and his anthropology is rooted in his belief that there is a human nature common to all. His much maligned belief in original sin was, at least in part, a recognition of a fundamental, innate and irresistible tendency of human nature: all human beings find themselves struggling unsuccessfully to master desires and impulses which evade or overcome control of the will. Lust becomes unruly and uncontrollable as a result of Adam and Eve's sin. The first human beings, by freely choosing to be disobedient, became disobedient to themselves in their own various members. Lust and other ungovernable human impulses subvert the will and corrupt the understanding, leading men and women into inevitable misery (*City of God* 14.24, 25). This fault of human nature was the result of divine punishment in Adam and Eve but has been passed to all succeeding generations in a way that is "natural" and "congenital" (*City of God* 13.3).

Neurobiology, like all other biological sciences, exists within an explicitly evolutionary framework, taking no note of ancient mythological treatments of human origins (such as Adam and Eve). But Augustine's view that human nature is universal and continues naturally through procreation is common to both evolutionary psychology and neurobiology. Theologically controversial, Augustine's observations surrounding "original sin" are woven through contemporary psychologies which are biologically grounded: these include the universal nature of desire and other non-rational motivations, their routine ability to escape or overcome conscious and rational control, and the manifold ways in which human nature is not in itself fully conducive to either high moral living or sustained happiness. Contemporary psychologies with such emphases include psychoanalytic psychology (Freud), evolutionary psychology (Buss) and neurobiologically grounded cognitive and affective science (Pinker, Panksepp).

Augustine equates this aspect of human nature with sin, the sort of sin that makes for chronic self-injury and unhappiness, an existential trail of bread crumbs which leads steadily away from God. And it is not difficult to summarize his treatment of this in recognizable terms which are congenial to biologically grounded psychology (as follows). Human beings, by nature, experience high levels of motivation toward specific rewards: sex; social status; certain types of food, drink, and drugs; novelty; acquisition of possessions; etc. These innately given positive motivations are deeply shaped by culture and the course of early development (as the *Confessions* show in sophisticated fashion). But at root they are biologically given and (along with fear) effective motivators which govern the behavior of humans across cultures.

While human beings tend to think of themselves as rational creatures who direct their behavior willfully according to conscious choices, their goals and behaviors are extensively determined by these non-rational motivation systems. They tend to use their intellects to rationalize their choices and attain their goals, rather than using their intellects to choose goals which are, in fact, rational. In the case of positive reward (mediated primarily through the dopamine system), human beings are "hard wired" to pursue goals which feel as if they will bring lasting happiness and satisfaction: the next meal, the next sexual partner, the next promotion, the next raise, the next drink, or the next book all promise to be the ultimate reward. But collective human experience and neuroscience have shown that there is no ultimate reward. Even the most intensively pleasurable experiences and the highest achievements bring feelings of joy and satisfaction which are fleetingly brief.

Rather than giving lasting happiness, the rewards which human beings preferentially seek create a painful, unsatisfied craving for the next and bigger reward. And the more quickly those rewards are attained, the more they take on an addictive quality. An overabundance of choice foods, alcohol and other drugs, sex and other rewards rapidly creates a state of restlessness and unhappiness (in addition to other negative consequences). Pleasurable, rewarding experiences inevitably rebound into stress and unhappiness, creating even more craving and dissatisfaction with ever-increasing internal demands for more and better rewards. Human beings who are lucky enough to attain their desires only occasionally exist in a state of mild but chronic longing and a sense that happiness may yet be theirs in the misty future of their dreams. Those who are unfortunate enough to gratify their desires repeatedly and predictably are likely to exist in a state of emptiness which borders on despair, as the ancient writer of Ecclesiastes so powerfully described. Addiction is merely nature's mocking caricature of the human condition governed by the reward system. While in addiction a single reward ultimately obliterates the pursuit of all others and destroys life, in unaddicted life a variegated web of small and large rewards pulls us from one hour to the next. Countless threads of desire for long- and short-term goals suspend humans between one set of forgotten past rewards and another future set which holds so much promise. Happiness and satisfaction are never attained but feel as if they are just out of reach. The last rewards are quickly forgotten in pursuit of the next. The "natural" human being, in this relatively stable state, is conscious of being neither happy nor unhappy. Only the low rumble of yearning for the next rewards of life, big and small, fills the mind, along with fears of their deprivations.

From Augustine's high perch, this state constitutes the fundamental human flaw. And consciousness of it constitutes the beginning of the spiritual life. As humans, we ignorantly pursue goals which, by their very nature, cannot satisfy. Such pursuit entangles us ever more deeply in webs of unhappiness and dissatisfaction. Consciously or unconsciously, we become the unsatisfied slaves of desire, trapped on a treadmill which is constantly accelerating. To become aware of this process, as Augustine did, opens the possibility of escape, the possibility of finding other goals and another way of life which may truly satisfy. And for him, this other way is the essence of true religion.

AUGUSTINE AND OTHER RELIGIONS

Augustine's answer to the problem of the human condition is unabashedly sectarian. Only Christ, scripture and the church catholic offer a legitimate way beyond. But his diagnosis of the human flaw is, as he well knew, broadly applicable. In the conclusion of this paper, I will discuss ways that his treatment may share points of contact with other religious traditions.

Augustine's own *Confessions* have enjoyed such sustained and nearly unparalleled popularity that it would not be especially adventurous to believe that many a reader has identified with his portrayal of himself and his own development. Augustine himself generalized much of his development and his experience in biblical and especially Pauline terminology—that is, there is no indication that he viewed his own struggles as unique. And neurobiologists, in their turn, assume that data obtained from scientific studies apply cross-culturally. Indeed, research on the dopamine system and the nature of reward and motivation applies across mammalian species, since much (though by no means all) of the research has been conducted with non-human mammals, including mice and monkeys.

My synthesis of development in regard to Augustine and the brain's reward system is, evidently enough, intended to apply cross-culturally. Whether it does is a matter which could ultimately be decided through empirical research, both psychological and neurobiological. David Buss' studies of human mate choice and sexual "strategies" provide an example of broadly applicable cross-cultural research conducted on a biologically informed basis (Buss, 97–186).

If such observations (or some related treatment of them) do apply, then it is possible that they represent one universal aspect of the human problems which religion addresses. And if they do represent a common aspect of human religious experience or reflection, then we should find this treated in a variety of religions from diverse cultures. It would, of course, be impossible to show this, even tentatively, in a brief and summary treatment. The questions and issues raised by any inter-religious dialogue (however modest) are immensely complex and certainly beyond the full expertise of any single person. I only mean to suggest here, through a few examples, that several religious treatments of desire and unhappiness may be amenable to a cross-cultural and biologically rooted examination and compared with Augustine's treatment of them.

Buddhism provides an obvious example of religious reflection upon the universal human condition. Buddhism is avowedly empirical and experiential in its approach, emphasizing experience and modes of living over speculative doctrine. And, interestingly enough, reflections on the role of desire play a fundamental part in some types of Buddhism. Here, I will simply note the well-known four noble truths of Buddhism: first, that all life is suffering; second, that the source of suffering is desire (or craving); third, that the cessation of suffering occurs through the cessation of desire; and fourth, that cessation of suffering can be obtained via the eight-fold path (Radhakrishnan and Moore, 274). Naturally, even questions of proper translation (of such terms as "desire" and "suffering") go beyond the scope of this paper. Yet a mere recitation of the four noble truths raises the question of whether an Augustinian, biologically grounded treatment of desire and its resulting misery overlaps with this perspective. Such a question might be continued in regard to the early collection, the *Dhammapada* (Radhakrishnan and Moore, 212–216, 338–340).

Hinduism, too, could be examined in this regard. I will cite another familiar and central source, the *Bhagavad-Gita* (hereafter *BG*). Although desire and craving are not as explicitly central to this treatment of religious life, they are closely connected to the notion of non-attachment, which is central to the work. In it, Prince Arjuna finds himself in an unresolvable dilemma— he and his allies face his own kinsmen, teachers and friends in battle. Krishna advises Arjuna to do his duty (indeed all of his duties, sacred and secular), but to do it with non-attachment. Non-attachment means a harmonious, non-possessive engagement in one's work and activities. One who is non-attached acts neither out of craving nor out of aversion. Such a one holds nothing back and forces nothing; the non-attached does not "rejoice or loathe" upon obtaining "good or evil" (Radhakrishnan and Moore, 111; *BG* ch. 2, v. 57).

What role has desire in non-attachment? Dwelling on sense objects (rather than on the Self in self-awareness) creates attachment to them: "from attachment springs desire, and from desire springs anger" (*BG* ch. 2, v. 62). And desire together with anger is the source of sin and misery (*BG* ch. 3, vv. 36–41). Freedom from desire (through mental awareness and control of the senses) is responsible for wisdom, peace, bliss and release from bondage (*BG* ch. 5, vv. 2–3; ch. 6, vv. 24–28; ch. 4, vv. 19–22; ch. 3, vv. 36–42; ch. 2, vv. 70–71). For desire itself creates the conditions of pain (*BG* ch. 5, v. 22). Those who are controlled by desires are demonic and deluded. "Bewildered by many thoughts, entangled in the meshes of delusion and addicted to the gratification of desires, they fall into a foul hell" (*BG* ch. 16, v. 16).

If desire plays a prominent and explicit role in some Hindu and Buddhist writings, its role is clearly more peripheral in the *Tao Te Ching*, the central text of Taoism. Since the Tao, by definition, defies explicit description (ch. 1), I will perhaps be forgiven for presenting only a vague treatment of the Tao and its specific relation to desire. The Tao (in some unutterable way) constitutes the deep interconnection, harmony and flow of all things. Human beings enjoy the possibility of recognizing and interweaving themselves with this harmony, or (more frequently) they may harm themselves and others by failing to see it and struggling against it. Desire, appropriately enough, comes into play here. For to see with desire is to see only "the manifestation," while to see without desire is to see the dark "mystery" of the Tao (ch. 1). Thus, human beings should temper or renounce desire and possessiveness of advancement, possessions, ideas and the like (chs. 19, 64). They should give up grasping, control, force, discontent and selfishness, and cultivate non-action, peacefulness and feminine yielding (chs. 44, 57). In this sense, "there is no greater sin than desire" (ch. 46), and "the sage seeks freedom from desire" (ch. 64). For desire and attachment only create the circumstances of pain and loss, competition and danger (chs. 44, 57).

From such fleeting and partial notes, I hope to raise the possibility that all of these religious narratives are alluding to a broad, common human experience, one which undergirds the great variety of cultural and religious expression. Naturally, this can only be argued if there is an underlying common human nature and if this aspect of human psychological functioning is linked to neurobiology in the way I have described. All of this, needless to say, remains unproven. But if it is accurate, then Augustine's personal narrative (of *Confessions*) and his related psychological theology of original sin and desire represent possible Western starting points for inter-religious dialogue and common ground in the psychology of religion.

CONCLUSION, OBJECTIONS, AND LIMITATIONS

I have argued in some detail that Augustine's developmental and religious psychology can be correlated and then synthesized with a contemporary neurobiological perspective. Furthermore, I have attempted to raise the question of whether Augustine's treatment of desire, habit, bondage and misery has correlates in other religions, correlates which reflect common human experience rooted in a common biology. Since such an argument is admittedly ambitious and suspect to both accurate criticism and misunderstanding, I will conclude with a discussion of several of its limitations.

First, this treatment may appear all too obvious, so obvious as to be of little use. Of course human beings are chronically dissatisfied creatures, chronically pursuing one gain after another, never satisfied with any particular gain. This is not only a commonplace observation of religion, literature and philosophy but part of everyday proverbial wisdom as well. How is it worthwhile or significant to single out Augustine and neurobiology? It is worthwhile because Augustine's treatment is insightful and articulate, not because it is unique. Any argument attempting to articulate some aspect of human nature can be expected, if successful, to address phenomena or ideas articulated in nearly all human cultures. But modern and post-modern scholarship have also revealed that it is all too easy to appropriate naively someone else's truth, distorting and doing violence to it in the process. Any attempt to discover cross-cultural commonalities of religious experience is therefore ambitious and only to be undertaken with great circumspection. Beginning with the more obvious seems prudent, under the circumstances. I regard discussions of the pre-enlightened, pre-religious, or "natural" state of human beings to be one of the more obvious starting points of discussion between students of various religions, one which may be less laden with diverse doctrines and obscure idiosyncrasies.

Secondly, the opposite may be argued. Many theologians and social scientists have rightly been suspicious of attempts to equate the content of different disciplines within the same culture, much less different cultures and religions. How can I so glibly assume that it is possible to span and meld such different types of discourse (neurobiological and Augustinian)? Is it possible, even likely, that these different discourses represent incommensurable points of view, even if they are all legitimate? I have attempted to interconnect the narratives of Augustine with those of neuroscientists. I have argued that this is justified because both contemporary neuroscientists and Augustine have articulated a belief in a common, biologically rooted human nature. And I have attempted to argue that both of these, in very different ways, are alluding to a common human experience. To do so is not to equate the two or reduce them to some third, supposedly superior narrative of my own.

Third (and in like manner), this discussion is likely to raise the specter of biological reductionism for some readers. Many social scientists and theologians have objected to crude biological treatments of religious and cultural experience, involving the assumptions that (1) psychological and religious experience is "nothing but" underlying biology, and (2) the biological realities underlying such experience determine it (as opposed to other determinates such as culture and individual choice). It is important to realize, however, that the majority of neuroscientists, psychiatrists and neurobiologically oriented philosophers have rejected both (1) biological reductionism and (2) biological determinism (also known as epiphenomenalism).

Generally speaking, neuroscientists (and other scientists) do not aim at reductionism but at linking together various "levels" of complexity and explanation. For example, physics can be utilized to explain but not predict chemistry, while chemistry can be utilized to explain but not predict biology, and so on. In regard to psychology and psychiatry, this is a difficult but necessary undertaking. Complex and interrelated levels of society, subjective experience, neural networks and underlying neural subsystems are all relevant to experience and behavior, at least as much as more basic levels of neurotransmitter and receptor function.

Psychology is in no position to explain or unify all of these in a grand theory, but neuroscientists, among other psychiatrists and psychologists, routinely attempt to link discrete levels of explanation or to attain what has been termed "integrative pluralism" (Kendler, 436). Pluralism, in this context, asserts that there are multiple legitimate scientific and non-scientific perspectives on any phenomenon, and integrative pluralism involves the attempt to incorporate and interlink divergent levels of analysis, without attempting to reduce one to another. Only such an approach can do justice to subjective experience, the importance of culture, and the complex but illuminating layers of neural interaction, all of which are ultimately necessary to provide adequate accounts of human behavior and experience. The goal of such efforts is consilience, the "'jumping together' of facts and fact-based theory across disciplines to create a common groundwork of explanation" (Wilson, 8). While the biologist Edward O. Wilson's famous vision is for a grand, ultimate synthesis of all knowledge, most neuroscientists are far more modest, seeking to link perspectives and levels of complexity in small islands of explanation, creating a "piecemeal integration" (Kendler, 433).

Thus, contemporary researchers and commentators on brain science are not, on the whole, reductionists. Neither are they epiphenomenalists. Epiphenominalism involves that belief that only lower level brain events determine mental contents and that mental life is mere "foam on the wave" of material brain events, having no causal significance of its own. This is to say that mind is a mere reflection of brain, and nothing more. Although this question remains more controversial than brute material reductionism, most psychiatrists, psychologists and neurobiologists believe that, "in ways we can observe but not yet fully understand" (Kendler, 434), subjective mental experience exerts causal effects upon the brain and the rest of the body.

Therefore, I am not attempting to assert that the dopamine system "determines" experiences of pleasure and desire. Rather, I am discussing the dopamine system and subjective reports of pleasure and desire as two perspectives which mutually illuminate the same phenomenon from very different perspectives. Neither "determines" the other because they are one, like two sides of the same coin. And there is no question of mere one-way determinism, as if only genes determine brain, and brain determines behavior (e.g., Gabbard, 648). Such a view involves a fundamental misunderstanding of the brain, which does not function as some isolated, insulated machine of outward-going causality. As Nobel laureate Eric Kandel has illustrated, the behavior of neurological systems exists in dynamic interaction with environmental and experiential factors (Kandel, 457ff.). Brains do create behavior, in their way, but behavior also shapes the brain, in many ways which can now be physically observed and measured. Brain science, and psychology in general, have moved beyond sterile arguments about "nature versus nurture." "All of 'nurture' is ultimately expressed as 'nature'," as Kandel put it (Kandel, 460). This complex interrelation and ultimate unity of one's nature and one's behavior (habits) constitute a fascinating aspect of human nature, one which I have here attempted to illustrate.

Finally, one might object that I am attempting to use brain science to prove that Augustine was right and therefore assuming neuroscience to be reality and Augustine's thought to be opinion. I hope that the preceding discussion of the limitations of this treatment has already addressed this possible objection. To put it another way: brain science, at least as it relates to humans, does not exist in some objectivist, materialist vacuum. To discuss neural networks or neurotransmitters without reference to human subjective experience and human behavior is ultimately meaningless. It is the effort to link and mutually illuminate subjective experience and objective neural patterns which is so worthwhile, stimulating and, I hope, enlightening. Brain science can only be legitimated as it progressively interweaves itself with human experience and behavior, without distorting or stunting the most sophisticated expressions of subjective life. In this sense, I assert, Augustine remains a powerful and much-needed interlocutor in the dialogue of religious psychology.

NOTES

1. The plight of these patients has been most famously described by neurologist Antonio Damasio in *Descartes' Error*. Damasio's treatment features the well-known case of Phineas

Gage, a nineteenth-century railroad employee who is one of the first and most dramatic documented cases of damage to this area.

2. For purposes of brevity, I have not mentioned the anterior cingulated cortex, adjacent to the frontal lobes but generally considered a part of the limbic, or emotional, system. The anterior cingulate is also critical for the reflective reward system. I have also implicitly grouped it with the frontal lobes in my discussion of Nora Volkow's work, below.

3. See *Enchiridion* (480; ch. 24) for a more general statement of the same process.

WORKS CITED

Aron, Arthur, Helen Fisher, Debra J. Mashek, Greg Strong, Haifang Li and Lucy L. Brown. "Reward, Motivation, and Emotion Systems Associated with Early-Stage Intense Romantic Love." *Journal of Neurophysiology* 94.1 (2005) 327–337.

Augustine. *City of God*. Trans. Henry Bettenson. Middlesex, England: Penguin Books, 1972.

———. *The Confessions of St. Augustine*. Trans. John K. Ryan. Garden City, New York: Image Books, 1960.

———. *On Continence*. Trans. C. L. Cornish. *The Nicene and Post-Nicene Church Fathers*. Ed. Philip Schaff. First Series, vol. 3, 714–741.

———. *Enchiridion*. Trans. J. F. Shaw. *The Nicene and Post-Nicene Church Fathers*. Ed. Philip Schaff. First Series, vol. 3, 449–552.

Brickman, P., D. Coates and R. Janoff-Bulman. "Lottery Winners and Accident Victims: Is Happiness Relative?" *Journal of Personality and Social Psychology* 36.8 (1978) 917–927.

Brown, Peter. *Augustine of Hippo: A Biography*. Berkeley and Los Angeles: University of California Press, 1967.

Buss, David. *Evolutionary Psychology: The New Science of the Mind*. Boston: Allyn and Bacon, 1990.

Chambers, R. Andrew, Jane R. Taylor and Marc N. Potenza. "Developmental Neurocircuitry of Motivation in Adolescence: A Critical Period of Addiction Vulnerability." *American Journal of Psychiatry* 160.6 (2003) 1041–1052.

Damasio, Antonio. *Descartes' Error: Emotion, Reason and the Human Brain*. New York: Harper Collins, 1994.

Diener, Ed, Richard E. Lucas and Christie Napa Scollon. "Beyond the Hedonic Treadmill. Revising the Adaptation Theory of Well-Being." *American Psychologist* 61.4 (2006) 305–314.

Erk, Susanne, Manfred Spitzer, Arthur P. Wunderlich, Lars Galley and Henrik Walter. "Cultural Objects Modulate Reward Circuitry." *NeuroReport* 13.18 (2002) 2499–2503.

Freud, Sigmund. *Civilization and Its Discontents. The Standard Edition of the Complete Psychological Works of Sigmund Freud, Volume XXI (1927–1931): The Future of an Illusion, Civilization and its Discontents, and Other Works*, trans. James Strachey. London: The Hogarth Press and the Institute of Psycho-analysis, 1961, 1–273.

Gabbard G. O. "Mind, brain, and personality disorders." *American Journal Psychiatry* 162.4 (2005) 648–655.

Graybiel, Ann M. "Building Action Repertoires: Memory and Learning Functions of the Basal Ganglia." *Current Opinion in Neurobiology* 5.6 (1995) 733–741.

Grosset, K. A., G. Macphee, G. Pal, D. Stewart, A. Watt, J. Davie and D. G. Grosset. "Problematic gambling on dopamine agonists: Not such a rarity." *Movement Disorders* 21.12 (2006) 2206–2208.

James, William. *The Principles of Psychology*. Vol. 1. New York: Dover Publications, 1950 (original 1890).

Kalivas, Peter W. and Nora D. Volkow. "The Neural Basis of Addiction: A Pathology of Motivation and Choice." *American Journal of Psychiatry* 162.8 (2005) 1403–1413.

Kandel, Eric R. "A New Intellectual Framework for Psychiatry." *American Journal of Psychiatry* 155.4 (1998) 457–469.

Kelley, Ann E. and Kent C. Berridge. "The Neuroscience of Natural Rewards: Relevance to Addictive Drugs." *The Journal of Neuroscience* 22.9 (2002) 3306–3311.

Kendler, Kenneth S. "Toward a philosophical structure for psychiatry." *American Journal of Psychiatry* 162.3 (2005) 433–440.

Knutson, Brian, Charles M. Adams, Grace W. Fong and Daniel Hommer. "Anticipation of Increasing Monetary Reward Selectively Recruits Nucleus Accumbens." *The Journal of Neuroscience*, 21.RC159 (2001) 1–5.

Koepp, M. J., R. N. Gunn, A. D. Lawrence, V. J. Cunningham, A. Dagher, T. Jones, D. J. Brooks, C. J. Bench and P. M. Grasby. "Evidence for Striatal Dopamine Release During a Video Game." *Nature*, vol. 393 (21 May 1998) 266–268.

Koob, George F. and Michel Le Moal. "Addiction and the Brain Antireward System." *Annual Review of Psychology* 59 (January 2008) 29–53.

Koob, George F. and Michel Le Moal. "Drug Abuse: Hedonic Homeostatic Dysregulation." *Science* 278.3 (1997) 52–58.

Koob, G. and M. J. Kreek. "Stress, Dysregulation of Drug Reward Pathways, and the Transition to Drug Dependence." *American Journal of Psychiatry* 164.8 (2007) 1149–1159.

Kundera, Milan. *Laughable Loves.* Trans. Suzanne Rappaport. Middlesex, England: Penguin Books, 1974.

Lao Tsu. *Tao Te Ching.* Trans. Gia-Fu Feng and Jane English. 1972. New York: Vintage Books, 1989.

Moran, Mark. "Drug Addiction Erodes 'Free Will' Over Time." *Psychiatric News* (8 July 2007) 16, 34.

Morgan, Drake, Kathleen A. Grant, H. Donald Gage, Robert H. Mach, Jay R. Kaplan, Osric Prioleau, Susan H Nader, Nancy Buchheimer, Richard L. Eherenkaufer and Michael A. Nader. "Social Dominance in Monkeys: Dopamine D2 Receptors and Cocaine Self-Administration." *Nature Neuroscience* 5.2 (2002) 169–174.

Nesse, Randolph M. and Kent C. Berridge. "Psychoactive Drug Use in Evolutionary Perspective." *Science* vol. 278 (3 October 1997) 63–66.

Nestler, Eric J. and David W. Self. "Neuropsychiatric Aspects of Ethanol and Other Chemical Dependencies." *The American Psychiatric Publishing Textbook of Neuropsychiatry and Behavioral Neurosciences.* 5th ed. Ed. Stuart C. Yudofsky and Robert E. Hales. Washington, D.C.: American Psychiatric Publishing, Inc., 2008, 881–905.

O'Donnell, James J. *Augustine: A New Biography.* New York: HarperCollins, 2005.

Panksepp, Jaak. *Affective Neuroscience: The Foundations of Human and Animal Emotions.* Oxford: Oxford University Press, 1998.

Pies, Ronald. "Should DSM-V Designate 'Internet Addiction' a Mental Disorder?" *Psychiatry (Edgmont)* 6.2 (2009) 31–37.

Pinker, Steven. *How the Mind Works.* New York: W. W. Norton & Co., 1997.

Radhakrishnan, Sarvepalli and Charles A. Moore, eds. *A Sourcebook in Indian Philosophy.* Princeton: Princeton University Press, 1957.

Schultz, Wolfram. "Predictive Reward Signal of Dopamine Neurons." *The Journal of Neurophysiology* 80.1 (1998) 1–27.

Spitzer, Manfred. *The Mind within the Net: Models of Learning, Thinking and Acting.* Cambridge, MA: The MIT Press, 1999.

Stahl, Stephen. *Stahl's Essential Psychopharmacology.* Cambridge: Cambridge University Press, 2008.

Volkow, Nora D. and Roy A Wise. "How Can Drug Addiction Help Us Understand Obesity?" *Nature Neuroscience* 8.5 (2005) 555–560.

Wilson, E. O. *Consilience: The Unity of Knowledge.* New York: Alfred A. Knopf, 1998.

Chapter Nine

Tears of Grief and Joy

Chronological Sequence and the Structure of Confessions, *Book 9*

Kim Paffenroth

In this chapter I will try to come to a fuller understanding of the structure of book nine of Augustine's *Confessions*, and in particular, to a clearer understanding of his confusion at his feelings over his mother's death (*Conf.* 9.12.29–9.13.34).[1] Indeed, Augustine's own confusion here is certainly not confined to himself but has understandably been shared by many of his readers: Why does the highly emotional Augustine, who so freely weeps at the death of his unnamed friend in book four (*Conf.* 4.4.7–4.6.11), hesitate to express his sorrow at his mother's death? Why does he find it so problematic? If one consults the secondary literature, one's perplexity is not immediately dispelled, for Augustine's critics have interpreted this passage in a number of ways: the epitome of Augustine as a divided, conflicted, alienated self;[2] Augustine turning his account of Monica's death into a rather Narcissistically self-referential story about himself;[3] a story of Augustine struggling to see the event in its proper perspective, first ineffectively denying his worldly attachments, then coming to see them in their proper relation to the eternal;[4] or a wrestling of Augustine's emotional, humane side with a rather inhuman, coldly ascetic attitude towards grief, a "ruthless . . . indifference" of Augustine and his contemporaries.[5]

Although not specifically addressing Augustine's grief and his confusion over it, there are also allegorical interpretations of his account of Monica's death, either as the climax of book nine and parallel to the allegorical interpretation of the Sabbath in book thirteen of the *Confessions* (*Conf.* 13.35.50–13.36.51);[6] or as an allegory of Augustine's love for his mother, the church.[7] Although this passage, like any other in Augustine, may have multiple meanings and functions, certainly the impression is that at this point there is a general confusion over Augustine's confusion. I think that an answer to this can be found by examining more closely the structure of book nine: in particular, by examining Augustine's use of interruptions in the chronological order of the narrated events.[8] By using these flashbacks and flash-forwards Augustine highlights for his readers his evolving attitudes towards death, grief, and love, thereby illuminating the climactic instance of all three, the death of Monica.

Augustine begins book nine quite typically with a praise of God,[9] in particular emphasizing Monica and himself as the servants of God: "O Lord, I am your servant; I am your servant and the son of your handmaid" (*Conf.* 9.1.1).[10] He then narrates the events that occurred next in the chronological sequence of his life, his final weeks as a professor of rhetoric and his intention to resign from that post (*Conf.* 9.2.2–9.2.4). The next event that should be narrated, if Augustine were still simply following the chronological sequence, should be the beginning of the vintage vacation and the end of his teaching; but this in fact is not mentioned until chapter four (*Conf.* 9.4.7). Instead, the next chapter narrates events that occur long after, events that in fact occur outside of the time frame of the autobiographical narrative of the *Confessions*. These are the conversions and deaths of Verecundus and Nebridius (*Conf.* 9.3.5–9.3.6). Augustine then resumes the proper chronological sequence of his story, narrating the beginning of the vintage vacation (*Conf.* 9.4.7); his retreat with his friends to Cassiciacum (*Conf.* 9.4.7–9.4.12); his formal resignation from his post (*Conf.* 9.5.13); and the baptisms of Alypius, Adeodatus, and himself (*Conf.* 9.6.14). But during the account of his baptism, Augustine again departs on another flash-forward to recount briefly the subsequent life and death of Adeodatus, more events outside of the time frame of the *Confessions* (*Conf.* 9.6.14).[11]

Several obvious similarities are to be noted between the chronological breaks so far in book nine. They are both accounts of deaths. They are both flash-forwards. In particular, they are flash-forwards to events that occur outside of the time frame of the *Confessions*. It could be said then that if the *Confessions* were strictly a story told in chronological sequence within a particular time frame, then these stories would not have been included. Their inclusion here by Augustine therefore seems especially deliberate. Augustine has violated both the order and the time frame of his story because it is important to his purpose to include accounts of these deaths.[12] A comparison between these accounts and the mention of Patricius' death (*Conf.* 3.4.7) and the more lengthy account of the death of Augustine's unnamed friend (*Conf.* 4.4.7–4.6.11) will help to uncover his purpose and meaning here.

Similar to these accounts, Patricius' death is also mentioned out of its proper place in the chronological sequence of the *Confessions*.[13] But dissimilar to these accounts, it is a flashback. More importantly, it is a flashback to an event that did in fact occur within the time frame of the *Confessions*: if Augustine had wanted to, he could have included it in its appropriate place. Therefore, the fact that Patricius' death is narrated so briefly and out of its proper chronological sequence is quite rightly taken as an indication of Augustine's ambiguous or indifferent feelings towards his father.[14] But as noted, with the deaths of Verecundus, Nebridius, and Adeodatus, the situation here is just the opposite: if Augustine had been following the chronology of his story and its time frame, there would have been no place to put these accounts. Rather, he deliberately makes a place for them despite this fact. Therefore, being told out of chronological sequence serves to highlight the importance of these three deaths for Augustine, not to minimize them.

Further, the events surrounding all three deaths in book nine should also be noted. Each of the three deaths is recounted in the context of the person's conversion, another comment missing from Augustine's first mention of his father's death.[15] Augustine makes a place for these accounts in book nine in order to assure the reader that Verecundus, Nebridius, and Adeodatus subsequently died in a state of grace. Such a happy conclusion could not otherwise have been known, since by the end of the time frame of the autobiographical part of the *Confessions* the first two are not yet Christians. As for Adeodatus, although he is a Christian, it would seem that because he is baptized in his youth, Augustine would surely fear he might fall into the same traps that he himself did: this would then be the background for his insistence that "you took his life away from the earth, and now I remember him with a more peaceful mind, for I have no fear for anything in his childhood or youth, and none at all for him as a man" (*Conf.* 9.6.14). By narrating their deaths, Augustine has shown us the conclusions to these three characters' own journeys to faith. In this and similar ways, it seems that the *Confessions* are not always so exclusively focused on Augustine himself as some have maintained:[16] these two accounts do not seem to advance Augustine's own story at all, but rather give us the completion of the stories of his friends and son, stories with importance and interest for us in their own right. They show us Augustine's genuine concern and love for them. The climaxes to their stories having been told, the three characters are dismissed from the narrative to make room for the similar climax to Monica's story.[17]

Augustine's insistence in these accounts that the three men died in a state of grace and are now safe with God, as well as his deep affection for the three, make the accounts very similar to that of the death of the unnamed friend in book four. Augustine describes the friend's deathbed conversion as bringing him to God quite similarly to how he describes Nebridius' state: of his friend he writes, "But he was snatched away from my madness, so that he might be kept with you for my consolation" (*Conf.* 4.4.8); and of Nebridius, "Now he lives in Abraham's bosom" (*Conf.* 9.3.6; cf. Luke 16:22).

The difference between books four and nine is striking, however, in Augustine's reaction to the deaths. In book four, he is paralyzed by despair: "most heavily there weighed upon me both weariness of life and fear of dying . . . my life was a horror to me" (*Conf.* 4.6.11). But in book nine, he can feel joy for his lost loved ones while remembering fondly the times he shared with them. Of Nebridius, Augustine says, "There he lives, in that place of which he asked so many questions of me, a poor, ignorant man. No longer does he put his ear to my mouth, but he puts his spiritual mouth to your fountain, and in accordance with his desire he drinks in wisdom, as much as he can, endlessly happy" (*Conf.* 9.3.6); and of Adeodatus, "I had experience of many still more wonderful things in him. To me his power of mind was a source of awe. Who except you is the worker of such marvels?" (*Conf.* 9.6.14). By narrating their deaths when he could have omitted them, Augustine shows his readers that he has now come to an appropriate understanding of love and grief. No longer absolutizing his loved ones in the almost idolatrous way he had the friend of book four, Augustine can accept them in life as gifts from God, while still loving them for their own sakes; and he can accept their deaths as not ending the loving and eternal relationship that still exists between them: "But blessed is the man who loves you [God], and his friend in you. . . . For he alone loses no dear one to whom all are dear in him who is not lost" (*Conf.* 4.9.14).[18]

After a very brief return to the proper chronological sequence in narrating his actual baptism (*Conf.* 9.6.14), Augustine next inserts a lengthy series of flashbacks (*Conf.* 9.7.15–9.9.22). The first of these is a description of the persecution under Justina and the rediscovery and translation of the relics of Sts. Gervasius and Protasius (*Conf.* 9.7.15–9.7.16). The episode is not particularly well integrated into the narrative and seems like more of an afterthought than the other chronological interruptions of book nine.[19] It is, moreover, a flashback to an event within the time frame of the *Confessions*, and therefore, like the death of Patricius, could have been narrated in its proper place. Being inserted here as an afterthought does make it seem that, like the death of Patricius, the events around the persecution under Justina did not particularly move Augustine at the time. He says as much when he notes that at the time he was "still cold to the warmth of your Spirit" (*Conf.* 9.7.15), though he did note the commotion in the city. But unlike the death of Patricius, the events of 386 did affect Augustine the following year at his baptism. By narrating these stories out of sequence, Augustine shows that they were not relevant to him until 387.

Augustine connects the events of 386 to his baptism because at his baptism he was overcome with tears at the singing in the church: "How greatly did I weep during hymns and canticles, keenly affected by the voices of your sweet-singing Church! Those voices flowed into my ears, and your truth was distilled into my heart, and from that truth holy emotions overflowed, and the tears ran down, and amid those tears all was well with me" (*Conf.* 9.6.14). The following flashbacks then narrate how it was that singing had become traditional in the Church in Milan. But more importantly, they show the significance of Augustine's tears at his baptism. He cries at the singing because he can remember a time, painfully recent, when the singing did not move him, even though it affected everyone else, especially his mother: "Therein, living in prayer, my mother, your handmaid, held a first place amid these cares and watchings," while Augustine himself was "still cold to the warmth of your spirit" (*Conf.* 9.7.15). His tears at his baptism contain an element of shame at his having not abandoned his former life sooner, even when the goal was within his grasp: "Yet even then, when the odor of your ointments was so fragrant, we did not run after you. Therefore, I wept the more at the singing of your hymns" (*Conf.* 9.7.16). But at the same time, his tears show Augustine's joy now that he has found God, however belatedly: "For long had I sighed after you, and at length I breathed in you, as far as breath may enter into this house of grass" (*Conf.* 9.7.16).[20] Only from these flashbacks can we see that Augustine's tears at his baptism are simultaneously tears with which he grieves over his previous alienation from God and rejoices at his present (and now permanent) communion with him.

In the next section, Augustine gives a lengthy flashback to Monica's earlier life (*Conf.* 9.8.17–9.9.22). As with Augustine's confusion over his feelings at her death, the exact reason for the inclusion of this little biography here is variously interpreted: "fond but highly selective memories of her" that eventually turn the story back to the real subject, Augustine himself;[21] a fitting final tribute to her;[22] or Monica as illustrative of the proper Christian life, either in contrast with Augustine's earlier sinfulness[23] or as an example for him now to follow.[24] Without necessarily denying these interpretations,[25] I think that they do not fully explain this flashback. In particular, all these interpretations tend to emphasize the positive, praising aspects of Augustine's story of Monica and therefore have somewhat minimized the significance of his including here the story of her drinking as a child. Since it is this part of the story that I think is most important for our understanding of Augustine's tears, I will save its treatment until last and begin with the latter parts of Augustine's story of Monica.

This little biography is divided into two parts: the first, on Monica's childhood (*Conf.* 9.8.17–9.8.18); and the second, on her life with Patricius (*Conf.* 9.9.19–9.9.22). In the second part Augustine praises Monica for her patience in the face of Patricius' adultery and violent temper: "She endured offenses against her marriage bed in such wise that she never had a quarrel with her husband over this matter. . . . But in addition to this, just as he was remarkable for kindness, so also was he given to violent anger. However, she had learned to avoid resisting her husband when he was angry, not only by deeds but even by words" (*Conf.* 9.9.19). Her patience similarly protected her from the ill will of her mother-in-law and the servants: "By her good services and by perseverance in patience and meekness, she also won over her mother-in-law who at first was stirred up against her by the whispered stories of malicious servants" (*Conf.* 9.9.20). Augustine goes on to praise her for her irenic influence over others, as she brings peace between any who are in disagreement: "wherever she could she showed herself to be a great peacemaker between persons who were at odds and in disagreement" (*Conf.* 9.9.21). Finally, he says that in her piety and devotion to others "she took care as though she had been mother to us all, and she served us as though she had been a daughter to all of us" (*Conf.* 9.9.22).

Several points should be noted about this part of the flashback. As with the immediately preceding flashback to the events around the persecution under Justina, the events narrated here have occurred (at least in part) during the time frame of the *Confessions* and could have been narrated somewhere else. But it should also be noted that unlike any of the other chronological interruptions we have examined, this passage, despite being one of the longer, is the most general:[26] with the possible exception of the incident with Monica's mother-in-law, no specific event is related, and no relation to any point in Augustine's life is given. In a way, the passage's generality means that it could have been included anywhere but at the same time nowhere, because it has no connection to any specific event in the narrative on which to "hang" it. It could only be used as it is at this point, as an epitome and generalization of everything we have learned about Monica earlier in the *Confessions*, and an epitome of her life is certainly most appropriate here at the end of it. Her long suffering patience at her wayward son is shown here as analogous to her patience with her wayward husband. Her concern for Augustine's salvation that we have seen throughout the *Confessions* is shown here as also applying to her husband and is even generalized to everyone: she was like a mother to all.[27] Indeed, the imagery of pain in childbirth mentioned earlier in relation to Augustine himself is here extended to all her children: "I cannot tell clearly enough what love she had for me, and how with greater anguish she brought me forth in spirit than she had given me birth in the flesh" (*Conf.* 5.9.16); "she had brought up children, being as often in labor in birth of them as she saw them straying from you" (*Conf.* 9.9.22). This part of the flashback, in which Monica is once again presented as the ideal mother, is most of a piece with the descriptions of her throughout the rest of the *Confessions*.[28] As a passage that really adds little new to our understanding of Monica, but only elaborates or epitomizes what we have already seen numerous times throughout the book, I do not find this part of the flashback surprising or problematic: it seems to function, as some of the interpretations cited above indicate, as a fairly straightforward tribute to her by Augustine.

It is the immediately preceding flashback to Monica as a child (*Conf.* 9.8.17–9.8.18) that seems surprising and significant. With Augustine's description of Monica's childhood drinking problem (*Conf.* 9.8.18) we have probably the only place in the *Confessions* in which we see Monica as flawed and sinful. (Although she is ultimately, indeed quite readily, turned back to the right path, she is here presented as sinful nonetheless.) No longer the perfect mother and the perfect believer that she is uniformly presented as in the rest of the *Confessions*,[29] she is seen here for the only time as someone in need of the exact same correction that Augustine himself has struggled to get and to receive throughout the book. Although not precisely parallel (it is, after all, not theft), Monica's youthful offense is here described in a way similar to the pear tree incident (*Conf.* 2.4.9–2.10.18), in that neither is motivated by desire for the object obtained, but rather by love of the sinful act of obtaining it: "Nor did I wish to enjoy that thing which I desired to gain by theft, but rather to enjoy the actual theft and the sin of theft" (*Conf.* 2.4.9); "She did this not out of a desire for drink, but from a sort of excess of those youthful spirits" (*Conf.* 9.8.18). Monica, whom Augustine so often contrasts to his own sinful self, is here shown as having once been exactly like him.

Like the earlier flash-forwards to the conversions and deaths of Verecundus, Nebridius, and Adeodatus, this episode obviously takes place outside of the time frame of the *Confessions*. It again seems that Augustine has included it here when he could have omitted it. Further, to give such a negative story about Monica in a flashback that is otherwise a typical and predictable praise of her patience and piety also makes this passage stand out as incongruous, deliberate, and potentially significant.

We are finally in a position to analyze Augustine's confusion over his weeping at Monica's death with which we began this paper. Following the flashback to Monica's life, Augustine resumes the proper chronological sequence of his story, telling of their vision together at Ostia (*Conf.* 9.10.23–9.10.26) and then Monica's death (*Conf.* 9.11.27–9.11.28). There follows a long section (*Conf.* 9.12.29–9.13.34) that constantly mentions Augustine's confusion over his grief and his unwillingness to cry for his mother. Again, why does he feel such confusion? A consideration of the types of weeping Augustine has described so far in the *Confessions* will help illuminate this.

First, the scene is described quite similarly to the death of the friend in book four. Augustine uses the same image of the two as one soul in two bodies: "For I thought that my soul and his soul were but one soul in two bodies" (*Conf.* 4.6.11); "For out of her life and mine one life had been made" (*Conf.* 9.12.30).[30] As noted, Augustine weeps freely at that earlier death, but they are clearly tears of despair, made without any hope for the friend's survival: "I marveled that other men should live, because he, whom I had loved as if he would never die, was dead. . . . Perhaps because of this I feared

to die, lest he whom I had loved so much should wholly die" (*Conf.* 4.6.11).
As Augustine indicates, such tears would certainly not be appropriate at
Monica's death but would only confuse and torment him more: "We did not
think it fitting to solemnize that funeral with tearful cries and groans, for it is
often the custom to bewail by such means the wretched lot of those who die,
or even their complete extinction. But she did not die in misery, nor did she
meet with total death" (*Conf.* 9.12.29).[31] If tears mean hopelessness, then
Augustine's refusal to shed such tears at Monica's death would surely make
sense.

But tears of despair over the physical death of someone are not the most
frequent tears in the *Confessions*. These would seem to be Monica's tears
over her son, living and dying in sin:[32] "Graciously you heard her, and you
did not despise her tears when they flowed down from her eyes and watered
the earth beneath, in whatsoever place she prayed" (*Conf.* 3.11.19); "For
when I would be washed clean by that water, then also would be dried up
those rivers flowing down from my mother's eyes, by which, before you and
in my behalf, she daily watered the ground beneath her face" (*Conf.* 5.8.15).
Augustine is in fact called "the son of such tears" (*Conf.* 3.12.21), and he
reminds us of them again in book nine, calling Monica "that mother now
dead to my eyes who for so many years had wept for me so that I might live
in your eyes" (*Conf.* 9.12.33). Monica's tears for Augustine the unreformed
sinner are portrayed throughout the book as positive and highly efficacious.
As shown above, such tears can also be turned, when the sinner repents, into
the kind of tears combining grief and joy that Augustine sheds at his own
baptism: "the tears ran down, and amid those tears all was well with me"
(*Conf.* 9.6.14). These tears of grief and joy, which Augustine has shown he
can shed for himself, are liberating and not problematic. But when Monica
died, would Augustine have been immediately ready to shed such tears for
her? Given the consistently idealized portrayal of her in the *Confessions*, the
answer would clearly seem to be no. How could he weep for Monica as she
had wept for him, when he sees himself as the foulest of sinners and her as
the perfect mother and believer?

It is at this point that the difference between the times when the events of
the *Confessions* occurred and when they were written down becomes clear
and sheds light on Augustine's confusion. At the time of Monica's death,
Augustine was deeply confused because he could not readily weep for her as
for another repentant sinner who had come to God. As shown above, Augustine seems to have felt no such confusion when Nebridius and Adeodatus
died several years later,[33] partly because he had by that time come to a better
understanding of death and grief, but also because they had never been for
him idealized figures like Monica. It is only by the time of the writing of the
Confessions that Augustine clearly sees Monica as another flawed human
being in need of God's grace, and he shows this particularly by the inclusion

of the story of her childhood drinking problem, an episode that surely did not occur to him at the actual time of Monica's death. In this story Augustine emphasizes God's part in Monica's correction: "My God, what did you do at that time? How did you cure her? Whence did you heal her? Was it not that you brought out of another soul, a hard and sharp reproach, like a surgeon's knife out of your secret stores, and by one stroke you cut away all that foul matter?" (*Conf.* 9.8.18). The larger-than-life Monica of the rest of the *Confessions* is here reduced years later to a more realistic and, for Augustine and his readers, a more manageable size: a little girl who sinned and needed God's help to stop sinning. Only with this story in which Monica is portrayed as exactly like Augustine himself can he now see his tears as comforting and not painful: "I took comfort in weeping in your sight over her and for her, over myself and for myself. I gave way to the tears that I had held back, so that they poured forth as much as they wished. I spread them beneath my heart, and it rested upon them, for at my heart were placed your ears, not the ears of a mere man" (*Conf.* 9.12.33). Only with this realization that Monica too required a repentance instigated and sustained by God's action can Augustine experience his tears rightly, not as signs of despair or weakness, but as signs of both grief and joy, proper expressions of a proper love.[34]

NOTES

*Originally published in *Augustinian Studies* 28 (1997) 141–54. Reprinted with permission.

1. References to the *Confessions* will include book, chapter, and section number in parentheses. All quotations from the *Confessions* will be from John K. Ryan, *The Confessions of St. Augustine* (Garden City, NY: Doubleday and Co., 1960) unless otherwise noted.

2. Donald Capps, "Augustine's *Confessions*: The Scourge of Shame and the Silencing of Adeodatus," in *The Hunger of the Heart: Reflections on the* Confessions *of Augustine* (ed. Donald Capps and James E. Dittes; Society for the Scientific Study of Religion Monograph Series 8; West Lafayette, IN: Society for the Scientific Study of Religion, 1990) 69–92, esp. 83–92.

3. Margaret R. Miles, *Desire and Delight. A New Reading of Augustine's* Confessions (New York: Crossroad Publishing, 1991) 81–86; on Augustine's narcissism, see also Donald Capps, "Augustine as Narcissist: Of Grandiosity and Shame," in *The Hunger of the Heart: Reflections on the* Confessions *of Augustine* (eds. Donald Capps and James E. Dittes; Society for the Scientific Study of Religion Monograph Series 8; West Lafayette, IN: Society for the Scientific Study of Religion, 1990) 169–84.

4. Colin Starnes, *Augustine's Conversion: A Guide to the Argument of* Confessions *I–IX* (Waterloo, Ontario: Wilfrid Laurier University Press, 1990) 264–65.

5. John J. O'Meara, *The Young Augustine: The Growth of St. Augustine's Mind up to His Conversion* (London: Longmans, Green and Co., 1954) 204.

6. Robert McMahon, *Augustine's Prayerful Ascent: An Essay on the Literary Form of the* Confessions (Athens, GA: University of Georgia Press, 1989) 108–12.

7. William Mallard, *Language and Love. Introducing Augustine's Religious Thought Through the Confessions Story* (University Park, PA: Pennsylvania State University Press, 1994) 173–74.

8. What to consider as an interruption is of course subjective to some extent. I have not considered every instance of Augustine mentioning something that happened before or after the events in the immediate context (such as his mention in *Conf.* 9.2.4 that he had been having

chest pains since the previous summer), but only those interruptions that are extensive enough to be considered narratives or episodes on their own. Also, this method means that we will not consider to any extent the two most overworked sections of book nine: the retreat at Cassiciacum and the vision at Ostia. These two incidents are particularly prominent in Courcelle's classic work: see P. Courcelle, *Recherches sur les Confessions de saint Augustin* (Paris: E. de Boccard, 1950) 7–11, 202–10, 222–26. See also P. Henry, *La vision d'Ostie, sa place dans la vie et l'oeuvre de saint Augustin* (Paris: J. Vrin, 1938).

9. Cf. the similar beginnings to books one, five, six, and eight. The beginning to book six, with its description of Monica, is especially similar.

10. Ps 116:16; cf. Starnes, *Augustine's Conversion*, 247–48. "Handmaid" here could also possibly refer to the church, or both: see Mallard, *Language and Love*, 172.

11. Cf. the very different analysis of Capps, "Silencing of Adeodatus," 87–92, who argues that Augustine's brief mention of his son's death is not a proper account at all, but rather shows his continuing shame at Adeodatus' illegitimacy. It does not seem that the mention here is so brief, but is of an appropriate length for an event outside of the time frame of the main story. Also, Augustine's relation to Adeodatus in their dialogue *On the Teacher* seems much fuller and closer than Capps indicates in his analysis: I do not believe that based on it one could legitimately characterize Augustine's relation to his son as primarily consisting of shame. Cf. the analysis by Peter Brown, *Augustine of Hippo* (Berkeley and Los Angeles: University of California Press, 1967) 135, especially his quotation of Augustine from the *Opus imperfectum contra Julianum* (6, 22), his last work: "Surely what Cicero says [to his son] comes straight from the heart of all fathers, when he wrote: 'You are the only man of all men whom I would wish to surpass me in all things.'" (For the Latin, see J.-P. Migne, ed., *Patrologiae Cursus Completus, Series Latina* [Paris: 1841] vol. 45, col. 1551.)

12. Cf. McMahon, *Augustine's Prayerful Ascent*, 109, who notes the preponderance of accounts of death in book nine and their "violation of the 'natural order' of the narrative."

13. Augustine's mention of his father's death as an afterthought in just one clause does not seem an example of an interruption in the chronological sequence, such as the ones we have been examining, but it is similar in its being narrated out of sequence.

14. Cf. Brown, *Augustine of Hippo*, 30.

15. Though Augustine will finally mention it as part of his tribute to Monica (*Conf.* 9.9.22), giving credit to her for his father's conversion.

16. E.g., Miles and Capps, cited in note 3 above.

17. Verecundus and Nebridius disappear completely. Adeodatus is mentioned in *Conf.* 9.12.29 and 9.12.31, though his action is minimized. Again, cf. the very different analysis in Capps, "Silencing of Adeodatus," 87–92. I would take Adeodatus' silencing as rather more likely a device to keep the focus on Monica at this point. Without necessarily agreeing completely with his allegorical interpretation, cf. the similar conclusion of McMahon, *Augustine's Prayerful Ascent*, 110: "Though Adeodatus, in fact, died some time after Monica, his death is recorded before it. The prolepsis enables the author to create correspondences with the allegory of on God's 'eternal sabbath' in book 13, while placing Monica's death at the climax of book 9."

18. Cf. the conclusions in my "God in the Friend, or the Friend in God? The Meaning of Friendship for Augustine," *Augustinian Heritage* 38 (1992) 123–36.

19. Cf. Starnes, *Augustine's Conversion*, 254: "The last chapter before the eulogy to Monica occurred to Augustine as an afterthought at the time he was writing the *Confessions*." In light of what follows, however, Justina may be seen as a contrast with the faithful Monica; she may also be another example of the repentant sinner, though her conversion is only hinted at here.

20. Cf. Starnes, *Augustine's Conversion*, 256: "This is Augustine's expressed reason for including these episodes. They explain his joy in the psalms and hymns of the church by showing exactly where he had come from—where such things were of no concern or consolation."

21. Miles, *Desire and Delight*, 85–86.

22. Mallard, *Language and Love*, 173–74.

23. Starnes, *Augustine's Conversion*, 257–59.

24. Colin Starnes, "Augustine's Conversion and the Ninth Book of the *Confessions*," in *Augustine: From Rhetor to Theologian* (ed. Joanne McWilliam; Waterloo, Ontario: Wilfrid Laurier University Press, 1992) 51–65.

25. Again, a passage may certainly have more than one meaning or function in Augustine's work. I find both of Starnes' treatments of this passage the most satisfying of those listed here: see previous two notes.

26. Cf. the much shorter description of Adeodatus' life, which nonetheless contains the detail that he plays a part in Augustine's dialogue *On the Teacher* (*Conf.* 9.6.14). Monica herself is also a character in Augustine's *The Happy Life*, though he does not mention so here. Clearly, that aspect of their relationship is not relevant now.

27. Cf. Starnes, *Augustine's Conversion*, 258: "Her care for Augustine's salvation has been before us throughout the *Confessions* but the same was true for the rest of her family. . . . To her family and to all in the church she was ever 'the servant of your servants' (IX, ix, 22): a mother to all."

28. Cf. Brown, *Augustine of Hippo*, 30: "In Augustine's description of his early life, Monica appears, above all, as a relentless figure. . . . This all-absorbing mother, deeply injured by her son's rebellions, is the Monica we usually see through Augustine's eyes." Augustine's constant portrayal of Monica as idealized mother continues to lead to psychological analyses of him and his work: e.g., recently, Charles Kligerman, "A Psychoanalytic Study of the *Confessions* of St. Augustine"; David Bakan, "Augustine's *Confessions*: The Unentailed Self"; and James E. Dittes, "Continuities Between the Life and Thought of Augustine"; as well as the interesting critique by David Burrell, "Reading the *Confessions* of Augustine: The Case of Oedipal Analyses"; all four to be found in *The Hunger of the Heart: Reflections on the* Confessions *of Augustine* (ed. Donald Capps and James E. Dittes; Society for the Scientific Study of Religion Monograph Series 8; West Lafayette, IN: Society for the Scientific Study of Religion, 1990) pp. 95–108, 109–15, 117–31, 133–42.

29. Cf. Brown, *Augustine of Hippo*, 29: "Yet, the balanced picture of Monica which Augustine provides in Book Nine of his *Confessions*, dissolves during most of the early books."

30. Cf. Miles, *Desire and Delight*, 84.

31. Cf. Miles, *Desire and Delight*, 84: "At the time of Monica's death, however, he thinks that tears are theologically incorrect since Monica has died as a faithful Christian, in the hope of resurrection, so that, in fact, 'she was not altogether dead.'"

32. On Monica's weeping, see the discussion in Miles, *Desire and Delight*, 81–82. On the connection between prayer and weeping in Augustine, see J. Balogh, "Unbeachtetes in Augustins Konfessionen," *Didaskaleion* (n.s.) 4 (1926) 5–21.

33. Probably in 390: see Brown, *Augustine of Hippo*, 74, 135.

34. Cf. Brown, *Augustine of Hippo*, 164: "Monica, the idealized figure that had haunted Augustine's youth like an oracle of God, is subtly transformed, by Augustine's analysis of his present feelings on remembering her death, into an ordinary human being, an object of concern, a sinner like himself, equally in need of mercy."

Chapter Ten

On Seeing the Light

Assessing Psychoanalytic Interpretations of Vision in Augustine's Confessions

William B. Parsons

Looking back over the last century of psychological analyses of Augustine's journey of faith as recounted in his *Confessions*, it is clear that the lion's share belongs to those employing specifically psychoanalytic methodology and that the latter, even when employing its most reductive analyses, have piqued the most interest from those championing theological perspectives. In point of fact there exist multiple psychoanalytic books as well as essays in the dozens on Augustine.[1] It is fair to say no other theological figure has caused more spilt ink in psychoanalytic circles.

Despite critiques of the psycho-historical project and reservations concerning the ability to find the "historical" Augustine from historical, literary and theological perspectives, all too many psychoanalytic studies nevertheless conduct their business as usual. Pivotal episodes, events and psycho-religious reflections in the text (e.g., the pear episode, the bath episode, significant deaths [i.e., of Augustine's childhood friend, of Monica, of Adeotatus], his various "conversions," matters concerning his concubine and celibacy) are interpreted with respect to the sizable inventory of psychoanalytic nomenclature (e.g., Oedipal conflict, pre-Oedipal stages, fragmentation, identity crisis, idealization, guilt, shame, etc). This is no more evident than with respect to what I, in adhering to accepted modern nomenclature, would call Augustine's "mystical experience" at Ostia (*Conf.* 9.10). This essay aims at reconsidering the meaning and nature of such an epiphany for both our understanding of Augustine's religious journey and, more directly, a psychoanalytic audience which, perhaps affected by a cultural trend towards the spiritual (or as Robert Fuller would have it: "spiritual but not religious"[2]), has become more open to the possibility and importance of what William James liked to call the "More."

In order to properly assess psychoanalytic contributions to this topic from a balanced interdisciplinary perspective, and by way of both summarizing and then going beyond my previous two essays on this topic,[3] the present essay will proceed by way of five short sections. The first surveys extant psychoanalytic interpretations of Augustine's mysticism. The aim here is but simple summary designed to show exactly what psychoanalysis has made of Augustine's mysticism. The second section begins a critique of the latter by revisiting the history of psychoanalytic models for mysticism as they emerged from the Freud-Rolland correspondence. The aim here is to wean psychoanalysis away from the "received view" of what Freud thought and said about mysticism. I do so by documenting that Freud had not one but three different models for understanding mysticism and that none of them accords with the typical view of oceanic feelings being regressions to primary narcissism. This provides the ground for the third section, which begins the process of trying to understand precisely what the nature of Augustine's mysticism really was—his "case" so to speak. The initial move, in acknowledging that Augustine was a professor of the rhetorical arts before he was a Bishop, is to engage literary concerns in order to ascertain precisely why Monica was involved in the ascent at Ostia. If indeed Augustine's inclusion of Monica can be understood as part and parcel of his emerging "mystical theology," then any simple and unnuanced recourse to framing the inclusion of Monica as wholly free associative and symptomatic becomes problematic, as does any simple attempt to see vision as a regression to primary narcissism.

It is the latter conclusion that provides the springboard for section four, which broadens the search for Augustine's teaching on mystical ascents and experiences by delving into his subsequent ruminations on, in particular, intellectual visions, and the latter as they engage certain pivotal epistemological debates within the contemporary academic study of mysticism. It is here that we can truly say we have come to an understanding of the nature of Augustine's mysticism—a fact that all previous analyses have failed to achieve. Finally, with such critiques in hand, the last section sketches out a new orientation which considers how psychoanalysis might be best utilized in creating a more meaningful, less reductive appreciation of Augustine's visions. In sum, the call here is for a truly interdisciplinary approach to Augustine's mysticism—one in which "textologists," theologians, philosophers, literary theorists, historians and psychologists (including, of course, psychoanalysts) can work together to create a more fitting framework for understanding Augustine's mysticism.

THE PSYCHOANALYSIS OF VISION: THE MOTHER AT OSTIA

Extant psychoanalytic perspectives on Augustine's visions employ a range of Oedipal, pre-Oedipal and ego-psychological models, following essentially two lines of interpretation: one emphasizing Augustine's mysticism as regressive and defensive (the "classic" school); the other as healing and adaptive (the "adaptive" school). Both lines see the presence of Monica at Ostia as symptomatic, stressing the preponderance of the mother and the array of instinctual and relational developmental vicissitudes associated with her. One could also include a third approach, the "transformational," which is the approach championed in this essay and of which more will be said in the pages to follow.

Keeping for the moment to the first two approaches, the earliest (i.e., mid-20th century) studies championed the most reductive, Oedipal line of interpretation. Paradigmatic in this regard is Charles Kligerman's 1957 essay, which interprets the Ostia vision as essentially incestuous and erotic:

> Augustine relates in equally masterly fashion quite a different sort of experience. He tells how they leaned together in a window overlooking the garden "discoursing together, alone, very sweetly" what the eternal life would be like. He goes on to describe a mystical ecstatic experience he shares with his mother which in rhythm, flow and imagery strike the reader as passionately orgiastic.[4]

Kligerman's analysis is paradigmatic for it impacted subsequent psychoanalytic studies to a determinative degree. For example, Phillip Woollcott and Paul Pruyser each a central player in the psychological analyses of Augustine, warmly cite Kligerman's interpretation as essentially correct.[5] James Dittes goes further by linking Monica to Augustine's turn to the mystical worldview of Neo-Platonism. For Dittes Augustine's development was such that it left him in a central conflict: that of being dependent or being autonomous. His "conversion" to Neo-Platonism and to a Christianity that finds its denouement in a Christianized Neo-Platonic ascent with the "Mother" at Ostia is but an expression of the psychic ascendancy of his need for dependence. Monica and Augustine are emotionally and symbolically "one" in the vision. To use Dittes's terminology, "Mom-ism" rules Augustine's vision at Ostia.[6]

Variations on this line of argument can be found in later studies of Augustine. Both Capps and William Beers turn to pre-Oedipal theory, utilizing Kohut's self-psychology in elaborating on the developmental basis of Augustine's ascent at Ostia. Echoing Dittes, Capps thinks Augustine never had Monica's approval for acts of independence. The "fusion" found in the Ostia vision is interlocked with the developmental fact that Augustine was never given that empathic response from Monica which would have allowed him to feel good about acts of independence.[7] For Beers, Augustine's archaic narcissistic structures were never integrated in a phase-appropriate developmental manner. The Ostia vision reflects both this developmental snag and its later Oedipal manifestation:

> Augustine soared to his longed for idealized mother imago. . . . The fact that the mystical area is beyond language (i.e., silent) suggests the pre-structural, pre-symbolic, and pre-linguistic realm of dedifferentiated narcissism. And, the reference to carnal pleasure suggests a degree of "telescoping" of narcissistic forms and energies onto later oedipal themes.[8]

The pre-Oedipal rendering of vision continues into most contemporary studies, many of which treat Augustine's visions as being of an adaptive, healing order. Dittes's second and much later study of Augustine, for example, begins to move in this direction by seeing in Augustine's mystical visions the encounter with a God who will not fail him. The central issue here is Erikson's epigenetic understanding of the pre-Oedipal stage as constituting the basic dilemma of "trust vs. mistrust." It is in his visions of God that Augustine "discovers God to be trustworthy."[9] Like Beers, Volney Gay has a Kohutian take on the vision at Ostia. He notes that "Mother and son engaged in a kind of spiritual ecstasy that unifies them in a common bond of selfobject merger with God" and that the presence of God "corresponds directly to the universal human need to find, somewhere, another who knows us to our depths, recognizes our faults, yet loves us completely."[10] Again, one could cite the attempt to utilize Ana-Maria Rizzuto's Winnicottian notion of an evolving "God-representation," particularly the dialectical relation she holds to exist between what she calls the relational, developmentally based "images" of God and the more conscious, rational "conceptual" aspects of the God-representation, to argue that Augustine's mystical experience was therapeutic and adaptive. From the perspective of this model Augustine's ascent to the "Light," with its maternal overtones, instigated an ego-syntonic release of the pre-Oedipal "images" of the God-representation—images which were then fortified through exposure to and integration of the "conceptual" aspects of the God-representation (namely, that of a Christian Neo-Platonism). This dialectical interplay between image and concept, mediated through the therapeutic auspices of fatherly sponsors like Ambrose, resulted in a dramatic shift in the evolution of Augustine's God-representation, leading to a more cohesive, integrated self and stable identity.[11]

OVERTURNING ORTHODOXY: FREUD AND MYSTICISM

What were above dubbed the "classic" and "adaptive" psychoanalytic approaches to mysticism find their historical moorings in Freud's correspondence with Romain Rolland concerning the meaning and interpretation of the famous oceanic feeling.[12] The "received view" of their dialogue frames oceanic feelings as examples of Jamesian transient mystical experiences of unity, now psychoanalytically rendered as regressions to that initial developmental phase Freud called "primary narcissism." Oceanic feelings, while themselves potentially neutral, are, when co-opted by religious institutions, framed as defensive, even pathological. Additionally oceanic feelings, based on the mother, cannot displace the true origin of religion, the latter based on the culturally superior role of the Father and the wish for guidance and protection. So the Freudian contribution to the psychoanalytic theory of mysticism has stood for greater part of the last century. Subsequent psychoanalytic analyses of mysticism have been but variations of the essential lines laid down by the received view. Indeed, with respect to contemporary debates in the academic study of mysticism, one can speak of a "psychoanalytic perennialism": varieties found in mystical texts reflect but religio-cultural overlays and variations of universal developmental phases.

However, the received view is at best misleading. Freud struggled with the problem of mysticism throughout his career, offering three models for varying mystical phenomena. The oceanic feeling, typically framed as a mystical "experience" was, in fact, an enduring mystical state. Rolland specifies it as such in his letters to Freud, stating that he felt it as a "constant state (like a sheet of water which I feel flushing under the bark)."[13] In turn, Freud understood it as such as well, for in summarizing the contents of Rolland's letter in the first chapter of *Civilization and Its Discontents* he describes Rolland's oceanic feeling as "a peculiar feeling, which he himself is never without."[14] This mystical phenomenon was not, then, an instance of the typical Jamesian transient mystical experience. Indeed, if one turns to Rolland's substantial oeuvre, one finds that he distinguished between mystical experience proper (which, in his own case at least, was phenomenologically similar to what R. C. Zaehner dubbed "nature" or "pan-en-henic" mystical experiences) and the later, more advanced, enduring, statelike oceanic feeling (which, without implying exact equivalence, is phenomenologically closer to the similarly more advanced and enduring mystical state Sri Ramana Maharshi refers to as *sahaj samadhi*).[15] Freud interpreted the enduring state of the oceanic feeling as the preservation of (and not regression to) the limitless ego feeling of the infant which, in some cases, is never extinguished but remains alongside the more narrowly demarcated adult ego.

Freud offered a different model for the mystical experience proper. At the end of the first chapter of *Civilization and Its Discontents*, Freud turned away from the statelike oceanic feeling to address the relation between mystical practices and episodic mystical experience. He refers to "another friend of mine" who had assured him that through the "practices of Yoga" and by "fixing the attention on bodily functions and by peculiar methods of breathing," one could evoke "sensations and coenaesthesias . . . which he regards as regressions to primordial states of mind."[16] Freud goes on to state: "It would not be hard to find connections here with a number of obscure modifications of mental life, such as trances and ecstasies." Significantly, instead of offering a full analysis of such phenomena, Freud simply exclaims: "But I am moved to exclaim in the words of Schiller's diver: 'Let him rejoice who breathes up here in the roseate light'!"[17]

Freud used the Schiller poem, as he had done in 1904, to compare mystical practices and the wisdom they unearthed, to that of psychoanalysis.[18] He reaffirms this in 1933 where one finds Freud employing a similar interpretative move. This becomes apparent when, at the end of Lecture 31 of his *New Introductory Lectures*, one looks at the imagery and linguistic construction of the "psychoanalytic motto" (namely, *Wo Es war, soll Ich werden*, or "where Id was, there Ego shall be"). In describing what it is that psychoanalytic therapy does, Freud clothes his remarks in typically poetic terms, speaking of rivers and oceans, of reclaiming land from the sea, and of Faust, Exodus and Genesis. Then, drawing an analogy between psychoanalysis and mystical intuition, Freud remarks that "certain mystical practices" could pierce the usual barriers between the Id and Ego, so that one could gain insight into "the depths of the ego and . . . the id which were otherwise inaccessible."[19] Casting doubt that "ultimate truths" and "salvation" could be had by such a route, he nevertheless went on to say: "it may be admitted that the therapeutic efforts of psychoanalysis have chosen a similar line of approach."[20]

Finally in 1938, in what can be called his "last" theory of mysticism, Freud ventures that mysticism is to be understood as "the obscure self-perception of the realm outside the ego, of the id."[21] The meaning of this becomes clear in his *Moses and Monotheism* where Freud states that the content of the "primordial layers" of the unconscious unearthed in religious ecstasy go beyond that of one's personal memories, developmental traumas and fixations and unique history. Rather, in coming alarmingly close to Jung, Freud states that what both motivates and is uncovered in religious ecstasy is the contents of the universal memory-traces which define the content of our phylogenetically transmitted "archaic heritage," the most recognizable of the latter being that of the "primal deed" (the repeated murder of the alpha ape-father).[22]

The lesson of the above amounts to more than a simple corrective to the received view. With respect to the psychoanalytic contribution to the comparative study of mysticism it asks of any psychoanalytically inclined researcher to make sure to delineate the exact characteristics of the mystical phenomena in question. Not all "mysticism" is the same: some phenomena may differ not simply in degree but in kind. The task of proper reconstruction, then, is vital to the subsequent task of deciding what psychoanalytic model is best suited to address the characteristics of the specific phenomena under consideration. This is no less true with respect to Augustine's teaching on vision. Once the latter is properly reconstructed and contextualized we can consider the adequacy of another set of psychoanalytic models which emerged from the Freud-Rolland correspondence: what I call the "transformative."[23]

RECONSTRUCTING THE TEXT: LITERARY PERSPECTIVES

Literary-critical methods have noted that Augustine's narrative is composed out of not only actual existential life-experiences but also elements taken from scripture, philosophy and literature. In contrast to Kligerman's claim that the *Confessions* can be read as revealing fantasies and free associative material, literary perspectives stress that Augustine was educated, as he himself says, to realize the cultural ideal of the "orator," to "become master of the spoken word . . . to learn the art of words, to acquire that eloquence that is essential to persuade men of your case, to unroll your opinions before them" (*Conf.* 1.16). What this means, as has been traditionally argued by Pierre Courcelle, Leo Ferrari and Robert McMahon and more recently with respect to the psychoanalytic literature on Augustine by Diane Jonte-Pace, Paul Elledge, Richard Fenn and Roger Johnson, is that Augustine's narrative in the *Confessions* must be taken for what it is: an intentional, constructed work of art which borrows heavily from literary sources.[24] In portraying his own self, Augustine undoubtedly utilized some of his own personal experiences. But in the last analysis the *Confessions* portrays a "fictionalized self, an allegorically and rhetorically constructed self, rather than a literal self."[25] Augustine used his own life experiences in conjunction with literary sources to construct an archetypal self which transcends his own biography, speaks to the universal human condition and functions as a religious, edifying discourse concerning the nature, limits and possibilities of human transformation. Augustine's teaching, his "theology," is found transmitted through a rhetorically crafted historical narrative. In rhetorically weaving his narrative, Augustine "makes the truth" and hence sublates the distinctions between autobiography, theology and history.[26] This perspective mitigates the attempt to isolate the "real," "historical" Augustine "behind" the text. It argues that psychology is better off engaging Augustine's narrative on its archetypical level, his "teaching" as it were. This does not wholly undercut or render useless the psychohistorical enterprise. The issue is how to engage the problems of the constructed subject and what is clearly the use of borrowed literary units in narrating a life history.

In the case of the vision at Ostia, we need to gain some insight into Augustine's rhetorical intent in including Monica. For Kligerman, as well as for many psychoanalysts and scholars of comparative mysticism, a dyadic mystical experience is very rare. It is easy, then, to see the inclusion of Monica and the language and imagery employed in the ascent as free-associative and symptomatic. While one cannot entirely rule out such a perspective, an analysis of the rhetorical structure of the text gives one pause to reconsider. Kligerman's reference to the inclusion of Monica and Augustine's description of the event ("he tells how they leaned together in a window overlooking the garden 'discoursing together, alone, very sweetly' what the eternal life would be like") has a specific meaning for Augustine: it denotes how a Christian mystical vision is different from a philosophic (i.e., Neo-Platonic) one. Augustine's and Monica's communion with God at Ostia emphasizes that the beatific vision is both specifically Christian and invariably social. As McGinn points out, Augustine's reference to the window overlooking the garden is a reference to the church: the garden would have been a "walled" (enclosed) one. Since Augustine linked the church with the "enclosed garden" of Song of Songs, it seems reasonable to conclude that Augustine's rhetorical inclusion of a "walled garden" was meant to emphasize the role of the church in the mystical ascent to God. [27]

This line of reasoning is given further sophistication when it is noted that Monica takes an active role in the ascent upwards. That is, Monica and Augustine were engaged in conversation—conversation which led them to eventually "touch" the One. Certainly the notion of not only a *communal* ascent but also one in which an *unlearned woman* is taking an active part would have been foreign to Plotinus. [28] Indeed, in the Dialogues written at Cassiciacum (*De ordine*; *De beata vita*) Monica is portrayed as actively engaging in religious discussions. In *De ordine* Augustine goes so far as to portray himself as Monica's disciple, exclaiming that her thoughts are so profound that he forgot her gender, thinking that "we had some great man in our midst"! Most significantly, in *De beata vita* Monica is framed as having the key to philosophy not so much because she was learned (rather, she was relatively unsophisticated with respect to knowledge about philosophy) but because she was completely devoted to God. Faith, hope and charity are the theological virtues that lead to happiness—happiness which in its fullest sense is reserved for those in the afterlife. In contrast to the Plotinian stress on the learned, intellectual life, then, Monica is presented as one who is capable of coming to the deepest truths of wisdom by reliance on faith in and study of scripture. [29] In sum, one can discern in these Dialogues two models of spirituality: the elite, learned, male, and philosophically sophisticated way of Plotinus and the humble, devotional way of Monica and the common Christian. As Kim Power notes, it is in the vision at Ostia that the two are both present and reconciled:

> By the time he wrote the *Confessiones*, Augustine had resolved his conflict between philosophy and faith, coming to the conclusion that the life of faith

and the experience of God could illuminate the mind as brightly as philosophy. Monica is the exemplar of the faith route to God, as Augustine is of the philosophic. The Ostia vision is irrefutable proof of the resolution of his conflict. . . . This experience of joint ecstasy erases all distance between mother and son . . . the fact that Monica and Augustine shared the same joy suggest he is intending to convey a Christian rather than philosophic vision.[30]

This makes a certain amount of sense for, in his capacity as the bishop of Hippo when he wrote his *Confessions*, Augustine would want to stress the communal, christocentric and ecclesiastical dimensions of mysticism. By stressing the role of a relatively unlearned but wholly devoted woman in the communal ascent upwards, Augustine accomplished his aim in a sophisticated, rhetorically elegant and edifying manner.

RECONSTRUCTING THE TEXT: THEOLOGICAL PERSPECTIVES

Augustine's views on vision extend beyond the confines of the seemingly autobiographical texts of the *Confessions* to multiple texts of the next two decades of his life. While the more intricate details offered in these texts are beyond the province of this essay, certain notable teachings are of import for the purpose at hand. First, we can focus simply on the actual language Augustine used. Orthodox psychoanalytic interpretations of Augustine's mysticism depend on the language of union, the presence of the Mother, and the concepts of regression, Oedipus and primary narcissism. But it is of import that in Augustine's description of the ascent and "experience" of the Divine the term "union" is not found. Indeed, as McGinn notes, the category of "union," often seen as being the essence and goal of Christian mysticism, is not found in many Christian texts:

> The essential note—or, better, goal—of mysticism may be conceived of as a particular kind of encounter between God and the human . . . This goal, essential characteristic, or defining note has most often been seen as the experience of some form of union with God, particularly a union of absorption or identity in which the individual personality is lost. If we define mysticism in this sense, there are actually so few mystics in the history of Christianity that one wonders why Christians use the qualifier "mystical" so often . . . it may also be argued that union with God is not the most central category for understanding mysticism . . . I have come to find the term "presence" a more central and more useful category for grasping the unifying note in the varieties of Christian mysticism.[31]

McGinn notes that the lack of the language of union is particularly true of Augustine, who was perfectly aware of such terminology and its use in Greek texts (notably the language linked to *henosis*).[32] But, contra Plotinus, Augustine's Christian teaching valorized the difference between God and the soul, as well as the need for God's grace in elevating the soul to the vision of its creator.[33]

McGinn goes on to observe that while Augustine thought the direct experience of God was possible in this life, he also believed that such an event was indescribable. In other words, for Augustine God is, in His essence, essentially unknowable: there is an apophatic dimension to Augustine's mysticism. On the other hand, Augustine does make use of a variety of images, terms, and metaphors to point to (but not definitively capture) the nature of the *visio Dei*. Many of these are taken from the language of the senses (seeing, hearing, tactile sensations like touching, tasting, etc.). This "form of synaesthia" and smorgasbord of images were thus "strategies meant to suggest and not to circumscribe the inexpressible."[34] These "mystical senses," moreover, are operative in the ascent narratives found in the *Confessions* where not "union" but "touching" God is favored.[35] As Augustine recounts in his ascent at Ostia: "and while we were thus talking . . . with all the effort of our heart did we for one instant attain to touch it" (*Conf.* 9.10). An orthodox psychoanalytic perspective may counter that such linguistic technicalities do not trump the standard regressive thesis and the presence of the Mother. Indeed, as is the case with many post-Freudian analyses, the issue simply becomes one of "degrees" of regression. Nevertheless, these "linguistic technicalities," alongside the evidence from literary perspectives we have adduced, make it increasingly difficult to subscribe wholesale to the orthodox view.

Augustine's teaching on what makes this "touching" possible, namely, the state of ecstasy, brings home a more forceful point vis-à-vis psychoanalysis. This teaching can be made accessible to those socialized into the "language" of the therapeutic understanding of the nature of the self in the following way. We know that Augustine's ascent was in some sense a descent into the wells of consciousness. We also know that his inward search for God led him to the field of *memoria* and to reflections on the will where he elaborates on psychological phenomena that many think prefigured later formulations of various psychological systems (e.g., the "stomach" of the mind, the divided will and chain of habit, the darkness and opaqueness of desire, the vicissitudes of desires in dreams[36]). But we also know that in his ascent he was led not only deep within himself but also above the summit of his soul, there to see the light of the Divine. Augustine laid down specific details of this encounter of "touching" and knowing. For example, the latter is made possible by the fact that one is literally rapt out of the body. As Andrew Louth notes, Augustine's ascent narratives are commensurate with his later, more detailed definition of ecstasy, which is as follows: "the attention of the mind is wholly turned away and withdrawn . . . from the bodily senses . . . then whatever bodies may be present are not seen with the open eyes, nor any voices heard at all . . . this ecstasy is sudden and fleeting, and draws out the whole force of the soul."[37] In other words, at the apex of his ascents in the *Confessions* Augustine touches and knows God by dint of an altered state (theologically rendered as due to grace and God's love) framed as an instant of ecstasy and rapture. The movement, as McGinn notes, is both *enstatic* and *ecstatic*: "Augustine taught that 'to go within is to go above,' that is, the 'enstatic' movement into the soul's ground would lead to a discovery of the God within who is infinitely more than the soul, and hence to an 'ecstatic' movement beyond the self—*Intus Deus altus est*, 'The God within is the God above.'"[38] Furthermore, and importantly, Augustine taught that in being raptured out of the self and in accessing this ecstatic level of vision one must, at least for the duration of vision, be in a state of virtual death (Augustine cites scripture in this regard, namely, Exodus 33:12ff where it is stated that no one can see God's face and live). It is only by dint of this partial (but not total) removal to the next life that this vision of the light takes place.[39]

At this apex level of the ascent there is, of course, a radical departure from traditionally understood psychoanalytic understandings of the self. One dives not merely into the depths of memory but "deeper than the deepest recesses of the soul" and indeed "above the soul" where, with the "eye" of the soul, one perceives the divine light. To better understand the noetic dimension apparent in this "touching" of God we must go to several of Augustine's later texts, notably his Letter #147 to Paulina, Sermon 52, his Homilies on the Psalms, Homilies on the Gospel of John, and Book 12 of his *Literal Meaning of Genesis* (in which he analyzes St. Paul's ascent to the third heaven and Paradise in 2 Corinthians 12:2-4). These texts make clear his teaching on the conditions and nature of this vision. Briefly summarized, in these texts Augustine develops his famous threefold typology of vision: 1) corporeal (or bodily); 2) spiritual (or imaginative); and 3) intellectual. The three are related in a hierarchical fashion (as Augustine puts it "spiritual vision is more excellent than corporeal, and intellectual vision is more excellent than spiritual"[40]), and only in intellectual vision is there "no deception."[41] In corporeal visions one has the "vision" of external objects given to us by the senses. It is called corporeal "because it is perceived through the body and presented to the senses of the body."[42] Spiritual or imaginative visions, on the other hand, are those referring to an imaginative recollection or imprint (as in a dream): "the image of an absent body."[43] It thus refers to the imagination, and to corporeal images in the mind. However, in intellectual visions the knowledge gleaned is completely divorced from the elements of bodily sensations and imaginative visions. Intellectual visions are of two kinds. The first pertains to incorporeal religious truths, e.g., the virtues ("charity, joy, peace, longanimity, kindness, goodness, faith, meekness, continency"[44]) that are not linked to sensation and physical objects but are "known" insofar as they are illuminated by the divine light. In the second kind one sees the Light itself: "the brightness of the Lord is seen, not through a symbolic or corporeal vision . . . but through a direct vision . . . In such a vision God speaks face to face to him whom he has made worthy of this communion."[45] In distinguishing between the two kinds of intellectual visions Augustine once again utilizes language reminiscent of the ascents in the *Confessions*:

> But distinct from these objects (of the first type of intellectual visions) is the light by which the soul is illumined, in order that it may see and truly understand everything, either in itself or in the light. For the light is God Himself . . . and when (the soul) tries to behold the Light, it trembles in its weakness and finds itself unable to do so. Yet from this source comes all the understanding it is able to attain. When, therefore, it is thus carried off and, after being withdrawn from the senses of the body, is made present to this vision in a more perfect manner . . . it also sees above itself that Light.[46]

This kind of intellectual vision, as one might surmise, is the highest vision granted to humans. Again recalling the *Confessions*, Augustine states that such a vision is necessarily brief (due to sin). In the brief, ecstatic experiences of God one is raptured out of the self and its usual mode of knowing. An intellectual vision of the light and substance of God, then, is much closer to an angelic mode of knowing. Theologically rendered, one needs the help of God to be lifted up to see this light, and, in so doing, one is removed from "normal" modes of corporeal sensing and knowing.

This description of what constitutes an intellectual vision underscores its philosophically problematic nature. In the case of Augustine the Light, framed as being the ground of reason and understanding, is not bound by space and time and is of a different ontological substance. The encounter with God is perhaps, as Kenney suggests, one of "direct acquaintance."[47] All this should not, however, serve to deny that Augustine had some very definite views on the conditions and possibility, however philosophically problematic they may be, of intellectual visions.

The question remains as to who is capable of accessing this level of vision. Augustine holds that such a vision was attained by at least Moses and Paul (and one can assume others[48]) and while he does not list himself as a beneficiary of this highest of visions, it is evident that his reflections are autobiographical. Certainly much of what he says is commensurate with the ascent narratives of the *Confessions*. Nevertheless, it should be noted that while there is general consensus that Augustine experienced "something" at Milan and Ostia, theological debates have accrued over whether what Augustine experienced was the "highest" intellectual vision of God's substance.[49] While many do think that he was so graced, the end of the debate, as may be predicted by its status as being already over a century old, does not appear to be in sight. This essay sides with those who favor Augustine's accessing of the highest level of intellectual vision. Nevertheless, such an opinion is not a necessary condition of our argument. What is beyond dispute is what Augustine's teachings were, and it is this avenue of thought that will pay dividends as we use the transformational psychoanalytic approach in our attempt to restructure psychoanalytic analyses of Augustine's visions.

ONCE AGAIN: ON PSYCHOANALYSIS AND SEEING THE LIGHT

As noted earlier the "transformational" is a third psychoanalytic approach to mysticism, which has developed alongside the classic and the adaptive and which is open to the notion that mystical experiences access the "More." Such an approach, which banks off and extends Freud's cursory reflections on how mystical practices and ecstasies access deep regions of the unconscious, points to the possibility that archaic, mystical levels of consciousness cannot be explained solely with respect to developmental phases or labeled with the pejorative overtones of concepts like regression and defensiveness. Examples would be Erikson's reference to the "unborn core of creation"—a phrase indebted to Angelus Silesius and elaborated in Erikson's later work in terms of the numinosity of the "I"; Bion's concept of "O", understood as the ideal aim of the therapeutic encounter, and framed as "the absolute truth, the godhead, the infinite, the thing-in-itself"; and Lacan's notions of jouissance and the Real.[50] With respect to Augustine, Dixon utilizes this approach when she notes that the noetic element which one finds in the vision (where Augustine and Monica "extended their reach and in a flash of mental energy attained the eternal wisdom that abides beyond all things") "sounds like an evocation of what Kohut called 'cosmic narcissism.'"[51] The latter, states Kohut, is a "transformation of narcissism" which goes well beyond the confines of the analytic session, evincing a mature engagement with the inevitable existential fact of death.

While acknowledging that these approaches are advances on those employed by the classic and adaptive schools, the contribution of this essay is to sketch out how transformational psychoanalytic models might integrate the insights of cognitive neuroscience. We can begin by calling attention to what, paralleling Augustine's ascent narratives, can be called a "psychoanalytic ascent motif." In his monograph *Group Psychology and the Analysis of the Ego* Freud, drawing once again on great thinkers of the Western past, and in rebuttal of those who sought to dismiss his views of sexuality as narrow and reductive, unpacked what he referred to as "the wider sense" of his use of the term "Eros." This passage is significant for not only does it demonstrate the psychoanalytic ascent motif but does so in a way that recalls figures who influenced Augustine:

> Libido is an expression taken from the theory of the emotions. . . . We call by
> that name the energy . . . of those instincts which have to do with all that may
> be comprised under the word "love." The nucleus of what we mean by love
> naturally consists . . . in sexual love. . . . But we do not separate from this . . .
> on the one hand, self-love, and on the other, love for parents and children,
> friendship and love for humanity in general, and also devotion to concrete
> objects and to abstract ideas. Our justification lies in the fact that psycho-
> analytic research has taught us that all these tendencies are an expression of
> the same instinctual impulses. . . . We are of the opinion, then, that language
> has carried out an entirely justifiable piece of unification in creating the word
> "love" with its numerous uses. . . . By coming to this decision, psycho-analysis
> has let loose a storm of indignation. . . . Yet it has done nothing original in
> taking love in this "wider" sense. In its origin, function and relation to sexual
> love, the "Eros" of the philosopher Plato coincides exactly with the love-force,
> the libido of psychoanalysis . . . and when the apostle Paul, in his famous
> epistle to the Corinthians, praises love above all else, he certainly understands
> it in the same "wider sense." But this only shows that men do not always take
> their great thinkers seriously, even when they profess most to admire them. [52]

We have seen that both Plato (through Plotinus) and Paul had a definitive impact on Augustine's teaching on mystical ascents. Not simply in the above passage but throughout his works it is clear that Freud was also influenced by Plato. For example, relying on Plato's *Phaedrus*, he was fond of likening his structural model of the mind in works like *The Ego and the Id* to a chariot: the rider (*das Ich*; translated in English as the "ego") was always at pains to control the noble (*das Uber-Ich*; English, "superego") and ignoble (*das Es*; "id") horses. And one hears echoes of the fundamental tenets of Plato's philosophy and its theory of anamnesis in psychoanalytic therapy (e.g., the end [self-knowledge], the means [asking questions], the assumptions [the answers are within] and the form [dialogue]). If, in following the work of James Tabor, we can say that Augustine creatively misread Paul, being ig-norant of the context within which the ascent of 2 Corinthians was penned and instead (mis)reading Paul in light of a Christian Neo-Platonism, then surely Freud can be similarly cast as reframing both Plato and Paul as intui-tive forerunners of psychoanalysis. [53]

Along these lines, as intimated above, psychoanalytic scholars would point out that the "psychoanalytic ascent motif" is dependent on sublimation. The latter becomes the lever for redirecting sexual love to "higher aims" like the love of abstract ideas. One could go on to observe that what limits Freud's ascent upwards is the chain which tied sublimation to the downward pull of the instincts. In Freud one has the psychoanalytic equivalent of the doctrine so integral to the thought of Augustine: that of original sin. Unlike Plato, Freud's steeds were neither winged nor capable of flight to the "Sea of Beauty." With regard to the reach of love upwards, and the ability of the mind to pierce the darkness below, Freud's theory is limited in comparison with Plato and Augustine. Indeed, Freud's psychology was oriented towards the this-worldly concerns of alleviating neurotic suffering, facilitating adaptation to social reality and increasing the capacity for *lieben und arbeiten* (love and work). Nevertheless, it is interesting that in all this he did find an intellectual space for theorizing about mystical intuition. And it is here that a "transformational" psychoanalytic approach could further Freud's more cursory reflections on ascent.

A transformational model that "fits" the case of Augustine lies in the work of Arthur Deikman. Utilizing empirical data concerning subjects in contemplative meditation, the textual evidence of mystics from multiple traditions and, in adopting the formulations of psychoanalytic ego psychology (specifically the concept of deautomatization as initially coined by Hartmann and elaborated by Gill and Brenman to account for the undoing of ego functions during hypnosis), Deikman came to theorize anew about the nature of the altered state induced by prayer and meditation. Deikman's use of deautomatization holds that as human development proceeds our perceptual, motor and behavioral systems undergo a slow process of automatization until they operate on a "second-nature" or "automatic" level. For example, seemingly unconscious or preconscious phenomena like perceptual focusing or audio processing, infant and childhood tasks like walking and talking, or learned routines like tying one's shoes and driving are all functions that, while once requiring attentional energy and concentration, are considered at the adult level to be routine. As one matures, one invests less intentional energy on such functions, allowing for the allocation of energy saved to new and more complex tasks like abstract reasoning. So in first learning to drive an automobile one's attention is entirely devoted to steering; later one can engage in abstract problem solving to the extent that miles on the highway have passed without notice.

A potential drawback of the process of automatization, according to Deikman, is that certain archaic modes of perceiving and relating may be left in a nascent state or even abandoned in favor of an environmental and socialization process that favors, if not demands, the cultivation of cognitive modes of operation which actively engage the sense-world. Such "archaic modes" of cognition, thinks Deikman, are awakened as a result of mystical practices. Thus it is that with respect to mystical experiences Deikman, in going beyond Freud's reflections on what we earlier referred to as the "psychoanalytic motto," says the following:

> Such experiences are the result of the operation of a new perceptual capacity response to the dimensions of the stimulus array previously ignored or blocked from awareness. For such mystics, renunciation has weakened and temporarily removed the ordinary objects of consciousness as a focus of awareness. Contemplative meditation has undone the logical organization of consciousness.

At the same time, the mystic is intensely motivated to perceive something. If undeveloped or unutilized perceptual capacities do exist, it seems likely that they would be mobilized and come into operation under such conditions. [54]

Deikman's "ascent motif," then, proceeds as follows: detachment and removal of ties to the sense world, a return inwards and contemplation (which leads to deautomatization, a prominent feature of which is the silencing of thoughts) and the opening and cultivation of new modes of knowledge—modes which become operative in part because the mystic is intensely motivated.

Deikman's theorizing, much of which engaged not simply ego-psychology but also the emerging empirical studies of brain hemispheric functioning in the 1960s, is similarly commensurate with contemporary advances in neuro-cognitive research. For example, recent studies of the psychophysiology of mystical experience agree that contemplative practices produce discernable shifts in the neurological ground of ordinary conscious awareness. [55] James Austin's study of Zen, in part based on his own mystical experience of timelessness and eternity in which the "insinuations of selfhood" vanished, agrees with Deikman that contemplative activity functions "to desynchronize habitual states of consciousness and open the brain-mind system up to the creation of new modes of awareness." [56]

Going further, of particular import along these lines is Augustine's teaching concerning the psycho-physiological conditions of the highest form of intellectual visions. Augustine taught that vision required not only a turn inwards and the gradual silencing of all images but a distinct physiological condition: that of virtual death. This leads one to consider the contributions of brain science research concerning near-death experiences (NDEs). While Raymond Moody's initial attempt at establishing "core" characteristics of virtual death experiences has been challenged through the past three decades, giving rise to an ever-changing laundry list of what qualifies as an NDE, one constant is the characteristic experience of a divine Light. [57] In pairing virtual death with the presence of the light Augustine was hardly alone, as there is now a substantial comparative literature correlating the physiological condition of near-death with mystic vision. [58] In this regard it is intriguing, given Augustine's interpretative gloss on St. Paul's heavenly journey, that Paul Badham (without any indication of knowing of Augustine's interpretation of the Pauline text) also sees 2 Corinthians 12 as indicative of someone who had a physiological condition of virtual death and, as such, experienced something at least analogous to contemporary NDEs. [59]

We can conclude with two important qualifications. First, as with the changing laundry lists of the characteristics of NDEs, multiple theories, leading to numerous debates, have been offered as explanations, ranging from the effects of hypoxia/hypercarbia (too little oxygen/too much carbon dioxide), ketamine (anesthetic), and endorphins (naturally occurring "pleasure" chemicals in the brain) to the role of states of depersonalization/derealization, limbic lobe stimulation and dying-brain syndrome to studies on the effect of virtual death on the brain's visual cortex, on nervous system functioning and on hallucinatory activity.[60] Certainly the general tenor of such studies tends to champion how NDEs can be accounted for by naturalistic causes. Yet one cannot, as famously argued by Carol Zaleski, entirely rule out other causes, even those of a religious kind. Indeed as Zaleski puts it, the plethora of explanations and counter-explanations is by now so expansive and contested that it is reasonable to conclude "that the final outcome will be a draw."[61] Indeed, there may be many conditions—religious, physiological, psychological—which are complicit in the production of an NDE. Secondly, research on NDEs do not necessarily buttress the claims of perennialism. As Zaleski, mirroring contemporary debates over the constructed nature of mysticism, notes:

> We cannot simply peel away the literary wrapper and put our hands on an unembellished event. Even when a vision actually did occur, it is likely to have been reworked many times before being recorded. The vision is a collaborative effort . . . one cannot point to the moment when the vision changed from a matter of personal confession into a public project; rather, it is built up in layers placed over one another like a series of transparencies . . . even the hypothetical bottom layer—the visionary's own experience—has a collective aspect . . . His very experience of the other world is shaped by expectations, both conscious and subliminal, that he shares with his peers, and he draws upon a common treasury of images from scripture, folklore or literary tradition, and religious art.[62]

This conclusion is supported by Kelly Bulkeley's recent reflections on mysticism and neurocognitive research.[63] In other words a constructivist take on the NDE literature must, as with its decidedly Kantian stance vis-à-vis the noumenon, simply bracket such deep encounters with the "More" as both inaccessible to empirical confirmation *and* philosophically problematic. Any claim to seeing a divine light, as with Augustine, is not necessarily indicative of a common core of all mystical experiences. It must be taken as but one part of what recent theological studies, in adopting a constructivist stance and refusing to isolate Augustine's episodic visions from their rootage in a total religious matrix, have framed as Augustine's "mystical theology." The psychoanalytic counterpoint to the constructivist emphasis on Augustine's mystical theology lies in understanding the latter as an instance, in again following Rizzuto, of his evolving "God-representation."[64]

The final matter is the extent to which the analysis offered here is portable. If one accepts the notion that the term "mysticism" designates not a single religious phenomena but multiple ones, linked by certain family resemblances but differing in degree and perhaps in kind, then certainly one could not state, a priori, that any "case" one might seek to interpret would necessarily fall along the lines suggested here. In any event, the simple recourse to understanding all mysticism as composed of "oceanic feelings" and interpreting them as regressions to primary narcissism is gone—hopefully forever. What is more portable, I think, is for those employing psychoanalytic methodology to acknowledge the need for a truly interdisciplinary approach, an example of which is employed in this essay, when confronted with mystical phenomena. We need to accrue many, many more cases, each understood in its own unique context, before we can start making any broad assertions about the nature and meaning of mysticism.

NOTES

1. Two good places to start would be: 1) Donald Capps and James Dittes (eds.), *The Hunger of the Heart: Reflections on the* Confessions *of Augustine* (West Lafayette, IN: Society for the Scientific Study of Religion Monograph Series #8, 1990), which reprints dozens of essays with summaries of dozens more; and 2) Sandra Lee Dixon, *Augustine: The Scattered and Gathered Self.* (St. Louis, MO: Chalice Press, 1999), the most interdisciplinary psychoanalytic study to date. Both books also contain extensive bibliographic references which, put together, comprise the most important psychological analyses of Augustine over the last century. My own contribution to this literature lies in two previous essays: "St. Augustine: 'Common-man' or 'Intuitive Psychologist'?" (*Journal of Psychohistory*, 1990, 18[2] 155–179) and "Psychoanalysis and Mysticism: The Case of St. Augustine" (in Jacob Belzen and Antoon Geels, eds., *Mysticism: A Variety of Psychological Perspectives* [Amsterdam: Rodopi, 2003], pp. 151–178). The present article is meant to be a companion piece to both of these previous essays. Some of the formulations and wording in the present article appeared in my "Psychoanalysis and Mysticism: The Case of St. Augustine," and my thanks to Rodopi Press for permission to cite from that article. The difference between the latter article and the present one lies in my elaboration of the specifics of Augustine's teaching on mysticism and the extension of my methodological focus to include the literature on brain science and near-death studies.

2. Robert Fuller, *Spiritual but not Religious* (New York: Oxford, 2001).

3. As cited above in note 1. The three essays can be read chronologically as indicating the progression of my thinking on how to build bridges between psychoanalysis and the mysticism of Augustine.

4. See Charles Kligerman, "A Psychoanalytic study of the *Confessions* of St. Augustine," in *Hunger of the Heart*, p. 107.

5. See Phillip Woollcott, "Some Considerations of Creativity and Religious Experience in St. Augustine of Hippo," in *Journal for the Scientific Study of Religion*, 1966 (5) 273–283; Donald Capps, "Augustine as Narcissist: Of Grandiosity and Shame," in *Hunger of the Heart*, pp. 172–184; Paul W. Pruyser, "Augustine: Psychoanalytic Examination," in *Hunger of the Heart*, pp. 32–38.

6. See Dittes, "Continuities between the Life and Thought of Augustine," in *Hunger of the Heart.*

7. See Dittes, "Continuities Between the Life and Thought of Augustine," in *Hunger of the Heart*, p. 122.

8. William Beers, "The Confessions of Augustine: Narcissistic Elements," in *American Imago*, 45: 1 (Spring 1988) 107.

9. See James Dittes, "Augustine: Search for a Fail-Safe God to Trust," in *Hunger of the Heart*, p. 259. W. Paul Elledge, "Embracing Augustine: Reach, Restraint and Romantic Reso-

lution in the Confessions," in *Hunger of the Heart*, pp. 265–288, similarly sees issues of basic trust in Augustine's mysticism.

10. See Volney Gay, "Augustine: The Reader as Self-Object," in *Hunger of the Heart*, pp. 200–201.

11. As I have done in my earlier article, "Augustine: 'Common-Man' or 'Intuitive Psychologist'?"

12. For this correspondence as well as the history of the classic and adaptive schools, see my *The Enigma of the Oceanic Feeling* (New York: Oxford, 1999).

13. See Parsons, *The Enigma of the Oceanic Feeling*, pp. 36–37.

14. Freud, *Civilization and Its Discontents*, p. 11.

15. See Parsons, *The Enigma of the Oceanic Feeling*, chapter 5.

16. Freud, *Civilization and Its Discontents*, p. 19.

17. Ibid., p. 20. Friedrich Schiller, "Der Taucher" ("The Diver").

18. See Parsons, *The Enigma of the Oceanic Feeling*, pp. 44ff.

19. Ibid., p. 79.

20. Ibid.

21. See Freud, *Moses and Monotheism*, in *Standard Edition*, vol. 23: 300.

22. Ibid., pp. 133ff. I have elaborated on this at length in a presently unpublished article under editorial consideration entitled, "Freud's Last Theory of Mysticism: The Return of the (phylogenic) Repressed."

23. See Parsons, *The Enigma of the Oceanic Feeling*, esp. chapter 6.

24. See Pierre Courcelle, *Recherches sur les 'Confessions' de S. Augustin* (Paris: Éditions de Boccard, 1968); Robert McMahon, *Augustine's Prayerful Ascent: An Essay on the Literary Form of the* Confessions (Athens, GA: The University of Georgia Press, 1990); Diane Jonte-Pace, "Augustine on the Couch: Psychohistorical (Mis)readings of the *Confessions*" *Religion* 23 (1993) 71–83; Leo C. Ferrari, "Paul at the Conversion of Augustine," *Augustinian Studies* 11 (1980) 5–20; Roger Johnson, "Comments on *Hunger of the Heart: Reflections on the* Confessions *of Augustine*" (unpublished manuscript; paper delivered at AAR national meeting, Chicago, 1990); and the articles by Paul W. Elledge, "Embracing Augustine"; and Richard Fenn, "Magic in Language and Ritual: Notes on the *Confessions* of Augustine," *Journal for the Scientific Study of Religion* 25:1 (March 1986) 77–91.

25. See Jonte-Pace, "Augustine on the Couch," p. 72.

26. For my use of the term "makes the truth" see John Cavadini's review of James J. O'Donnell's work on the *Confessions* ("Making Truth: A New Commentary on Augustine's *Confessions*" *Religious Studies Review* 21: 4 [1995] 291–298).

27. Bernard McGinn, *The Foundations of Mysticism*, pp. 234–235.

28. See John Peter Kenney, *The Mysticism of Saint Augustine*, chapter 8.

29. See Paul Henry, *The Path to Transcendence: From Philosophy to Mysticism in Saint Augustine* (Pittsburgh, PA: Pickwick Press, 1981), chapter 5.

30. See Kim Power, *Veiled Desire*, pp. 88–89.

31. McGinn, *The Foundations of Mysticism*, pp. xvi–xvii.

32. Ibid., p. 242.

33. Ibid., see chapter 7.

34. Ibid., p. 253.

35. Ibid. See pp. 237, 253, 255.

36. I have made this point in my "Augustine: 'Common-man' or 'Intuitive Psychologist'?"

37. Andrew Louth, *The Origins of the Christian Mystical Tradition: from Plato to Plotinus* (London: Oxford University Press, 1981) p. 137.

38. McGinn, *Foundations of Mysticism*, p. 242.

39. J. P. Kenney has made this point forcefully in his *The Mysticism of Saint Augustine* (New York: Routledge, 2005) pp. 130–136.

40. Augustine, *Literal Meaning of Genesis*, 12.24.53.

41. Ibid., 12.14.29.

42. Ibid., 12.7.16.

43. Ibid.

44. Ibid., 12.24.50; emphasis omitted.

45. Ibid., 12.26.54.

46. Ibid., 12.31.59.

47. See Kenney, *The Mysticism of St. Augustine*, p. 143.

48. See McGinn, *The Foundations of Mysticism,* chapter 7.

49. The debate was initiated, as André Mandouze has ably catalogued, as early as 1863. See McGinn, *The Foundations of Mysticism*, pp. 230ff. I have been unable to find any sustained engagement with this ongoing debate in the psychoanalytic literature on Augustine. Abbot E. Cuthbert Butler, in his classic *Western Mysticism* (New York: Dutton, 1923), was perhaps the most strident in his view that Augustine had experienced the highest form of intellectual vision.

50. See Parsons, *The Enigma of the Oceanic Feeling*, pp. 134ff.

51. See Dixon, *Augustine: The Scattered and Gathered Self*, p. 159.

52. Sigmund Freud, *Group Psychology and the Analysis of the Ego*, pp. 22–23.

53. See James Tabor, *Things Unutterable: Paul's Ascent to Paradise in Its Graeco-Roman, Judaic and Early Christian Context* (Lanham, MD: University Press of America, 1986). Tabor reads the ascent of Paul to the 3rd heaven and Paradise as making sense within the Jewish mystical milieu of his time (Merkavah mysticism). Paradise, in this reading, refers to the 7th heaven of the Jewish Merkavah cosmology.

54. Arthur Deikman, "Deautomatization and the Mystic Experience," in *Understanding Mysticism*, ed. R. Woods (Garden City, NY: Image Books, 1980), p. 258.

55. See Kelly Bulkeley, *The Wondering Brain* (New York: Routledge, 2005), chapter 4.

56. Ibid., pp. 155, 157.

57. See Mark Fox, *Religion, Spirituality and the Near-Death Experience* (London and New York: Routledge, 2003).

58. Ibid.

59. See Paul Badham, "Religious and Near-Death Experience in Relation to Belief in a Future Life," *Mortality* 2:1 (March 1997) 11–12.

60. See Fox, *Religion, Spirituality and the Near-Death Experience*.

61. Carol Zaleski, *Otherworld Journeys* (New York: Oxford, 1987), p. 180.

62. Ibid., p. 86.

63. Bulkeley, *The Wondering Brain: Thinking about Religion with and beyond Cognitive Neuroscience* (New York: Routledge, 2005), chapter 4.

64. As I have argued in my previous two essays on Augustine (see note 1 above).

Chapter Eleven

Augustine's Extraordinary Theory of Memory

Raymond J. Shaw

INTRODUCTION

Through reflection, an insightful mind can deduce many of the characteristics of memory. It is clear that we forget, that some incidents in our childhood stand out more than others, and that remembering often brings with it vivid images related to our past. Nobody would dispute that Augustine had an insightful mind, and he applied that mind to the understanding of memory—most clearly, of course, in Book 10 of *The Confessions*.[1] His writings on memory could be described as a theory of memory that he developed through introspective reflection. When compared to the understanding of memory that has been developed through decades of extensive experimentation in modern psychology,[2] Augustine's theory is extraordinary. Much of what Augustine says about memory meshes well with contemporary theorizing about cognition. So this chapter begins with a description of Augustine's theory, in relation to contemporary work, focusing on different kinds of memory that he clearly identified and discriminated. Augustine also either explicitly described several interesting memory phenomena or writes about memory in a way that shows an awareness of them.

In evaluating Augustine's theory in light of contemporary theories, all three logical possibilities are present: Augustine shares some ideas with contemporary thought, Augustine missed some important aspects of memory as we understand it today, and Augustine's writings contain some noteworthy ideas we do not have in current theory. Much of what is different between Augustine's theory and those of contemporary cognitive psychologists is the result of differences in method. Conscious awareness of memory is a poor basis for judging how memory works (cf. Tulving, "Episodic memory," 1505). Indeed, some theorists have utilized the metaphor of an iceberg (e.g., Masson & Graf, 8) to express the idea that what we are consciously aware of is dwarfed by what we are not aware of. Augustine's theory of memory is therefore limited by his method of introspective reflection on his own awareness, and what he missed is a consequence of those limits. However, there are also some aspects of his understanding of memory that we have missed. Most notable in that latter category are some thoughts about memory for emotional experiences. While there is much excellent research on emotion and memory, the approach taken today is driven by different concerns than Augustine's questions about it. A second topic we have missed was of brief interest in contemporary psychology—research on the method of loci. Implicit in Augustine's description of memory is a reliance on the metaphors relevant to a method of memorization that was a common tool of rhetoric in his time.

Finally, in examining Augustine's understanding of memory with a modern eye, several possibilities for new research using modern methods arises, and the chapter ends with a brief outline of such ideas.

AUGUSTINE'S THEORY OF MEMORY

Contemporary memory researchers have made a veritable industry of splitting memory into different kinds. One critical distinction between kinds is between short-term and long-term memory. Different theorists describe that distinction in a variety of ways, but in brief, one can think of short-term memory as what one is currently thinking about, and long-term memory as what one remembers but is not thinking about at the moment. That distinction is generally agreed upon by contemporary memory theorists, but a variety of names appears in the psychological literature for the distinction: primary and secondary (James, 646–648; Waugh & Norman, 89); short-term and long-term (Atkinson & Shiffrin); and working memory / working attention instead of short-term memory (Baddeley & Hitch, 47–89; Baddeley, 152). Within long-term memory, however, there are additional distinctions between kinds, and there is not as much agreement. Augustine's writing in *Confessions* and in *The Trinity* more or less assumes a version of the primary versus secondary memory sort, and he writes in detail about three kinds of long-term memory.

Primary Versus Secondary Memory

In *Confessions*, Augustine certainly characterizes memories as either being present in his mind or stored away until they are needed, consistent with the notions of primary and secondary memory (Waugh & Norman, 69). For example, he writes, "there are remembered items that come to hand easily and in ordered sequence as soon as they are summoned, the earlier members giving way to those that follow and returning to their storage-places, ready to be retrieved next time I need them" (*Conf.* 10.8.12); and "the huge repository of the memory . . . welcomes and keeps all these things, to be recalled and brought out for use when needed" (*Conf.* 10.8.13). In describing how he recalls memory for sensations, he says, "I am simply passing them in review before my mind by remembering them" (*Conf.* 10.8.13). In *The Trinity*, at first Augustine seems to back off of the idea of these two aspects of memory: "For memory is of things past, not of things present. Some writers upon the virtues, including Cicero, have analysed prudence into the three elements of memory, understanding and foresight, assigning memory to what is past, understanding to what is present, and foresight to what is future" (*de Trin.* 14.14). However, calling one aspect memory and another understanding, along with a third, foresight, appears to be a rhetorical act in service of arguing for a trinitarian mind, which is his larger point in the context of *The Trinity*. There is an echo of considering present consciousness as something other than truly memory in modern times as well, however. In describing the difference between primary and secondary memory, James writes, "Memory proper, or secondary memory as it might be styled, is the knowledge of a former state of mind after it has already once dropped from consciousness . . . with the additional consciousness that we have thought or experienced it before" (James, 648). Both Augustine and James show a preference for secondary memory as being more truly "memory"; they share an ambivalence about primary memory being called memory. James clearly equates primary memory with "consciousness" and "the immediately present moment" (James, 646–647), Augustine seems to equate "understanding" with the present moment in *The Trinity*: "We can perceive, in various ways, what is present to our senses or our understanding: what is absent but was once present" (*de Trin.* 15.13). Memories of the past are brought back into consciousness (James) or our understanding (Augustine, *The Trinity*) or our attention (Augustine, *Conf.* 11.28.37; see below), and the parallel to the modern concept of primary memory is clear.

KINDS OF LONG-TERM MEMORY

Some of the most interesting distinctions that memory theorists spend their time making are among kinds of long-term memories. As I indicated, making these distinctions (and criticizing the number of distinctions made by others) is a veritable industry in psychology. Tulving, a prominent memory theorist over the last 50 years, once wrote a paper titled, "How many memory systems are there?" His own answer over the years has ranged from two ("Episodic and Semantic," 385) to three ("How many," 387) to five ("Concepts," 11) and other theorists have argued for anything from one on up. Squire classifies a variety of kinds of memories into two main categories, declarative and nondeclarative, with each having multiple subtypes (Squire, 173). Among those who split things up, there are clear disagreements about the specifics of how to do that. However, two types that appear in nearly every theory are often referred to as episodic (memory for personally experienced events) and semantic (memory for, or knowledge of facts) after Tulving.

Like modern and especially contemporary psychologists, Augustine splits secondary memory into different types in Book 10 of *the Confessions*. The most notable distinction is between memory for personally experienced events and memory for (or knowledge of) facts or "Truths." His description is astonishingly comparable to Tulving's descriptions of episodic and semantic memory.

Augustine's description of memory begins with the idea that "the fields and vast mansions of memory" contain "innumerable images brought in there" through perception (*Conf.* 10.8.12). Some of those images come easily to mind, some through effort. He describes "The huge repository of the memory, with its secret and unimaginable caverns [that] welcomes and keeps all these things, to be recalled and brought out for use when needed" (*Conf.* 10.8.13). The "immense court of my memory," he writes, has all that he can bring to mind, "together with everything that I have ever been able to perceive" (*Conf.* 10.8.14). He then distinguishes a different aspect of memory: "The immense spaces of my memory harbor even more than these, however. Here too are all those things which I received through a liberal education and have not yet forgotten; . . . everything I know about literature, or skill in debate, or how many kinds of questions can be logically formulated, lodges indeed in my memory, but not like an image" that results from a perceptual experience (*Conf.* 10.9.16). Further, "the memory also stores countless truths and laws of mathematics and mensuration, no single one of which was impressed upon it by bodily sense, for they have no color, sound, or smell, nor have they been tasted or handled" (*Conf.* 10.12.19). Augustine's two types of memory differ in terms of their association with perceptual experiences.

At the simplest level, Tulving describes episodic memory as "memory for personally experienced events or remembering what happened where and when," and semantic memory as "memory for general facts of the world" ("Episodic Memory," 1506). Tulving also notes that "semantic memory is the memory necessary for the use of language. It is a mental thesaurus, organized knowledge a person possesses about words and other verbal symbols, their meaning and referents, about relations among them, and about rules, formulas, and algorithms for the manipulation of these symbols, concepts, and relations. Semantic memory does not register perceptible properties of inputs, but rather cognitive referents of inputs" ("Episodic and Semantic," 386). Note the similarity of Augustine's notion that the "countless truths and laws" have no perceptual properties, and Tulving's notion that "semantic memory does not register perceptible properties." Tulving also writes about the importance of perceptual properties of episodic memories: "Retrieval of information of this kind from episodic memory is successful if the person can describe the perceptible properties of the event in question and more or less accurately specify its temporal relations to other events" ("Episodic and Semantic," 388).

As Tulving's understanding of memory advanced over his career, he added a critical way to distinguish episodic from semantic memory in terms of the nature of consciousness associated with each. Semantic memory carries with it an experience of "noetic (knowing) consciousness . . . [that] makes possible introspective awareness of the internal and external world" ("How many," 388). In short, one knows something, and knows that one knows it. Episodic memory, in contrast has a "necessary correlate" of "Autonoetic (self-knowing) consciousness . . . [that] allows an individual to become aware of his or her own identity and existence in subjective time that extends from the past through the present to the future. It provides the familiar phenomenal flavor of recollective experience characterized by 'pastness' and subjective veridicality" ("How many," 388). Augustine writes that "in the immense court of my memory . . . I come to meet myself. I recall myself, what I did, when and where I acted in a certain way, and how I felt about so acting" (*Conf.* 10.8.14). Likewise, when he describes memory for facts, or knowledge, his description indicates that there is no sense of personal experience, no "self" in his knowledge of them. He is not explicit about states of consciousness, as Tulving is, but his distinction between these kinds of memory is made on grounds that are related to their association with self during acquisition. There are no *specific* events or images associated with knowledge, but such images are the hallmarks of experienced events for Augustine.

A second critical element of episodic memory for Tulving is its connection to personal time. As noted earlier, episodic memory is about answering questions of "what happened where and when"; Augustine recalls himself, he writes, "what I did, when and where I acted in a certain way." In recent writing, Tulving develops the notion of "chronesthesia," which he defines as a "form of consciousness that allows individuals to think about the subjective time in which they live and that makes it possible for them to 'mentally travel' in such time" ("Chronosthesia," 311). Autonoetic consciousness is also described in terms of such mental time travel, including into the future. As described earlier, at one point in his writing, in *The Trinity*, Augustine appears to reject the notion of memory as being about anything other than the past, reserving present and future for other mental capacities. However, in *Confessions*, he writes of his secondary / episodic memory that "I can draw on this abundant store to form imaginary pictures . . . and weave these together with images from the past, and so evoke future actions, occurrences or hopes, and on all these as well I can meditate as though they were present to me" (*Conf.* 10.8.14). Past, present, and future come together as one present reality in Augustine's mind, consistent with Tulving's chronesthesia.

EMOTIONAL MEMORY

While Augustine's theory of memory is remarkably similar to Tulving's, it does differ in an important way. Augustine distinguishes a third type of memory that is not a part of contemporary memory theory. He identifies memory for emotional states as different from episodic and semantic memory. The thrust of his distinction is that he can "remember having been happy, without feeling happy now," for example (*Conf.* 10.14.21). At another point, he enumerates places in memory (acknowledging that they are not really *places*) and writes, "I came to those regions of memory to which I had committed my emotional states" (*Conf.* 10.24.36). At yet another point, he clearly makes a list of three kinds, one of which is emotions: "See, in the measureless plains and vaults and caves of my memory, immeasurably full of countless kinds of things which are there either through their images (as with material things), or by being themselves present (as is the knowledge acquired through a liberal education), or by registering themselves and making their mark in some indefinable way (as with emotional states which the memory retains even when the mind is not actually experiencing them)" (*Conf.* 10.17.26).

There are, thus, three types of memories in Augustine's theory:

> 1. Those for which there are associated images (of experiences or of experienced things)
>   i. [episodic]
> 2. Those for which there is no sense of an experience of the memory [semantic]; and
> 3. Those for which there is a disconnection between what is remembered and what is experienced while remembering [emotions].

These distinctions are clearly made on the basis of the nature of the conscious experience associated with each one, in a way that is surprisingly reminiscent of Tulving's basis for distinguishing types of memory (although the net result is strikingly different). Tulving would clearly place the third type in his version of episodic memory.

Research on the nature of emotion and memory in contemporary cognitive psychology does not address the question that plagues Augustine: How can I remember being happy but not necessarily be happy when I remember it? In the context of empirical research, contemporary workers would frame that question as, "What is the effect of a prior, remembered emotion on one's current emotional state?" Contemporary researchers, however, have most extensively examined the reverse: "What is the effect of current emotional state on what one remembers?" (e.g., Levine & Pizarro, 537). More generally, contemporary research on memory and emotion has addressed questions relatively unrelated to Augustine's interests. Broadly speaking, emotion researchers have asked two questions about memory: "Are memories for emotions accurate?"; and, "What does someone remember while feeling a particular emotion?"

Levine, Safer, and Lench note that some theorists argue that emotions per se are not stored in memory, "but must be reconstructed based on knowledge concerning the circumstances in which the emotion was experienced. According to this view," they continue, "when asked to remember emotions, people retrieve not the fleeting emotional experience but a redescription of it based on memory for relevant details concerning the event (episodic knowledge) or based on beliefs about how one is likely to have felt (semantic knowledge)" (Levine, Safer, and Lench, 272). In other words, such theorists would characterize Augustine's third type of memory as just reconstructions from the other two types. Indeed, Levine and Pizarro summarize research showing that in remembering emotional states, even important ones like those experienced on hearing about the events of September 11, 2001, people remember their feelings in ways that are "partially reconstructed based on their current appraisals of events" (Levine & Pizarro, 533). Research on memory for highly emotional events shows people's memory is not nearly as good as they believe it to be (Neisser & Harsch), with people claiming much higher confidence about accuracy of such memories compared to memories of everyday events (e.g., Talarico & Rubin, 455–461).

A version of this view—that recollection of former emotional states is reconstructed—is described by Levine, Safer, and Lench (272), who note that people "experience a similar but new emotion in the present," citing James who describes the recall of emotions as "we can produce, not remembrances of the old grief or rapture, but new griefs and raptures, by summing up a lively thought of their exciting cause" (James, vol. 2, 474). In short, most research suggests that we either do not commit our emotional states to memory, or that if we do so, our recollection of them is not likely to be veridical.

However, Levine and her colleagues note that some theorists argue that emotions are "stored permanently and accurately" (Levine, Safer, and Lench, 272), based on other kinds of evidence. They develop a compromise position about memories for emotions, ultimately arguing that what one is consciously aware of when remembering an earlier emotional state is an episodic reconstruction, but at the same time, particularly for highly charged emotional events, one is unconsciously re-experiencing the emotion (Levine, Safer, and Lench, 273). Ultimately, they agree with Augustine's view of a special kind of memory storage for emotions themselves that is different from the storage of verbalized memories. It is, however, not accessible to declarative or verbal consciousness.

An additional few studies have partly addressed Augustine's question however. The issue for Augustine, again, is that the recollection of an emotional state does not re-create or reenact it, that he does not feel the emotion again when he brings it back to mind, in stark contrast to the other kinds of memories he describes. Some researchers have examined a very specialized version of this question by exploring an element of "mood regulation" in which people "repair sad moods" by recalling happy memories. For example, Joorman and Siemer report that at least for non-depressed individuals, recalling happy memories made them happier (Joorman & Siemer, 179) consistent with the idea that remembering a prior emotional state can affect the present emotional state, in contrast to Augustine's sense that the recall of emotional states does not bring those emotional states back. So the evidence suggests that emotional memory is special, and that while Augustine separates it from other kinds of memories, he may have missed it because of his method of introspective reflection, which is necessarily verbal and based on declarative memory.

MEMORY PHENOMENA

Augustine's writings illustrate a number of other memory phenomena, theoretical issues, or characteristics that are worth noting: the metaphor of storage and retrieval; the temporal perception or identification of the psychological present (relevant to episodic memory); redintegration, or the retrieval of a memory based on partial information; and the use of what has been referred to as the method of loci (Bower, 496), or the method of places (Carruthers).

Encoding, Storage, and Retrieval

One of the more fascinating characteristics of Augustine's description of memory, in light of contemporary theories, is his use of a storage metaphor. Repeatedly, Augustine uses wonderful language to describe memory: fields and vast mansions; remote crannies; secret and unimaginable caverns; an immense court; an abundant store; a vast, infinite recess; concealed hollows; plains and vaults and caves; a wide land without boundaries. All these fantastic places are described as filled with things which are memories, as if they are some kind of objects. Those objects (generally images) are described as being retrieved, as examined, as brought out into the light of day, or as commanded to present themselves. The metaphor is one of storage and retrieval.

A contemporary struggle with this storage and retrieval metaphor rages (e.g., Tulving, "Episodic Memory," 1506). Contemporary theorists also speak of a third component, as a set of three memory processes that are vulnerable to error—encoding, storage, and retrieval. Encoding is a process whereby the experienced events "out there" are translated into a kind of mental language for storage. Information could be lost because of encoding biases or errors; memories may also decay as they sit in storage, and we may have problems remembering during the retrieval processes, because the process may fail to "find" the memory of interest.

Augustine most clearly speaks of storage and retrieval, but he also (more subtly) writes about the encoding process. He uses language very consistent with the idea of some kind of translation: "The sense-impressions themselves do not find their way in, however; it is the images of things perceived by the senses that are available to the person who recalls them" (*Conf.* 10.8.13). And included in memory are "the modified images we produce when by our thinking we magnify or diminish or in any way alter the information our senses have reported" (*Conf.* 10.8.12).

Tulving writes that memory researchers talk of encoding, or placing items into memory, using the metaphor of a "store" that "holds" those memories. "Once the remembered stuff ('memories') has been effectively acquired, or stored, it can be used ('retrieved') at will" ("Episodic Memory," 1506). Augustine writes of how, after having retrieved some memories, they return "to their storage places, ready to be retrieved next time I need them" (*Conf.* 10.8.12). But Tulving notes also that retrieval is the challenge: his use of "at will" in the quote above is ironic to some degree. "Retrieval consists in a complex and elaborate set of processes; it is not simply a matter of 'reading the contents of memory store" ("Episodic Memory," 1506). He then describes examples of retrieval failures, situations in which it is clear that a memory exists, but the person cannot access it or retrieve it under certain circumstances. So Augustine's description seems naive at first. However, he does (at *Conf.* 10.8.12) also describe examples of difficulty of retrieval.

Time perception

In Book 11 of *Confessions*, Augustine ponders the notion of time and our perception of it. Perceiving ourselves in time—past, present, and future—is a critical element of Tulving's episodic memory, and in Augustine's memory as well. Contemporary research on the perception of time wrestles with a number of possible ways of understanding it. Block notes that "if an event or sequence of events lasts more than a few seconds, people experience what most theorists call the *psychological present* or *conscious present*" (Block, 5). Block cites James's metaphor for the psychological present of sitting on a saddle looking in two directions in time, the past and the future. Block continues: "Controversy about the upper limit of the psychological present continues, especially concerning what this implies about the attention and memory systems that may underlie the phenomenon" (Block, 5). Block notes that other researchers differ on their estimates of the upper limit of the extent of the psychological present, ranging from five to eight seconds at the most. Block also describes a variety of research that suggests a minimum perceptible "moment" of a tenth of a second (Block, 3).

Augustine likewise wrestles with this notion of the psychological present in language that parallels Block's note about the roles of attention and memory in forming a psychological present. Augustine's language evokes the notion of a psychological present: "In you, my mind, I measure time. . . . What I measure is the impression which passing phenomena leave in you, which abides after they have passed by: That is what I measure as a present reality" (*Conf.* 11.27.36). And then he discusses the roles of attention and memory in perceiving that present reality:

> [T]here are three realities in the mind. . . . The mind expects, and attends, and remembers, so that what it expects passes by way of what it attends to into what it remembers . . . . [A]n expectation of future events does exist in the mind . . . the memory of past events still lives on in the mind. And who would deny that the present has no duration, since it passes in an instant? Yet our attention does endure, and through our attention what is still to be makes its way into the state where it is no more. (*Conf.* 11.28.37)

The enduring attention, and the memory of the passing phenomena, combine to make a psychological present. Another interesting parallel with contemporary thought is that Baddeley, after many years of research, has written that working memory (his term for primary memory) might have been better labeled working attention (Baddeley, 152), consistent with Augustine's use of "attention" as another name for awareness of the present moment.

REDINTEGRATION

Some cognitive psychologists today study the concept of redintegration, a process by which partial information about a to-be-remembered word is used to reconstruct the whole word, using knowledge stored in semantic memory (Nairne, 286). Augustine describes this process as well, when he discusses a situation in which we have forgotten something, and we search our memory for it. After searching for it, it turns up, and we recognize it. He writes,

> [W]e could not recognize it if we did not remember it. Yet we had undoubtedly forgotten. Is this the explanation: that the thing had not fallen out of the memory entirely? Can it be that the part which was retained gave a clue to the part which had vanished, because the memory was aware that some item was

absent from the full complement it was used to turning over and, feeling itself to be lame and lacking something that normally belonged to it, demanded that the missing element be restored? (*Conf.* 10.19.28)

METHOD OF PLACES

Professional orators in the Roman Empire, like Augustine, were thoroughly trained in rhetoric, and there are some central texts that are likely to have been encountered by Augustine. One important work was *De Inventione* by Cicero, and another often attributed to Cicero was called *Rhetorica ad Herrenium*. This latter was a "textbook that describes an art of memory based upon the building plan of a familiar house in whose rooms and recesses an orator should 'place' images that recall to him the material he plans to talk about" (Carruthers, 7). According to Carruthers, this "architectural technique" was brought to contemporary light by Frances Yates in her classic text, *The Art of Memory*. The invention of the method is a story well known to cognitive psychologists, and it is often referred to as "the method of loci." The story goes something like the following: An orator, named Simonides, attended a dinner, with many people seated around a table. During the feast, an earthquake shook the building down on the people, killing all but the orator, who was lucky enough to have been called outside just moments before. Their bodies were so mangled that nobody could identify most of the bodies. However, the orator was able to tell exactly who everyone was, because he remembered where everyone was seated, by having an image of them in their places around the table.

Orators who used this method worked hard to develop a collection of places (loci) and the art of crafting images that would remind them of what they wanted to know, and to include in their speeches. This method of memorization has been studied by contemporary psychologists (e.g., Bower, 496). After teaching people what to do, and helping them form a series of locations, we might give subjects in an experiment a list of words. They then associate each word in the list with one location, by forming an image of the word in that location in their mind's eye. For example, one can imagine the sequence of locations from house to office, and associate the front door of the house with the first word, the first corner near the house with the second, a particular house on the next block with the third, a store along the route with the fourth, and so on. To recall the list of words, the individual would mentally drive along, looking at each location and, "seeing" the word that is associated with it, accurately recall the word list in order.

Much of Augustine's description of memory appears to be based on this art of memory, this architectural technique. For example, his first metaphor for memory in Book 10 of *Confessions*, cited earlier, is "fields and vast *mansions* where are treasured innumerable images brought in there" (*Conf.*

10.8.12, emphasis added). This is exactly the architectural technique described. He also talks of walking through the fields and caverns of his memory and finding what he wants "in orderly sequence . . . the earlier members giving way to those that follow and returning to their storage places, ready to be retrieved next time I need them. All of which happens when I recite anything from memory" (*Conf.* 10.8.12). But very little research on this persisted for long in contemporary psychology. What research there is shows that it is a powerful technique for remembering. (More on this below.)

EVALUATION OF AUGUSTINE'S UNDERSTANDING OF MEMORY

In evaluating Augustine's description of memory and associated phenomena in light of contemporary psychology, it is possible to identify three categories: ideas that we share; ideas Augustine is missing; and ideas that we are missing.

In the shared category, the episodic/semantic distinction, as described above, is an astonishing parallel. It is astonishing not only because he distinguishes experienced events from knowledge, but because of the strong parallels in terms of the details of each that he describes. The basic distinction is fairly obvious in a sense, but the details of both the episodic and semantic types of memory are not. The notion of episodic memories as having one's self in them; as having a past, present, and future component; and the role of images, all sound straight out of Tulving's writings. Likewise, semantic memories having no particular location in time, and no imagery, are directly parallel to Tulving's descriptions.

Another shared concern is with the perception of time, a critical component of episodic memory. Augustine's struggle to understand what constitutes an episode or event continues today. And, of course, Augustine's description of memory processes evokes the concept of redintegration, as described above. The details of common aspects and types of memory in Augustine's writing is extraordinary, considering the decades of research that led to similar findings and theorizing in contemporary cognitive psychology compared to one person's reflections.

Augustine, however, is missing some critical aspects of memory. Two in particular are worth mentioning. First, memory is not always as accurate as it feels subjectively. Augustine mostly talks about memories as veridical representations of life's experiences. Second, contemporary researchers have discovered that much of memory does not involve conscious awareness, something missing entirely from Augustine's descriptions. Each of these is addressed in turn.

Johnson notes that "the fundamental question" for memory theories to address is "the relation between what we remember and what 'really' happened" (Johnson, 82). Further she describes a category of memory theories as coming from a position of "naive realism," in which memory is a store of experienced events, as they happened. Of course, as she points out, such a view cannot "account for the sometimes dramatic errors and distortions in memory" (Johnson, 83). Augustine's memory theorizing comes entirely from reflecting on his own experiences, which naturally leads to a lack of awareness of the possibility that those memories might not be accurate. Indeed, Augustine describes memories of perceptual experiences as "preserved" in memory, "classified and distinct" (*Conf.* 10.8.13). And of things he learned in school, he writes, "Not only do I retain all those things in my memory: I can also keep in my memory the way in which I learned them" (*Conf.* 10.13.20). And memories are described as being "returned to their storage places, ready to be retrieved next time I need them" (*Conf.* 10.8.12).

Augustine does acknowledge forgetting: "Here too are all those things which I received through a liberal education and have not yet forgotten" (*Conf.* 10.9.16) and some memories of experiences can be "engulfed and buried in oblivion" (*Conf.* 10.8.12). But for most things he writes as though it can ultimately be retrieved: "I command something I want to present itself, and immediately certain things emerge, while others have to be pursued for some time and dug out from remote crannies" (*Conf.* 10.8.12; cf. *Conf.* 10.11.18). However, for the most part, he writes as though everything remembered is remembered as if it were "preserved" and completely veridical. The one exception is that he notes that among the memories of experiences are "hidden away the modified images we produce when by our thinking we magnify or diminish or in any way alter the information our senses have reported" (*Conf.* 10.8.12). Such alterations during the encoding process would not lead to veridical memories.

What we know from experimental examination of memory in contemporary research is that it is quite possible to falsely remember things that did not actually occur (the "dramatic errors and distortions" mentioned by Johnson, above). Tulving ("Episodic memory," 1507) describes a variety of kinds of false memories, in which people remember things that did not occur, and that they do so because that is a normal part of remembering, which involves reproduction, reconstruction, and even out-and-out construction of past events, with room for error rampant; he describes it as "fact," as opposed to theory or interpreted from data. While such "dramatic errors and distortions" are beyond what Augustine seems to describe, there is also strong evidence of biases and distortions involving "magnified," "diminished," or other alterations, as Augustine puts it so eloquently (e.g., the research on memory for emotion recall described earlier).

None of what Augustine misses in the category of false and distorted memory should be surprising, given that Augustine had only his own subjective awareness to evaluate memory. The research by Talarico and Rubin described earlier (along with many other studies) makes it clear that subjective judgment about accuracy is no basis for determining actual accuracy. As one author noted succinctly, "When memory changes the records in our heads, it doesn't tell us about it" (Kotre, 54). Indeed, Tulving's description of autonoetic consciousness cited earlier includes the claim that it carries with it a "subjective veridicality" when we recall some memory. Whether the memory is recalled accurately, autonoetic consciousness endows such memories with a feeling of being true.

The other aspect of memory that Augustine naturally missed falls into the category of "implicit processes," mental activity that occurs outside of conscious awareness. In Squire's delineation of types of memory, these are aspects of non-declarative memory, memories that cannot be verbalized. In Tulving's description of kinds of consciousness associated with kinds of memory, non-declarative remembering is associated with anoetic consciousness, or "unknowing" consciousness ("How many," 388) in which there is no introspective awareness of mental activity, there is just responding. When typing, skilled typists are not aware of having learned where the keys are, or even being able to describe how they type, they just do it. Implicit processes can be richer than physical skills, however, including things like reading. If a person reads a particular word, and then encounters that word again soon after, it is processed faster the second time, without any awareness of the repetition. The accurate retrieval of an emotional state as described by Levine, Safer, and Lench (273) is one such implicit process and would explain why Augustine does not feel that he relives emotional states when recalling them. Unless he regenerates the emotion through such implicit, non-verbal processes, he is only recalling a verbal, or declarative (or explicit) memory that does not carry with it the emotional state itself.

Augustine's account of memory has two elements that go beyond our own contemporary understanding worth discussion. First, the idea of re-experiencing emotional states as he frames the question is rarely considered in contemporary research. Second, his description of memorial activities that seem to involve the method of places also goes beyond where contemporary research has explored.

Regarding the first of these, Augustine's question about the re-experiencing of former emotional states merits additional experimental research. A study could be designed in which subjects are placed into a neutral mood and then asked to recall events in which they felt particular emotions. They could be asked to recall strongly emotional events, and less strongly emotional states, and then to evaluate their current mood. While this has been done with unhappy or sad people recalling happy memories as mood repair (as described above), it would be interesting to see how that translated to other emotional states, to explore more fully the ideas about the characteristics of re-experienced emotions. Augustine's observations about memory for emotions can serve as a prompt for research that is timely for today, particularly given the extensive current interest in the study of happiness (e.g., Seligman).

Regarding the second, while interest in the method of loci or places waned in psychology, it may have done so because of an overemphasis on a version of it that focused too strongly on rigid veridicality. Carruthers writes that Frances Yates, who introduced the mnemonic technique to contemporary psychology in the 1960s, found it too rigid, unnecessarily complex, and difficult. But that was because, according to Carruthers, there was a sense that its purpose was to memorize and regurgitate memorized material in a rigid order, and that was how it was presented to psychology. Curiously, the ancient texts that describe the technique indicate that it could be used for memorizing either a sequence of concepts, or a specific sequence of words (as from a speech, for example). But we focus only on its usefulness for the latter case, which those same texts describe as much more difficult. They argued that it would be useful only for particularly valuable texts, not for every occasion. Indeed, they felt that for composition, it was better *not* to have exact words because not doing so allowed for real creativity and spontaneity. So psychology missed the point and rejected it for the wrong reasons.

Why might that be? First, over the centuries, the increasing availability of texts makes memorizing them seem less worthwhile, and the sheer number of texts available makes memorizing them all seem impossible, even for the best trained scholar. Let alone today the virtually immediate availability of nearly every text through computers, smart phones, and e-book readers.

Second, psychology in the twentieth century developed and fixed on our ability to reproduce stimuli perfectly. Throughout at least the first half of the twentieth century, psychology was dominated by the behaviorist view of the human organism as a passive recipient of stimulation: memory, in this view, is seen largely as an attempt to reproduce the stimulation accurately. Even though behaviorism largely passed away, the "cognitive revolution" that replaced it never lost that focus on and narrow view of what constituted accuracy. To understand memory more fully, psychology should learn to recognize the limitations of our metaphors, whether we think of memory as a storehouse, or a text, or a videotape, or as the Internet. A reconsideration of memory that recognized the broader uses and value of the method of places would lead to potentially valuable research on memory skill and technique.

CONCLUSION

Augustine, in contemplating the nature of God and his relationship with God, wrote eloquently and presciently in *Confessions* and in *The Trinity* about the mind, and especially his memory. A relatively large community of cognitive psychologists (and their psychological forebears who did not use that label for themselves) has spent decades engaged in extensive, careful, and insightful experimental research and theorizing on the nature of human memory. Both Augustine, through his introspective reflection, and today's scholars, through their empirical research, overlap extensively in their resulting descriptions of memory.

Augustine's thoughts on memory led him to distinguish between what he is thinking about in a particular moment, and what he remembers from the past as persisting without his thinking about it. Today's scholars call that distinction by a number of terms, including primary and secondary memory, but both they and Augustine describe the difference similarly. Most notable, perhaps, is that both Augustine and today's scholars reflect some ambivalence about whether the contents of current consciousness is actually a kind of memory, with "attention" as a shared alternative conception.

When thinking about the nature of long-term memory, Augustine distinguished three different categories: a perception-based memory for his own experiences; a knowledge-based memory for what he had learned; and memory for emotional states that nevertheless had an odd disconnect between memory for an emotional state and actually feeling that emotion. Today's scholars identify the first two but not the third as a special category, though recent research hints at a possible reason for why Augustine felt disconnected from emotions when he recalled a former emotional state. With regard to the first two kinds, the language used to describe both the nature of memory of each type, and the phenomenological experience associated with each type of memory, is extraordinary in its parallels with the descriptions given by Tulving today, especially given the different methods and amount of energy expended to generate those two sets of descriptions. Augustine also described a number of processes and characteristics of memory that are remarkable for their parallels with today's understanding of memory.

Augustine's "method" of introspective reflection to understand memory limited what he could be able to understand and describe to those aspects of memory that are accessible through conscious awareness, which today's scholars refer to as declarative memory. His method, because of the nature of memory, kept him from understanding the fallibility—the dramatic distortions and errors—of memory and the variety of implicit memory processes that might actually account for the bulk of human memory phenomena. However, his writing also suggests (at least) two areas that might be fruitful areas of research today, on the nature of emotional memory and the use of trained mnemonic techniques. The limitations of method did not limit Augustine's potential to inspire new ideas and advances in our understanding of memory even today.[3]

NOTES

1. All quotations from *Confessions* are from *The Confessions*, trans. Maria Boulding (Hyde Park, NY: New City Press, 2001). All quotations from *The Trinity* are from John Burnaby, *Augustine: The Later Works* (Philadelphia: Westminster, 1955).

2. I use the term "modern" to refer to the period from the late nineteenth century to the present day as a contrast with Augustine's time, not in the sense of modern versus postmodern. I use the term "contemporary" to refer to psychological theory from the late 1950s to the present day, reflecting the "Cognitive Revolution."

3. The author is grateful to Merrimack College's Center for Augustinian Study and Legacy for financially supporting the original forays into this topic; to Diane Shaw for her essential role as muse; to Joseph Kelley for his encouragement in the study of Augustine; and to Provost Michael Bell for his giving me time to complete the work and for additional inspiration.

WORKS CITED

Atkinson, Richard C., and Richard M. Shiffrin. "Human Memory: A Proposed System and its Control Processes." *The Psychology of Learning and Motivation: Advances in Research and Theory*. Ed. Kenneth W. Spence and Janet T. Spence. Vol. 2. New York: Academic Press, 1968. Pp. 89–195.

Baddeley, Alan D. "Working Memory or Working Attention?" *Attention: Selection, Awareness and Control*. Ed. Alan D. Baddeley and Lawrence Weiskrantz. New York: Oxford University Press, 1993. Pp. 152–170.

Baddeley, Alan D., and Graham J. Hitch. "Working Memory." *The Psychology of Learning and Motivation: Advances in Research and Theory*. Ed. Gordon H. Bower. Vol. 8. New York: Academic Press, 1974. Pp. 47–89.

Block, Richard A. "Models of Psychological Time." *Cognitive Models of Psychological Time*. Ed. Richard A. Block. Hillsdale, NJ: Erlbaum, 1990. Pp. 1–36.

Bower, Gordon H. "Analysis of a Mnemonic Device." *American Scientist* 58.5 (1970) 496–510.

Carruthers, Mary. *The Craft of Thought: Meditation, Rhetoric, and the Making of Images, 400–1200*. Cambridge: Cambridge University Press, 1998.

James, William. *The Principles of Psychology*. 1890. Vol. 1. New York: Henry Holt, 1896.

Johnson, Marcia K. "A Multiple-Entry, Modular Memory System." *The Psychology of Learning and Motivation: Advances in Research and Theory*. Ed. Gordon H. Bower. Vol. 17. New York: Academic Press, 1983. Pp. 81–123.

Joorman, Jutta, and Matthias Siemer. "Memory Accessibility, Mood Regulation, and Dysphoria: Difficulties in Repairing Sad Mood with Happy Memories?" *Journal of Abnormal Psychology* 113.2 (2004) 179–188.

Kotre, John. *White Gloves: How We Create Ourselves Through Memory*. New York: Norton, 1996.

Levine, Linda J., and David A. Pizarro. "Emotion and Memory Research: A Grumpy Review." *Social Cognition* 22.5 (2004) 530–554.

Levine, Linda J., Martin A. Safer, and Heather C. Lench. "Remembering and Misremembering Emotions." *Judgments Over Time: The Interplay of Thoughts, Feelings, and Behaviors*. Ed. Lawrence J. Sanna and Edward C. Chang. New York: Oxford University Press, 2006. Pp. 271–290.

Masson, Michael E. J., and Peter Graf. "Introduction: Looking Back and Into the Future." *Implicit Memory: New Directions in Cognition, Development, and Neuropsychology.* Ed. Peter Graf and Michael E. J. Masson. Hillsdale, NJ: Erlbaum, 1993. Pp. 1–11.

Nairne, James S. "A Functional Analysis of Primary Memory." *The Nature of Remembering: Essays in Honor of Robert G. Crowder.* Ed. Henry L. Roediger, James S. Nairne, Ian Neath, and Aimee Surprenant. Washington, D.C.: American Psychological Association, 2001. Pp. 283–296.

Neisser, Ulrich, and Nicole Harsch. "Phantom Flashbulbs: False Recollections of Hearing the News about *Challenger*." *Affect and Accuracy in Recall: Studies of "Flashbulb" Memories.* Ed. Eugene Winograd, and Ulrich Neisser. New York: Cambridge University Press, 1992. Pp. 9–31.

Seligman, Martin E. P. *Authentic Happiness: Using the New Positive Psychology to Realize Your Potential for Lasting Fulfillment.* New York: The Free Press, 2002.

Squire, Larry R. (2004). "Memory Systems of The Brain: A Brief History and Current Perspective." *Neurobiology of Learning and Memory* 82.3 (2004) 171–177.

Talarico, Jennifer M. and David C. Rubin. (2003). "Confidence, Not Consistency, Characterizes Flashbulb Memories." *Psychological Science* 14.5 (2003) 455–461.

Tulving, Endel. "Episodic and Semantic Memory." *Organization of Memory.* Ed. Endel Tulving and Wayne Donaldson. New York: Academic Press, 1972. Pp. 381–403.

———. "How Many Memory Systems Are There?" *American Psychologist* 40.4 (1985) 385–398.

———. "Concepts of Human Memory." *Memory: Organization and Locus of Change.* Ed. Larry R. Squire, Norman Weinberger, Gary Lynch, and James L. McGaugh. New York: Oxford University Press, 1991. Pp. 3–32.

———. "Episodic Memory and Common Sense: How Far Apart?" *Philosophical Transactions of the Royal Society, London,* B, 356.1413 (2001) 1505–1515.

———. "Chronesthesia: Awareness of Subjective Time." *Principles of Frontal Lobe Function.* Ed. Donald T. Stuss and Robert C. Knight. New York: Oxford University Press, 2002. Pp. 311–325.

Waugh, Nancy C. and Donald A. Norman. "Primary Memory." *Psychological Review* 72.2 (1965) 89–104.

Bibliography

Alexander, Franz G. and Sheldon T. Selesnick, *The History of Psychiatry: An Evaluation of Psychiatric Thought and Practice from Prehistoric Times to the Present*. New York: Harper & Row, 1966.

Ambrose. Letter 20 (printed as Letter 60). Trans. M. M. Beyenka. Fathers of the Church vol 26. Washington, DC: Catholic University Press of America, 2002.

Annas, Julia. *The Morality of Happiness*. New York: Oxford University Press, 1993.

Arendt, Hannah. *Between Past and Future: Eight Exercises in Political Thought*. New York: Penguin, 1993.

———. *Love and Saint Augustine*. Ed. J. V. Scott and J. C. Stark. Chicago: University of Chicago Press, 1996.

Armstrong, Richard H. *A Compulsion for Antiquity: Freud and the Ancient World*. Ithaca, NY: Cornell University Press, 2005.

Aron, Arthur, Helen Fisher, Debra J. Mashek, Greg Strong, Haifang Li and Lucy L. Brown. "Reward, Motivation, and Emotion Systems Associated with Early-Stage Intense Romantic Love." *Journal of Neurophysiology* 94.1 (2005) 327–337.

Atkinson, Clarissa. "'Your Servant, My Mother': The Figure of Saint Monica in the Ideology of Christian Motherhood." In *Immaculate and Powerful: The Female in Sacred Image and Social Reality*, edited By Clarissa W. Atkinson, Constance H. Buchanan and Margaret R. Miles. Boston: Beacon Press, 1985. Pp. 139–172.

Atkinson, Richard C. and Richard M. Shiffrin. "Human Memory: A Proposed System and its Control Processes." *The Psychology of Learning and Motivation: Advances in Research and Theory*. Ed. Kenneth W. Spence and Janet T. Spence. Vol. 2. New York: Academic Press, 1968. Pp. 89–195.

Augustine of Hippo. *Against the Academicians and The Teacher*. Trans. Peter King. Indianapolis, IN: Hackett, 1995.

———. "Care to Be Taken for the Dead." Translated by John A. Lacy. In Roy J. Deferrari, ed., *Saint Augustine: Treatises on Marriage and Other Subjects*. Fathers of the Church 27. New York: Fathers of the Church, 1955. Pp. 351–384. Latin Text: *Corpus Scriptorum Ecclesiasticorum Latinorum* 41, 625–626.

———. *Confessions*. Translated by Henry Chadwick. Oxford and New York: Oxford University Press, 1992.

———. *The Confessions of St. Augustine*. Trans. John K. Ryan. Garden City, NY: Image Books, 1960.

———. *Confessions*. Trans. Rex Warner. New York: Mentor-Omega, 1963.

———. *City of God*. Trans. Henry Bettenson. New York: Penguin, 1972.

———. *Ennarrationes in Psalmos* 85, *Corpus Christianorum Latinorum* 39.

———. *Enchiridion*. Trans. J. F. Shaw. *The Nicene and Post-Nicene Church Fathers*. Ed. Philip Schaff. First Series, vol 3. Pp. 449–552.

———. *The Happy Life*. Translated by Ludwig Schopp. Fathers of the Church, Vol. 5. New York: Cima Publishing Company, 1948. *De beata vita, Corpus Christianorum Latinorum* 29.

———. *The Literal Meaning of Genesis*. Vol. 2. Trans. and annotated by J. Taylor. New York: Newman, 1982.

———. *On Continence*. Trans. C. L. Cornish. *The Nicene and Post-Nicene Church Fathers*. Ed. Philip Schaff. First Series, vol. 3. Pp. 714–741.

———. *On the Gift of Perseverance*. Trans. Peter Holmes and Robert Ernest Wallis. Rev. with an Introduction by Benjamin B. Warfield. *Nicene and Post-Nicene Fathers of the Christian Church*. Ed. Philip Schaff, vol. 5, *Saint Augustin: Anti-Pelagian Writings*, pp. 521–552. Repr. ed. Grand Rapids, MI: W.B. Eerdmans, 1978. Latin text: *De dono perseverantiae* 20, 53, *Corpus Christianorum Latinorum* 29.

———. *Sermons. The Works of St. Augustine: A Translation for the 21st Century*. Trans. Edmund Hill. Edited by John E. Rotelle. Part 3/1–3/11. Hyde Park, NY: New City Press, 1990–1997.

———. *The Spirit and the Letter*. Trans. John Burnaby in *Augustine: Later Works*. Philadelphia: The Westminster Press, 1965.

———. *The Trinity*. Trans. Edmund Hill. New York: New City Press, 1998.

Ayres, Lewis. "The Christological Context of Augustine's *De Trinitate* XIII: Toward Relocating Books VIII–XV." *Augustinian Studies* 29:1 (1998) 111–139.

———. "The Discipline of Self-Knowledge in Augustine's *De Trinitate* Book X." In *The Passionate Intellect: Essays on the Transformation of Classical Traditions, Presented to Professor I. G. Kidd*. New Brunswick: Transaction Publishers, 1995. Pp. 261–296.

Babcock, William S. "Augustine and the Spirituality of Desire." *Augustinian Studies* 25 (1994) 179–199.

———. "*Cupiditas* and *Caritas*: The Early Augustine on Love and Human Fulfillment." In *The Ethics of St. Augustine*, edited by William S. Babcock. Atlanta, GA: Scholars Press, 1991. Pp. 39–66.

Baddeley, Alan D. "Working Memory or Working Attention?" *Attention: Selection, Awareness and Control*. Ed. Alan D. Baddeley and Lawrence Weiskrantz. New York: Oxford University Press, 1993. Pp. 152–170.

Baddeley, Alan D. and Graham J. Hitch. "Working Memory." *The Psychology of Learning and Motivation: Advances in Research and Theory*. Ed. Gordon H. Bower. Vol. 8. New York: Academic Press, 1974. Pp. 47–89.

Bakan, David. "Augustine's *Confessions*: The Unentailed Self." In *The Hunger of the Heart: Reflections on the* Confessions *of Augustine*, edited by Donald Capps and James E. Dittes. Society for the Scientific Study of Religion Monograph Series 8. West Lafayette, IN: Society for the Scientific Study of Religion, 1990. Pp. 109–115.

Balogh, J. "Unbeachtetes in Augustins Konfessionen." *Didaskaleion* (n.s.) 4 (1926) 5–21.

Balsdon, J.P.V.D. *Roman Women: Their History and Habits*. London: Bodley Head, 1962.

Balthasar, Hans Urs von. *Love Alone is Credible*. Trans. D. C. Schindler. San Francisco: Ignatius Press, 2004.

Bass, Alan. *Difference and Disavowal: The Trauma of Eros*. Stanford: Stanford University Press, 2000.

Beers, W. "The Confessions of St. Augustine: Narcissistic Elements." *American Imago* 45 (1988) 107–125.

Benjamin, Jessica. *The Bonds of Love: Psychoanalysis, Feminism, and the Problem of Domination*. New York: Pantheon, 1988.

———. *Like Subjects, Love Objects: Essays on Recognition and Sexual Difference*. New Haven: Yale University Press, 1995.

———. *The Shadow of the Other: Intersubjectivity and Gender in Psychoanalysis*. New Haven: Yale University Press, 1998.

Block, Richard A. "Models of Psychological Time." *Cognitive Models of Psychological Time*. Ed. Richard A. Block. Hillsdale, NJ: Erlbaum, 1990. Pp. 1–36.

Block, S. L. "St. Augustine: On Grief and Other Psychological Matters." *American Journal of Psychology* 122 (1966) 943–946.

Bonnichon, Marie-Odile. "Pourquoi 'sainte' Monique?" In *Histoire et culture chrétienne*, edited by Yves Ledure. Paris: Beauchesne, 1992. Pp. 23–56.

Børresen, Kari Elisabeth. *Subordination and Equivalence: The Nature and Role of Woman in Augustine and Thomas Aquinas*. Kampen: Kok Pharos, 1995.

Bouyer, L. "Mysticism: An Essay on the History of the Word." In *Understanding Mysticism*, edited by R. Woods. Garden City, NJ: Image Books, 1980. Pp. 42–55.

Bower, Gordon H. "Analysis of a Mnemonic Device." *American Scientist* 58.5 (1970) 496–510.

Bowery, Anne-Marie. "Monica: The Feminine Face of Christ." In *Interpretations of Augustine*, edited by Judith Chelius Stark. University Park: Pennsylvania State University Press, 2007. Pp. 69–95.

Brändle, Rudolph and Walter Neidhart. "Lebensgeschichte und Theologie: Ein Beitrag zur psychohistorischen Interpretation Augustins." *Theologische Zeitschrift* 40 (1984) 157–180.

Brennan, Teresa. *The Interpretation of the Flesh: Freud and Femininity*. New York: Routledge, 1992.

Breyfogle, Todd. "Intellectus," in *Augustine Through the Ages: An Encyclopedia*. Allan Fitzgerald, O.S.A., edited by Grand Rapids: Eerdmans, 1999. Pp. 452–454.

———. "Memory and Imagination in Augustine's *Confessions*." In *Literary Imagination, Ancient and Modern: Essays in Honor of David Grene*, edited byTodd Breyfogle. Chicago: University of Chicago Press, 1999. Pp. 139–154.

Brickman, P., D. Coates and R. Janoff-Bulman. "Lottery Winners and Accident Victims: Is Happiness Relative?" *Journal of Personality and Social Psychology* 36.8 (1978) 917–927.

Brown, Peter. *Augustine of Hippo: A Biography*. Berkeley and Los Angeles: University of California Press, 1967; new ed. 2000.

———. *The Body and Society: Men, Women, and Sexual Renunciation in Early Christianity*. New York: Columbia University Press, 1988.

Browning, Don S. "The Psychoanalytic Interpretation of Augustine's *Confessions*." In *Psychoanalysis and Religion*, edited by Joseph H. Smith and Susan Handelman. Psychiatry and the Humanities. Baltimore and London: Johns Hopkins University Press, 1990.

Bubacz, B. *St. Augustine's Theory of Knowledge*. Lewiston, NY: Edwin Mellen Press, 1981.

Bulkeley, K. *The Wondering Brain*. New York: Routledge, 2005.

Burnell, Peter. *The Augustinian Person*. Washington, DC: The Catholic University Press, 2005.

Burrell, David. "Reading *The Confessions* of Augustine: An Exercise in Theological Understanding." *The Journal of Religion* 50 (1970) 327–351.

———. "Reading the *Confessions* of Augustine: The Case of Oedipal Analyses." In *The Hunger of the Heart: Reflections on the* Confessions *of Augustine*, edited by Donald Capps and James E. Dittes. Society for the Scientific Study of Religion Monograph Series 8. West Lafayette, IN: Society for the Scientific Study of Religion, 1990. Pp. 133–142.

Burrus, Virginia and Catherine Keller. "Confessing Monica." In *Feminist Interpretations of Augustine*, edited by Judith Chelius Stark. University Park, PA: Pennsylvania State University Press, 2007. Pp. 119–145.

Buss, David. *Evolutionary Psychology: The New Science of the Mind*. Boston: Allyn and Bacon, 1990.

Butler, C. *Western Mysticism*. New York: Dutton, 1923.

Capps, Donald. "Augustine as Narcissist: Of Grandiosity and Shame." In *The Hunger of the Heart: Reflections on the* Confessions *of Augustine*, edited by Donald Capps and James E. Dittes. Society for the Scientific Study of Religion Monograph Series 8. West Lafayette, IN: Society for the Scientific Study of Religion, 1990. Pp. 169–184.

———. "Augustine's *Confessions*: The Scourge of Shame and the Silencing of Adeodatus." In *The Hunger of the Heart: Reflections on the* Confessions *of Augustine*, edited by Donald Capps and James E. Dittes. Society for the Scientific Study of Religion Monograph Series 8. West Lafayette, IN: Society for the Scientific Study of Religion, 1990. Pp. 69–92.

———. "Augustine's *Confessions*: Self-reproach and the Melancholy Self." *Pastoral Psychology*, 55 (2007) 571–591.

————. "Augustine's *Confessions*: The Story of a Divided Self and the Process of Its Unification." *Pastoral Psychology* 55 (2007) 551–569.

Capps, Donald and James E. Dittes, eds. *The Hunger of the Heart: Reflections on the Confessions of Augustine.* West Lafayette, IN: Society for the Scientific Study of Religion, 1990.

Carruthers, Mary. *The Craft of Thought: Meditation, Rhetoric, and the Making of Images, 400–1200.* Cambridge: Cambridge University Press, 1998.

Cavadini, John C. "The Darkest Enigma: Reconsidering the Self in Augustine's Thought." *Augustinian Studies* 38 (2007) 119–132.

————. "Feeling Right: Augustine on the Passions and Sexual Desire." *Augustinian Studies* 36 (2005) 195–217.

————. "Making Truth: A New Commentary on Augustine's Confessions." *Religious Studies Review* 21.4 (1995) 291–298.

————. "The Structure and Intention of Augustine's *De Trinitate*." *Augustinian Studies* 23 (1992) 103–123.

Chambers, R. Andrew, Jane R. Taylor and Marc N. Potenza. "Developmental Neurocircuitry of Motivation in Adolescence: A Critical Period of Addiction Vulnerability." *American Journal of Psychiatry* 160.6 (2003) 1041–1052.

Charry, Ellen T. "Augustine of Hippo: Father of Christian Psychology." *Anglican Theological Review* 88:4 (2006) 575–589.

Chidester, D. "The Symbolism of Learning in St. Augustine." *Harvard Theological Review* 76 (1983) 73–90.

Clark, Elizabeth. *History, Theory, Text: Historians and the Linguistic Turn.* Cambridge and London: Harvard University Press, 2004.

Clark, Elizabeth. "Rewriting Early Christian History: Augustine's Representations of Monica." In *Portraits of Spiritual Authority: Religious Power in Early Christianity, Byzantium and the Christian Orient*, edited by Jan Willem Drijvers and John W. Watt. *Religions in the Graeco-Roman World*, ed. R. Van Den Broek, H. J. W. Drijvers, H. S. Versnel, vol. 137. Leiden: Brill, 1999. Pp. 14–21.

Clark, Gillian. *Augustine, the* Confessions. Cambridge and New York: Cambridge University Press, 1993.

Cooper, John M., ed. *Plato: Complete Works.* Indianapolis: Hackett Publishing, 1997.

Courcelle, Pierre Paul. *Connais-toi toi-même; de Socrate à saint Bernard.* 3 vols. Paris: Études augustiniennes, 1974–1975.

————. *Recherches sur les* Confessions *de saint Augustin.* Paris: E. de Boccard, 1950.

Crews, Frederick C. *Unauthorized Freud: Doubters Confront a Legend.* New York: Viking, 1998.

Daley, Lawrence J. "St. Augustine's *Confessions* and Erik Erikson's *Young Man Luther*: Conversion as 'Identity Crisis'." *Augustiniana* 31 (1981) 183–196.

Daly, Lawrence J. "Psychohistory and St. Augustine's Conversion Process." *Augustiniana* 28 (1978) 231–254.

Damasio, Antonio R. *Descartes' Error: Emotion, Reason and the Human Brain.* New York: Harper Collins, 1994.

————. *The Feeling of What Happens: Body and Emotion in the Making of Consciousness.* New York: Harcourt, Brace and Company, 1999.

Davidson, Arnold I. *The Emergence of Sexuality: Historical Epistemology and the Formation of Concepts.* Cambridge, MA: Harvard University Press, 2001.

Deikman, A. "Deautomatization and the Mystic Experience." In *Understanding Mysticism*, edited by R. Woods. Garden City, NJ: Image Books. Pp. 240–260.

Diener, Ed, Richard E. Lucas and Christie Napa Scollon. "Beyond the Hedonic Treadmill. Revising the Adaptation Theory of Well-Being." *American Psychologist* 61.4 (2006) 305–314.

Dihle, Albrecht. *The Theory of the Will in Classical Antiquity.* Berkeley: University of California Press, 1982.

Dittes, James E. "Augustine: Search for a Fail-Safe God to Trust." In *The Hunger of the Heart: Reflections on the* Confessions *of Augustine*, edited by Donald Capps and James E. Dittes.

Society for the Scientific Study of Religion Monograph Series 8. West Lafayette, IN: Society for the Scientific Study of Religion, 1990. Pp. 255–264.

————. "Continuities Between the Life and Thought of Augustine." *Journal for the Scientific Study of Religion* 5.1 (1965) 130–40. Reprinted in *The Hunger of the Heart: Reflections on the* Confessions *of Augustine*, edited by Donald Capps and James E. Dittes. Society for the Scientific Study of Religion Monograph Series 8. West Lafayette, IN: Society for the Scientific Study of Religion, 1990. Pp. 117–131.

Dixon, Sandra L. *Augustine: The Scattered and Gathered Self.* St. Louis: Chalice Press, 1999.

————. "The Many Layers of Meaning in Moral Arguments: A Self Psychological Case Study of Augustine's Arguments for Coercion." Ph.D. diss., University of Chicago, 1993.

Dodds, E. R. "Augustine's Confessions: A Study of Spiritual Maladjustment." *Hibbert Journal* 26 (1928) 459–473. Repr. in *The Hunger of the Heart: Reflections on the* Confessions *of Augustine*, edited by Donald Capps and James E. Dittes. Society for the Scientific Study of Religion Monograph Series 8. West Lafayette, IN: Society for the Scientific Study of Religion, 1990. Pp. 41–54.

Dupuy, J. P., ed. *Self-Deception and Paradoxes of Rationality.* Stanford: CSLI Publications, 1998.

Elledge, P. "Embracing Augustine, Reach, Restraint and Romantic Resolution in the Confessions." In *The Hunger of the Heart: Reflections on the Confessions of Augustine*, edited by Donald Capps and James E. Dittes. Society for the Scientific Study of Religion Monograph Series 8. West Lafayette, IN: Society for the Scientific Study of Religion, 1990. Pp. 265–288.

Erk, Susanne, Manfred Spitzer, Arthur P.Wunderlich, Lars Galley and Henrik Walter. "Cultural Objects Modulate Reward Circuitry." *NeuroReport* 13.18 (2002) 2499–2503.

Fenn, Richard. "Magic in Language and Ritual: Notes on Augustine's *Confessions.*" *Journal for the Scientific Study of Religion* 25 (1986) 77–91.

Ferrari, L. "Paul at the Conversion of Augustine." *Augustinian Studies* 11 (1980) 5–20.

————. "The Theme of the Prodigal Son in Augustine's *Confessions.*" *Recherches Augustiniennes* 12 (1977) 105–118.

Flasch, Kurt. *Augustin: Einführung in sein Denken.* Stuttgart: Reclam, 1994.

Foucault, Michel. *Abnormal: Lectures at the Collège de France, 1974–1975.* New York: Picador, 1999.

Fredriksen, Paula. "Augustine and his Analysts: The Possibility of a Psychohistory." *Soundings* 61 (1978) 206–227.

————. *Augustine on Romans.* Chico CA: Scholars Press, 1982.

Freud, Sigmund. *Civilization and Its Discontents.* Translated by James Strachey. New York: W. W. Norton, 1989.

————. *Group Psychology and the Analysis of the Ego.* New York: W. W. Norton, 1959.

————. *On Narcissism.* In *Standard Edition of the Complete Psychological Works of Sigmund Freud.* Translated and edited by James Strachey. Vol. 14. London: Hogarth Press, 1961/ 1914. Pp. 69–102.

————. *Origin and Development of Psychoanalysis.* Trans. Harry W. Chase. N.p.: Nu Vision, 2007.

————. *Standard Edition of the Complete Works of Sigmund Freud.* Ed. James Strachey. London: Hogarth Press, 1968.

Gabbard G. O. "Mind, brain, and personality disorders." *American Journal Psychiatry* 162.4 (2005) 648–655.

Gay, Volney. "Augustine: The Reader as Self-Object." *Journal for the Scientific Study of Religion* 25 (1986) 64–76. Repr. in *The Hunger of the Heart: Reflections on the* Confessions *of Augustine*, edited by Donald Capps and James E. Dittes. Society for the Scientific Study of Religion Monograph Series 8. West Lafayette, IN: Society for the Scientific Study of Religion, 1990. Pp. 185–202.

Gilson, Etienne. *The Christian Philosophy of Saint Augustine.* Trans. L. E. M. Lynch. New York: Random House, 1960.

Graybiel, Ann M. "Building Action Repertoires: Memory and Learning Functions of the Basal Ganglia." *Current Opinion in Neurobiology* 5.6 (1995) 733–741.

Grosset, K. A., G. Macphee, G. Pal, D. Stewart, A. Watt, J. Davie, and D. G. Grosset. "Problematic gambling on dopamine agonists: Not such a rarity." *Movement Disorders* 21.12 (2006) 2206–2208.

Gusdorf, G. "Conditions and Limits of Autobiography." In *Autobiography: Essays Theoretical and Critical*, edited by J. Olney. Princeton: Princeton University Press, 1980.

Hadot, Ilsetraut. "The Spiritual Guide." In *Classical Mediterranean Spirituality: Egyptian, Greek, and Roman*, edited by A. H. Armstrong. New York: Crossroad, 1986. Pp. 436–459.

Hadot, Pierre. *Philosophy as a Way of Life: Spiritual Exercises From Socrates to Foucault.* Ed. Arnold Davidson. Trans. Michael Chase. Oxford: Blackwell, 1995.

———. *The Veil of Isis: An Essay on the History of the Idea of Nature.* Trans. Michael Chase. Cambridge, MA: Belknap Press of Harvard University Press, 2006.

———. *What is Ancient Philosophy?* Trans. Michael Chase. Cambridge: Harvard University Press, 2002.

Hamman, A.-G. *La vie quotidienne en Afrique du Nord au temps de saint Augustin.* Nouvelle éd. Paris: Hachette, 1979.

Hankey, Wayne J. "'Knowing as We Are Known' in *Confessions* 10 and Other Philosophical, Augustinian and Christian Obedience to the Delphic *Gnothi Seauton* from Socrates to Modernity." *Augustinian Studies* 34 (2003) 23–48.

Hawkins, Anne Hunsaker. "St. Augustine: Archetypes of Family." In Don Capps and James E. Dittes, eds., *Hunger of the Heart: Reflections on the* Confessions *of Augustine.* Society for the Scientific Study of Religion Monograph Series 8. West Lafayette, IN: Society for the Scientific Study of Religion, 1990. Pp. 239–254.

Hazelton, R. "The Devotional Life." In *A Companion to the Study of St. Augustine*, edited by R. W. Battenhouse. New York: Oxford University Press, 1955.

Henry, P. *La vision d'Ostie, sa place dans la vie et l'oeuvre de saint Augustin.* Paris: J. Vrin, 1938.

Herrera, Robert A. "St. Augustine's *Confessions*: A Prelude to Psychoanalytic Theory." *Augustiniana* 39 (1989) 462–473.

Homans, Peter. *The Ability to Mourn: Disillusionment and the Social Origins of Psychoanalysis.* Chicago and London: University of Chicago Press, 1989.

James, William. *The Principles of Psychology.* Vol. 1. New York: Dover Publications, 1950 (original, 1890).

Johnson, Marcia K. "A Multiple-Entry, Modular Memory System." *The Psychology of Learning and Motivation: Advances in Research and Theory.* Ed. Gordon H. Bower. Vol. 17. New York: Academic Press, 1983. Pp. 81–123.

Johnson, R. "Comments on *Hunger of the Heart: Reflections on the* Confessions *of Augustine.*" Unpublished manuscript. Paper delivered at AAR national meeting, Chicago, 1990.

Jonte-Pace, Diane. "Augustine on the Couch: Psychohistorical (Mis)readings of the *Confessions.*" *Religion* 23 (1993) 71–83.

———. *Speaking the Unspeakable: Religion, Misogyny, and the Uncanny Mother in Freud's Cultural Texts.* Berkeley: University of California Press, 2005.

Jonte-Pace, Diane, and William B. Parsons, eds. *Religion and Psychology: Mapping the Terrain.* New York: Routledge, 2001.

Joorman, Jutta and Matthias Siemer. "Memory Accessibility, Mood Regulation, and Dysphoria: Difficulties in Repairing Sad Mood with Happy Memories?" *Journal of Abnormal Psychology* 113.2 (2004) 179–188.

Jung, Carl Gustav. "Psychological Aspects of the Mother Archetype," and "The Phenomenology of the Spirit in Fairytales." In *The Archetypes and the Collective Unconscious.* Trans. RFC Hull. *The Collected Works of CG Jung,* 20 Vols. Ed. Herbert Read et al. London: Routledge and Kegan Paul, 1968.

———. "The Syzygy: Anima and Animus." In *Aion, Collected Works.* Trans. R. F. C. Hull. Bollingen Series 20, Vol. 9, Pt. 2. Princeton, NJ: Princeton University Press, 1959.

Jung, Carl Gustav and Carl Kerényi. "The Psychology of the Child Archetype." In *Essays in a Science of Mythology.* Trans. R. F. C. Hull. Bollingen Series 22, 2nd ed. Princeton, NJ: Princeton University Press, 1969.

Kalivas, Peter W. and Nora D. Volkow. "The Neural Basis of Addiction: A Pathology of Motivation and Choice." *American Journal of Psychiatry* 162.8 (2005) 1403–1413.

Kandel, Eric R. "A New Intellectual Framework for Psychiatry." *American Journal of Psychiatry* 155.4 (1998) 457–469.

Kaufman, Peter Iver. "Augustine, Martyrs, and Misery." *Church History* 63 (1994) 1–14.

Kelley, Ann E. and Kent C. Berridge. "The Neuroscience of Natural Rewards: Relevance to Addictive Drugs." *The Journal of Neuroscience* 22.9 (2002) 3306–3311.

Kendler, Kenneth S. "Toward a philosophical structure for psychiatry." *American Journal of Psychiatry* 162.3 (2005) 433–440.

Kenney, J. P. *The Mysticism of Saint Augustine*. New York: Routledge, 2005.

Kligerman, Charles. "A Psychoanalytic Study of the *Confessions* of St. Augustine." *Journal of the American Psychoanalytic Association* 5 (1957) 469–484. Reprinted in *The Hunger of the Heart: Reflections on the* Confessions *of Augustine*, edited by Donald Capps and James E. Dittes. Society for the Scientific Study of Religion Monograph Series 8. West Lafayette, IN: Society for the Scientific Study of Religion, 1990. Pp. 95–108.

Klöckener, Martin. "*De Cura pro mortuis gerenda.*" *Augustinian Studies* 2 (1996) 182–188.

Knutson, Brian, Charles M. Adams, Grace W. Fong and Daniel Hommer. "Anticipation of Increasing Monetary Reward Selectively Recruits Nucleus Accumbens." *The Journal of Neuroscience*, 21.RC159 (2001) 1–5.

Koepp, M. J., R. N. Gunn, A. D. Lawrence, V. J. Cunningham, A. Dagher, T. Jones, D. J. Brooks, C. J. Bench and P. M. Grasby. "Evidence for Striatal Dopamine Release During a Video Game." *Nature* vol. 393 (21 May 1998) 266–268.

Kohut, H. "Forms and Transformations of Narcissism." In *Search for the Self*. New York: International Universities Press, 1978. Pp. 427–460.

———. *The Kohut Seminars on Self Psychology and Psychotherapy with Adolescents and Young Adults*. Ed. Miriam Elson. New York and London: W. W. Norton, 1987.

———. *Self Psychology and the Humanities: Reflections on a New Psychoanalytic Approach*. New York and London: W.W. Norton, 1985.

Kolbet, Paul R. *Augustine and the Cure of Souls: Revising a Classical Ideal*. Notre Dame: University of Notre Dame Press, 2010.

Koob, George F. and Michel Le Moal. "Addiction and the Brain Antireward System." *Annual Review of Psychology* 59 (January 2008) 29–53.

———. "Drug Abuse: Hedonic Homeostatic Dysregulation." *Science* 278.3 (1997) 52–58.

Koob, G. and M. J. Kreek. "Stress, Dysregulation of Drug Reward Pathways, and the Transition to Drug Dependence." *American Journal of Psychiatry* 164.8 (2007) 1149–1159.

Kotila, Heikki. "Monica's Death in Augustine's *Confessions* IX.11–13." *Studia Patristica* 27 (1993) 337–341.

Kotre, John. *White Gloves: How We Create Ourselves Through Memory*. New York: Norton, 1996.

Kripal, Jeffrey. *Kali's Child: The Mystical and the Erotic in the Life and Teachings of Ramakrishna*. 2nd ed. Chicago and London: University of Chicago Press, 1995.

———. "Why the Tantrika is a Hero: Kali in the Psychoanalytic Tradition." In *Encountering Kali: In the Margins, at the Center, in the West*, edited by Rachel Fell McDermott and Jeffrey J. Kripal. Berkeley and Los Angeles: University of California Press, 2003. Pp. 196–222.

Kundera, Milan. *Laughable Loves*. Trans. Suzanne Rappaport. Middlesex, England: Penguin Books, 1974.

Lamberton, Robert. *Homer the Theologian: Neoplatonist Allegorical Reading and the Growth of the Epic Tradition*. The Transformation of the Classical Heritage 9. Berkeley: University of California, 1986.

Lao Tsu. *Tao Te Ching*. Trans. Gia-Fu Feng and Jane English. 1972. New York: Vintage Books, 1989.

Lancel, Serge. *St. Augustine*. Translated by Antonia Nevill. London: SCM Press, 2002.

Land-Closson, Linda. "Strings of Relationship and Community: A Dialogue between the Life of Bede Griffiths and the Theories of Jean Baker Miller." Ph. D. diss., Joint Ph.D. Program in Religious and Theological Studies of the Iliff School of Theology and the University of Denver, 2008.

LaPorte, Jean, and F. Ellen Weaver, "Augustine and Women: Relationships and Teachings." *Augustinian Studies* 12 (1981) 115–132.

Lawless, George P. "Interior Peace in the *Confessions* of St. Augustine." *Revue des Études Augustiniennes* 26 (1980) 49–61.

Legewie, Bernard. *Augustinus: Eine Psychographie*. Bonn: A. Marcus et E. Weber, 1925.

———. "Die körperliche Konstitution und die Krankheiten Augustins." In *Miscellanea Agostiniana. Testi e studi pubblicati a cura dell'ordine eremitano di s. Agostino nel XV centenario dalla morte del santo dottore* 2 (1931) 5–21.

Lenox-Conyngham, Andrew. "The Topography of the Basilica Conflict of A.D. 385/6 in Milan." *Historia* 31 (1982) 353–363.

Levine, Linda J. and David A. Pizarro. "Emotion and Memory Research: A Grumpy Review." *Social Cognition* 22.5 (2004) 530–554.

Levine, Linda J., Martin A. Safer and Heather C. Lench. "Remembering and Misremembering Emotions." *Judgments Over Time: The Interplay of Thoughts, Feelings, and Behaviors*. Ed. Lawrence J. Sanna and Edward C. Chang. New York: Oxford University Press, 2006. Pp. 271–290.

Lonergan, Bernard. *Insight: A Study of Human Understanding*. New York: Philosophical Library, 1970.

Louth, A. *The Origins of the Christian Mystical Tradition*. Oxford: Clarendon Press, 1981.

Madec, G. "Christus, scientia et sapientia nostra. Le principe de cohérence de la doctrine augustinienne." *Recherches augustiniennes* 10 (1975) 77–85.

Mallard, William. *Language and Love. Introducing Augustine's Religious Thought Through the* Confessions *Story*. University Park, PA: Pennsylvania State University Press, 1994.

Marcus, Paul and Alan Rosenberg, eds. *Psychoanalytic Versions of the Human Condition: Philosophies of Life and Their Impact on Practice*. New York: New York University Press, 1998.

Marrou, H. *Saint Augustin et la fin de la culture antique*. Paris: Éditions de Boccard, 1949.

Masson, Michael E. J. and Peter Graf. "Introduction: Looking Back and Into the Future." *Implicit Memory: New Directions in Cognition, Development, and Neuropsychology*. Ed. Peter Graf and Michael E. J. Masson. Hillsdale, NJ: Erlbaum, 1993. Pp. 1–11.

Matter, E. Ann, "Christ, God and Woman in the Thought of St Augustine." In *Augustine and His Critics: Essay in Honour of Gerald Bonner*, edited by Robert Dodaro and George Lawless. London and New York: Routledge, 2000. Pp. 164–175.

McGinn, B. *The Foundations of Mysticism: Origins to the Fifth Century*. New York: Crossroad, 1991.

McMahon, Robert. *Augustine's Prayerful Ascent: An Essay on the Literary Form of the* Confessions. Athens: University of Georgia Press, 1989.

Mele, A. R. "Real Self-Deception." *Behavioral and Brain Sciences* 20 (1997).

———. "Understanding and Explaining Real Self-Deception, *Self-Deception Unmasked*. Princeton: Princeton University Press, 2001. Pp. 127–136.

Miles, Margaret R. *Desire and Delight. A New Reading of Augustine's* Confessions. New York: Crossroad Publishing, 1991.

———. "Infancy, Parenting and Nourishment in Augustine's *Confessions*." In *The Hunger of the Heart: Reflections on the* Confessions *of Augustine*, edited by Donald Capps and James E. Dittes. Society for the Scientific Study of Religion Monograph Series 8. West Lafayette, IN: Society for the Scientific Study of Religion, 1990. Pp. 219–236.

Miller, Jean Baker. "The Development of Women's Sense of Self." In *Women's Spirituality: Resources for Christian Development*, edited by Joann Wolski Conn. New York and Mahwah, NJ: Paulist Press, 1996. Pp. 165–184.

Miller, Julie B. "To Remember Self, to Remember God: Augustine on Sexuality, Relationality, and the Trinity." In *Feminist Interpretations of Augustine*, edited by Judith Chelius Stark. University Park, PA: Pennsylvania State University Press, 2007. Pp. 243–279.

Minsky, Rosalind. *Psychoanalysis and Culture: Contemporary States of Mind*. New Brunswick: Rutgers University Press, 1998.

Mitchell, Juliet. *Psychoanalysis and Feminism: Freud, Reich, Laing, and Women*. New York: Vintage, 1975.

Moore, Rebecca. "O Mother, Where Art Thou? In Search of Saint Monnica." In *Feminist Interpretations of Augustine*, edited by Judith Chelius Stark. University Park, PA: Pennsylvania State University Press, 2007. Pp. 147–166.

Moran, Mark. "Drug Addiction Erodes 'Free Will' Over Time." *Psychiatric News* (8 July 2007) 16, 34.

Morgan, Drake, Kathleen A. Grant, H. Donald Gage, Robert H. Mach, Jay R. Kaplan, Osric Prioleau, Susan H Nader, Nancy Buchheimer, Richard L. Eherenkaufer and Michael A. Nader. "Social Dominance in Monkeys: Dopamine D2 Receptors and Cocaine Self-Administration." *Nature Neuroscience* 5.2 (2002) 169–174.

Nairne, James S. "A Functional Analysis of Primary Memory." *The Nature of Remembering: Essays in Honor of Robert G. Crowder*. Ed. Henry L. Roediger, James S. Nairne, Ian Neath and Aimee Surprenant. Washington, D.C.: American Psychological Association, 2001. Pp. 283–296.

Nash, Ronald H. *The Light of the Mind: St. Augustine's Theory of Knowledge*. Lexington: University of Kentucky Press, 1969.

Neiman, Susan. *Evil: An Alternative History of Philosophy*. Princeton: Princeton University Press, 2002.

———. *Moral Clarity: A Guide for Grown-Up Idealists*. New York: Harcourt, 2008.

Neisser, Ulrich, and Nicole Harsch. "Phantom Flashbulbs: False Recollections of Hearing the News about *Challenger*." *Affect and Accuracy in Recall: Studies of "Flashbulb" Memories*. Ed. Eugene Winograd, and Ulrich Neisser. New York: Cambridge University Press, 1992. Pp. 9–31.

Nesse, Randolph M. and Kent C. Berridge. "Psychoactive Drug Use in Evolutionary Perspective." *Science*, vol. 278 (3 October 1997) 63–66.

Nestler, Eric J. and David W. Self. "Neuropsychiatric Aspects of Ethanol and Other Chemical Dependencies." *The American Psychiatric Publishing Textbook of Neuropsychiatry and Behavioral Neurosciences*. 5th ed. Ed. Stuart C. Yudofsky and Robert E. Hales. Washington, D.C.: American Psychiatric Publishing, Inc., 2008. Pp. 881–905.

Newman, Robert J. "*Cotidie Meditare*: Theory and Practice of the *meditatio* in Imperial Stoicism." *Aufstieg und Niedergang der römischen Welt* 2.36.3 (1989) 1473–1517.

Nolan, R. W. "Psychohistory, Theory and Practice." *Massachusetts Review* 18 (1977) 295–322.

Nussbaum, Martha C. *The Therapy of Desire: Theory and Practice in Hellenistic Ethics*. Martin Classical Lectures, new series 2. Princeton: Princeton University Press, 1994.

Obeyesekere, Gananath. *Medusa's Hair: An Essay on Personal Symbols and Religious Experience*. Chicago and London: University of Chicago Press, 1981.

———. *The Work of Culture: Symbolic Transformation in Psychoanalysis and Anthropology*. Chicago and London: University of Chicago Press, 1990.

O'Connell, R. J. *St. Augustine's Early Theory of Man*. Cambridge: Harvard University Press, 1968.

———. *Imagination and Metaphysics in St. Augustine*. Milwaukee: Marquette University Press, 1986.

———. *The Origin of the Soul in St. Augustine's Later Works*. New York: Fordham University Press, 1987.

O'Daly, Gerard J. P. *Augustine's Philosophy of Mind*. Berkeley: University of California Press, 1987.

———. "Did St. Augustine Ever Believe in the Soul's Pre-existence?" *Augustinian Studies* 5 (1974) 227–235.

———. "Augustine and the Origin of Souls." In *Platonismus und Christentum. Festschrift für Heinrich Dörrie*. Munster: Aschendorffsche Verlagsbuchhandlung, 1983.

O'Donnell, James J. *Augustine: A New Biography*. New York: HarperCollins, 2005.

———. *Confessions*. 3 vols. Oxford: Clarendon Press, 1992.

———. *St. Augustine's Confessions: The Odyssey of Soul*. Cambridge: Harvard University Press, 1969.

O'Donovan, O. M. T. *The Problem of Self-Love in Saint Augustine.* New Haven: Yale University Press, 1980.

O'Meara, John J. *The Young Augustine: The Growth of St. Augustine's Mind up to His Conversion.* London: Longmans, Green and Co., 1954.

Paffenroth, Kim. "Book IX: The Emotional Heart of the *Confessions.*" In *A Reader's Companion to Augustine's Confessions,* edited by Kim Paffenroth and Robert P. Kennedy. Louisville, KY, and London: Westminster John Knox Press, 2003. Pp. 137–154.

———. "God in the Friend, or the Friend in God? The Meaning of Friendship for Augustine." *Augustinian Heritage* 38 (1992) 123–136.

Panksepp, Jaak. *Affective Neuroscience: The Foundations of Human and Animal Emotions.* Oxford: Oxford University Press, 1998.

Parsons, William B. "Augustine; Common-Man or Intuitive Psychologist?" *The Journal of Psychohistory* 18 (1990) 155–179.

———. *The Enigma of the Oceanic Feeling; Revisioning the Psychoanalytic Theory of Mysticism.* New York: Oxford University Press, 1999.

———. "Psychoanalysis and Mysticism: The Case of St. Augustine." In *Mysticism: A Variety of Psychological Perspectives,* edited by J. Belzen and A. Geels. Amsterdam: Rodopi, 2003. Pp. 151–178.

Pies, Ronald. "Should DSM-V Designate 'Internet Addiction' a Mental Disorder?" *Psychiatry (Edgmont)* 6.2 (2009) 31–37.

Pinker, Steven. *How the Mind Works.* New York: W. W. Norton & Co., 1997.

Pincherle, Augusto. "The *Confessions* of St. Augustine." *Augustinian Studies* 7 (1976) 119–133.

Plumer, Eric. *Augustine's Commentary on Galatians: Introduction, Text, Translation, and Notes.* Oxford: Oxford University Press, 2006.

———. "Book Six: Major Characters and Memorable Incidents." In *A Reader's Companion to Augustine's* Confessions, edited by Kim Paffenroth and Robert P. Kennedy. Louisville, KY, and London: Westminster John Knox Press, 2003. Pp. 89–105.

Possidius. *Vita Augustini. Patrologiae Latinae* 32. *Sancti Augustini Vita.* Edited and translated with an introduction by Herbert T. Weiskotten. Princeton: Princeton University Press, 1919.

Power, Kim. *Veiled Desire.* New York: Continuum, 1996.

Pruyser, Paul W. "Psychological Examination: Augustine." *Journal for the Scientific Study of Religion* 5 (1966) 284–289.

Quattrone, G. and A. Tversky. "Self-Deception and the Voter's Illusion." In *The Multiple Self,* edited by J. Elster. Cambridge, UK: Cambridge University Press, 1985. Pp. 35–57.

Radhakrishnan, Sarvepalli and Charles A. Moore, eds. *A Sourcebook in Indian Philosophy.* Princeton: Princeton University Press, 1957.

Ranke-Heinemann, Ulriche. *Eunuchen für das Himmelreich: Katholische Kirche und Sexualität.* Hamburg: Hoffmann und Campe, 1988.

Rees, Brinley Roderick. "The Conversion of St. Augustine." *Trivium* 14 (1979) 1–17.

Ricoeur, Paul. "Art and Freudian Systematics." In *The Conflict of Interpretations: Essays in Hermeneutics.* Translated by Willis Domingo. Edited by Don Ihde. Northwestern University Studies in Phenomenology and Existential Philosophy. Gen. ed. James M. Edie. Evanston, IL: Northwestern University Press, 1974. Pp. 196–208.

———. *Freud and Philosophy.* Translated by Denis Savage. New Haven and London: Yale University Press, 1970.

———. "The Model of the Text: Meaningful Action Considered as a Text." In *Interpretive Social Science: A Reader,* edited by Paul Rabinow and William M. Sullivan. Berkeley: University of California Press, 1979. Pp. 73–101.

Rigby, Paul. "Paul Ricoeur, Freudianism, and Augustine's *Confessions.*" *Journal of the American Academy of Religion* 53 (1985) 93–114. Repr. as "Augustine's *Confessions*: The Recognition of Fatherhood." In Donald Capps and James E. Dittes, eds. *The Hunger of the Heart: Reflections on the* Confessions *of Augustine.* Society for the Scientific Study of Religion Monograph Series 8. West Lafayette, IN: Society for the Scientific Study of Religion, 1990. Pp. 146–165.

Rist, John. "Faith and Reason." In *The Cambridge Companion to Augustine*, edited by Eleonore Stump and Norman Kretzmann. Cambridge: Cambridge University Press, 2001. Pp. 26–39.

Röckelein, C. Hedwig. "Psychohistorie(n) zur Religions und Kirchengeschichte." *Kirchliche Zeitgeschichte* 7 (1994) 11–25.

Schaps, David. "The Women Least Mentioned: Etiquette and Women's Names." *Classical Quarterly*, N.S. 27 (1977) 323–330.

Schindler, David C. "Freedom Beyond Our Choosing: Augustine on the Will and Its Objects." In *Augustine and Politics*, edited by John Doody, Kevin L. Hughes, and Kim Paffenroth. Lanham, MD: Lexington Books, 2005. Pp. 67–96.

Schultz, Wolfram. "Predictive Reward Signal of Dopamine Neurons." *The Journal of Neurophysiology* 80.1 (1998) 1–27.

Seelbach, Larissa Carina. *"Das weibliche Geschlecht ist ja kein Gebrechen . . .": die Frau und ihre Gottebenbildlichkeit bei Augustin*. Würzburg: Augustinus-Verlag, 2002.

———. "Psychoanalytische Deutungsversuche zur Persönlichkeit Augustins—Beispiele und Anfragen." *Theologie und Glaube* 93 (2003) 240–261.

Seligman, Martin E. P. *Authentic Happiness: Using the New Positive Psychology to Realize Your Potential for Lasting Fulfillment*. New York: The Free Press, 2002.

Shanzer, Danuta. "Pears Before Swine: Augustine, *Confessions*, 2.4.9." *Revue des études augustiniennes* 42 (1996) 45–55.

Shaw, Brent D. "The Family in Late Antiquity: The Experience of Augustine." *Past and Present* 115 (May 1987) 3–51.

Simon, William. *Postmodern Sexualities*. New York: Routledge, 1996.

Smail, Daniel Lord. *On Deep History and the Brain*. Berkeley: University of California Press, 2008.

Sorabji, Richard. *Emotion and Peace of Mind: From Stoic Agitation to Christian Temptation*. Oxford: Oxford University Press, 2000.

Spitzer, Manfred. *The Mind within the Net: Models of Learning, Thinking and Acting*. Cambridge, MA: The MIT Press, 1999.

Squire, Larry R. "Memory Systems of The Brain: A Brief History and Current Perspective." *Neurobiology of Learning and Memory* 82.3 (2004) 171–177.

Stahl, Stephen. *Stahl's Essential Psychopharmacology*. Cambridge: Cambridge University Press, 2008.

Stark, Judith Chelius, ed. *Feminist Interpretations of Augustine*. University Park, PA: Pennsylvania State University Press, 2007.

Starnes, Colin. *Augustine's Conversion: A Guide to the Argument of* Confessions *I–IX*. Waterloo, Ontario: Wilfrid Laurier University Press, 1990.

———. "Augustine's Conversion and the Ninth Book of the *Confessions*." In *Augustine: From Rhetor to Theologian*, edited by Joanne McWilliam. Waterloo, Ontario: Wilfrid Laurier University Press, 1992. Pp. 51–65.

Tabor, J. *Things Unutterable*. New York: University Press of America, 1986.

Talarico, Jennifer M. and David C. Rubin. "Confidence, Not Consistency, Characterizes Flashbulb Memories." *Psychological Science* 14.5 (2003) 455–461.

Taylor, Charles. *The Sources of the Self: The Making of the Modern Identity*. Cambridge: Harvard University Press, 1989.

TeSelle, Eugene. "Augustine as Client and as Theorist." *Journal for the Scientific Study of Religion* 25 (1986) 92–101.

———. *Augustine the Theologian*. London: Burns & Oates, 1970.

Thomas, Michael. "Das psychische Erlebnis im Werk von Augustinus." *Wissenschaft und Weisheit* 35 (1972) 137–164.

Truax, Jean A. "Augustine of Hippo: Defender of Women's Equality?" *Journal of Medieval History* 16 (1990) 279–299.

Tulving, Endel. "Episodic and Semantic Memory." In *Organization of Memory*. Ed. Endel Tulving and Wayne Donaldson. New York: Academic Press, 1972. Pp. 381–403.

———. "How Many Memory Systems Are There?" *American Psychologist* 40.4 (1985) 385–398.

———. "Concepts of Human Memory." *Memory: Organization and Locus of Change*. Ed. Larry R. Squire, Norman Weinberger, Gary Lynch and James L. McGaugh. New York: Oxford University Press, 1991. Pp. 3–32.

———. "Episodic Memory and Common Sense: How Far Apart?" *Philosophical Transactions of the Royal Society, London*, B, 356.1413 (2001) 1505–1515.

———. "Chronesthesia: Awareness of Subjective Time." *Principles of Frontal Lobe Function*. Ed. Donald T. Stuss and Robert C. Knight. New York: Oxford University Press, 2002. Pp. 311–325.

Van Herik, Judith. *Freud on Femininity and Faith*. Berkeley: University of California, 1982.

Vergil. *The Aeneid*. Trans. Allen Mandelbaum. New York: Bantam, 1971.

Volkow, Nora D. and Roy A Wise. "How Can Drug Addiction Help Us Understand Obesity?" *Nature Neuroscience* 8.5 (2005) 555–560.

Waugh, Nancy C. and Donald A. Norman. "Primary Memory." *Psychological Review* 72.2 (1965) 89–104.

Weintraub, Karl. *The Value of the Individual: Self and Circumstance in Autobiography*. Chicago and London: University of Chicago Press, 1978.

Welty, William M. "Discussion Method Teaching: How to Make It Work." *Change* (July/ August 1989) 41–49.

Werpehowski, William. "Weeping at the Death of Dido: Sorrow, Virtue, and Augustine's *Confessions*." *Journal of Religious Ethics* 19 (1991) 175–191.

West, Rebecca. *St. Augustine*. Chicago: Thomas More Press, 1982.

Wetzel, James. *Augustine and the Limits of Virtue*. Cambridge: Cambridge University Press, 1992.

———. "Body Double: Saint Augustine and the Sexualized Will." In *Weakness of Will from Plato to the Present*, edited by Tobias Hoffmann. Washington, D.C.: Catholic University of America Press, 2008. Pp. 58–81.

———. "Will and Interiority in Augustine: Travels in an Unlikely Place." *Augustinian Studies* 33 (2002) 139–160.

White, Stephen A. "Cicero and the Therapists." In *Cicero the Philosopher: Twelve Papers*, edited by J. G. F. Powell. Oxford: Oxford University Press, 1995. Pp. 219–246.

Williams, Rowan. "'Know Thyself': What Kind of an Injunction?" In *Philosophy, Religion and the Spiritual Life*, edited by Michael McGhee. Cambridge: Cambridge University Press, 1992. Pp. 211–227.

———. "Sapientia and the Trinity: Reflections on *De trinitate*." In Bernard Bruning, Mathijs Lamberigts and J. van Houtem, eds. *Collectanea Augustiniana: Mélanges T J van Bavel*. Vol. 1. Bibliotheca Ephemeridum Theologicarum Lovaniensium XCII–A. Louvain: Leuven University Press, 1990. Pp. 317–332.

Wills, Garry. *Saint Augustine*. New York: Lipper/Viking, 1999.

Wilson, E. O. *Consilience: The Unity of Knowledge*. New York: Alfred A. Knopf, 1998.

Winter, Sarah. *Freud and the Institution of Psychoanalytic Knowledge*. Stanford, CA: Stanford University Press, 1999.

Woollcott, Phillip. "Some Considerations of Creativity and Religious Experience in St. Augustine of Hippo." *Journal for the Scientific Study of Religion* 5 (1966) 273–283.

Zuzne, L. *Names in the History of Psychology*. New York: John Wiley and Sons, 1957.

Index

About the Contributors

Todd Breyfogle is Director of Seminars at the Aspen Institute. He holds degrees from Colorado College, Oxford University (where he studied as a Rhodes Scholar), and the University of Chicago's Committee on Social Thought (where he was a Century and Javits Fellow). Before joining the Aspen Institute, he taught in and directed the honors program at the University of Denver and was a visiting professor at the University of Tulsa. He is the editor of *Literary Imagination, Ancient and Modern: Essays in Honor of David Grene* (University of Chicago Press, 1999), has authored a number of articles ranging from Augustine to J. S. Bach to contemporary political theory, and is a co-editor of a five-volume commentary on Augustine's *City of God* for Oxford University Press.

Sandra Lee Dixon has written on Augustine and psychology from the points of view of Augustine's theological anthropology, as well as culture and psychology in a psychoanalytic mode, since her dissertation research at the Divinity School of the University of Chicago. She examined Augustine's arguments for the coercion of the Donatists' religious practice as part of her larger interest in the psychology of moral lives and the roles of religions in morality across the life span. She is Associate Professor of Psychology of Religion in the Department of Religious Studies at the University of Denver.

John Doody is Professor of Philosophy, Director of the Villanova Center for Liberal Education, and the Robert M. Birmingham Chair of Humanities at Villanova University.

Anne Hunsaker Hawkins is Professor of Humanities at the Penn State College of Medicine at the Milton S. Hershey Medical Center. She is the author of several books on medicine, literature, and spirituality.

Morton T. Kelsey was a professor at the University of Notre Dame and an Episcopalian priest. He studied with Carl Jung and was widely known for his books and lectures on meditation, spirituality, and dreams.

Paul R. Kolbet lives in Wellesley, Massachusetts, and is co-chair of the Augustine and Augustinianisms Group of the American Academy of Religion. He is the author of *Augustine and the Cure of Souls: Revising a Classical Ideal* (Notre Dame, IN: University of Notre Dame Press, 2010), co-editor (with Brian Daley) of *The Harp of Prophecy: Early Christian Interpretation of the Psalms* (Notre Dame, IN: University of Notre Dame Press [forthcoming]), and articles in *Ecclesiology, Harvard Theological Review, Journal of the American Academy of Religion, Modern Theology*, and *Studia Patristica*. He is currently writing a book on Origen of Alexandria.

Margaret R. Miles is Emeritus Professor of Historical Theology, The Graduate Theological Union, Berkeley. She taught at the Harvard University Divinity School from 1978–1996, and she was Dean and Dillenberger Professor of Historical Theology of the Graduate Theological Union, Berkeley, from 1996 until her retirement in 2002. Her latest books are *A Complex Delight: The Secularization of the Breast, 1350–1750* (University of California Press, 2008), and *The Word Made Flesh: A History of Christian Thought* (Blackwell, 2005).

Daniel Morehead is a psychiatrist in private practice. He is consulting psychiatrist at the Samaritan Center for Pastoral Counseling and clinical faculty for the University of Texas Southwestern–Austin Psychiatry Residency Program. Dr. Morehead has served as adjunct faculty for the Austin Presbyterian Theological Seminary and is former assistant residency director at the Karl Menninger School of Psychiatry, where he also trained in psychiatry. He is board certified in General Psychiatry, and Neuropsychiatry and Behavioral Sciences. He lives with his wife and three children in Austin, Texas.

Kim Paffenroth is Professor of Religious Studies at Iona College. He has written extensively on Augustine, the Bible, and on the interface between Christian belief and popular culture. In the last category, he produced *Gospel of the Living Dead: George Romero's Visions of Hell on Earth* (Baylor, 2006), which won the Bram Stoker Award and led Dr. Paffenroth to write several popular zombie novels.

William B. Parsons is Associate Professor of Religious Studies at Rice University. His publications include *The Enigma of the Oceanic Feeling, Religion and Psychology: Mapping the Terrain, Mourning Religion, Disciplining Freud on Religion, Teaching Mysticism* and dozens of essays in multiple journals and edited books. He has served as Chair of the Department of Religious Studies at Rice University, Director of the Rice University Humanities Research Center, Editor of *Religious Studies Review*, and has been a Fellow of the Institute for Advanced Studies (IAS) at Hebrew University.

Raymond J. Shaw earned his doctorate at the University of Toronto in 1990, where he studied attention, memory, and cognitive aging with Fergus Craik. He completed a post-doctoral fellowship in Cognitive Aging at the Georgia Institute of Technology and was on the faculty at West Virginia University. He is now Vice Provost and Associate Professor of Psychology at Merrimack College with interests in cognition, memory, positive psychology, and research methodology.

Lightning Source UK Ltd.
Milton Keynes UK
UKHW011458190123
415627UK00003B/17